INVITATION TO THE APOCRYPHA

Invitation
to the
Apocrypha

Daniel J. Harrington, S.J.

WILLIAM B. EERDMANS PUBLISHING COMPANY
GRAND RAPIDS, MICHIGAN / CAMBRIDGE, U.K.

Library of Congress Cataloging-in-Publication Data

Harrington, Daniel J.
Invitation to the Apocrypha / Daniel J. Harrington.
p.   cm.
ISBN 0-8028-4633-5 (pbk.: alk. paper)
1. Bible. O.T. Apocrypha Introductions.   I. Title.
BS1700.H37   1999
229'.061 — dc21   99-34518
CIP

The author and publisher gratefully acknowledge permission to adapt previously published material from the following sources:

"Introduction to the Canon." In *The New Interpreter's Bible,* vol. 1, p. 12. Nashville: Abingdon Press, 1994. Used by permission.

The Maccabean Revolt: Anatomy of a Biblical Revolution. Wilmington, Del.: Michael Glazier, 1988. Copyright held by Liturgical Press, Collegeville, Minn. Used by permission.

"Sirach." In *The International Bible Commentary,* edited by William R. Farmer, pp. 923-50. Collegeville, Minn.: Liturgical Press, 1998. Used by permission.

Contents

v

CONTENTS

Preface

The word *serendipity* refers to the making of a desirable discovery by accident (or, by divine providence). This introduction to the Old Testament Apocrypha had a serendipitous origin.

In May 1998 I had just finished teaching once more a course on suffering in the Bible and theology. In the course we work through key Old and New Testament texts as well as classic and modern theological essays on the mystery of suffering. The material helps students (and me) to integrate their biblical and theological studies with their personal and pastoral experiences. It is a privilege for me as the professor to take part in the discussions and to read the students' papers. I have offered the course several times, and often have wanted to write something on the topic. But what? I had planned vaguely to begin work on a writing project about suffering during the summer of 1998. However, I had no clear idea what shape it might take.

In late May I received a letter from Dr. Daniel C. Harlow, Editor of Biblical Studies at Wm. B. Eerdmans Publishing Company. In it he invited me to write a college and seminary level introduction to the Old Testament Apocrypha. This was an opportunity too good for me to refuse. For many years I have studied and taught these texts, written about them, and followed developments in scholarship on them. Here was the opportunity to bring together thirty-five years of work. And so the project on suffering would have to be pushed aside and put off for another time. Or so I thought.

As a way of getting started on my new project, I read through the

Old Testament Apocrypha again in the course of a weekend. And here is where serendipity (or divine providence) came in. One problem with the Old Testament Apocrypha is that they are an artificial collection of ancient Jewish books. They come from roughly the fourth century B.C.E. to the first century C.E. and originated in various places in the ancient world, in both the land of Israel and the Diaspora. How then can a teacher or a writer introduce college and seminary students to such a disparate corpus of books? As I read on, for the first time I began to recognize how the mystery of suffering might serve as an integrating principle for reading the Old Testament Apocrypha. Each of these books in its own way deals with the question of theodicy (How can an omnipotent and just God allow human suffering?) and provides its own perspectives on the mystery of suffering.

And so this invitation to read the Old Testament Apocrypha takes as its theological focus the mystery of suffering. It provides a guide for beginners to work through each book according to its distinctive literary presentation and in its historical context within Second Temple Judaism (sixth century B.C.E. to first century C.E.). My hope is that this introduction will contribute something fresh to the study of both the Old Testament Apocrypha and the mystery of suffering in the biblical tradition.

I am grateful to Dan Harlow for his unexpected invitation and for his good advice and encouragement in the early stages of writing. I am also thankful to two teachers, colleagues, and friends of many years: John Strugnell, for introducing me to the Old Testament Apocrypha in his course, and for our ongoing conversations about these books; and Lucien Richard, for showing me how to interpret the Bible, theology, and life from the perspective of the mystery of suffering.

CHAPTER 1

Reading the Old Testament Apocrypha

The books known in some circles as the Old Testament Apocrypha or Deuterocanonical books are sometimes called "books between the testaments." They stand between the Testaments in several different senses. In many editions of the Bible printed under Protestant auspices, these books appear in a separate section between the Old and the New Testaments. Moreover, these books were generally composed between the time of the last books in the Hebrew Bible (though some may antedate Daniel) and the New Testament books (though the various parts of 2 Esdras are contemporary with them or later). Also, these books provide a theological bridge between the Testaments in that they give a sample that illustrates how the traditions of the Hebrew Scriptures were carried forward, and they greatly illumine the world in which Jesus and the New Testament writers lived and worked. Of course, this sample needs to be supplemented by the Old Testament Pseudepigrapha, the Dead Sea Scrolls, the works of Josephus and Philo, and early rabbinic literature.

This guide to the Old Testament Apocrypha seeks to encourage and facilitate an intelligent and sympathetic reading of these texts as they appear in the New Revised Standard Version of the Bible. The NRSV enjoys a very wide circulation. Standing in the tradition of the King James Bible and the Revised Standard Version, it combines the best of modern textual scholarship and a serious effort to reflect modern English usage. It is published in many editions, and generally includes the Apocryphal or

Deuterocanonical books of the Old Testament situated between the Old Testament and New Testament. This collection of books is larger than the New Testament and about thirty percent the size of the Old Testament.

For Jews and Protestants these books are not part of the canon of Scripture, whereas for Catholics and Orthodox Christians most of them are canonical. In all the traditions, however, these books command relatively little attention. But as I hope to show, these books are worth serious reading and reflection. Though none of them may rival Genesis, Exodus, Isaiah, Job, Luke's Gospel, John's Gospel, or Romans in historical or theological significance, the collection does include literary gems (Tobit and Judith), an eloquent biblical-philosophical exhortation (Wisdom), a massive combination of traditional wisdom and the Torah (Sirach), two portraits of some decisive events in Jewish history (1 and 2 Maccabees), and a magnificent apocalypse from roughly the same time as the book of Revelation (2 Esdras 3–14/4 Ezra).

This introduction is intended more as a guide for those who want to read and study the books seriously for the first time than as a handbook for scholars and Bible professors. In this chapter I will introduce the books and provides suggestions on how best to read them. The treatments of each book in the following chapters contain four sections: *Basic Information* (who, when, where, what, why, and how?), *Content* (structure, content, and literary features), *Significance* (theological importance, issues in scholarship, and influence in Judaism and Christianity), and *Suggestions for Further Study* (books that can enable the reader to move to the next level).

In treating the individual books, I want to show their links to the Hebrew Bible, since many of these books take biblical texts as starting points for their content and style. I also intend to note their importance for understanding the New Testament. Another goal is to illustrate modern methods of studying biblical texts by applying them to the reading of these books (for example, narrative criticism for Tobit, and rhetorical criticism for Wisdom). And I want to introduce in an unobtrusive way the latest and best scholarship on these works, and to provide leads for further study.

The Apocryphal/Deuterocanonical books of the Old Testament are a collection or anthology of very diverse writings. They differ in their historical settings, literary forms, rhetorics, contents, and theological perspectives. They are a part of the much wider phenomenon of Second

Temple Judaism, and as such provide only a small sample of, but nonetheless an entry into, the world in which classical Judaism and early Christianity took shape. Since few Christians or Jews know these books well, study of them in the setting of ecumenical and interreligious dialogue may be especially fruitful.

In working through these books, I have chosen as a theological lens the problem of suffering. Almost every one of the writings touches in some way upon the mystery of suffering, which remains a major concern to all human beings and to all religious traditions. How can we say that God is omnipotent and just when innocent people are suffering? Are righteous people really rewarded, and wicked people really punished? If so, when and how? No one of these books provides *the* answer to such questions, nor are these issues always the most obvious focus of attention. But each book can make a contribution to our understanding of how the problem of suffering was handled in Second Temple Judaism, and may make us reflect on the adequacy of and enrich our own theological approaches today to this universal human experience.

Since the Old Testament Apocrypha are contained in all Catholic and most Protestant Bibles today, there are many good translations of these books. The books can be found there in many different orders. And one can devise one's own order of reading them: by genres (history, wisdom, prayers, etc.), by chronological or historical sequence or by place of origin (the Land of Israel, Alexandria in Egypt, the eastern Diaspora), or by canonical authority or theological significance. In this introduction I have taken the New Revised Standard Version as the base text, and have followed its order in those editions that present these books as a separate corpus between the Old and New Testaments. I do so because the NRSV is a good and readily available translation, and following its order may facilitate the use of this book in college and seminary courses and by Bible-study groups. But this introduction can be used with any modern translation, and the books can be read in whatever order seems most useful.

The Canonical Status of the Apocrypha

In Christian circles the Greek term *kanōn,* which means "rule" or "norm," has come to refer to an authoritative list of sacred books and their function as the rule or norm of faith and life. All Christians today accept as canonical the books of the Hebrew Bible. Bibles published under Roman

Catholic auspices contain in their Old Testament seven additional books — Tobit, Judith, Wisdom, Sirach, 1 and 2 Maccabees, and Baruch, as well as some additions to Daniel and Esther. These latter books were part of the manuscript traditions of the Greek (Septuagint) and Latin (Vulgate) Bibles. In Catholic Bibles they are interspersed among the uncontested books of the Hebrew Bible, while in many Protestant Bibles they appear as an appendix to the Old Testament.

The additional books are sometimes called Deuterocanonicals. This term evokes the debate about their place in the biblical canon, and sets them in opposition to the "Protocanonical" or uncontested books contained in the Hebrew Bible. They are also known as the "Apocrypha," a term that means "hidden" or "secret." There is some connection with a passage in 2 Esdras/4 Ezra 14:45-46, which distinguishes between "the twenty-four books" (the traditional number of books constituting the Hebrew canon) and "the seventy that were written last" that are to be given to the wise among the people but "hidden" from others. Other books — 1 and 2 Esdras, Letter of Jeremiah, Prayer of Manasseh, and 3 and 4 Maccabees — are sometimes included among the Old Testament Apocrypha in English Bibles, though they are not regarded as canonical by either Catholics or Protestants. The biblical canons of the various Orthodox churches contain books over and above what is in the Roman Catholic canon.

In presenting the Old Testament Apocrypha, the NRSV divides the books into four categories according to their canonical status in the churches: (1) books that are in the Roman Catholic, Greek, and Slavonic Bibles — Tobit, Judith, Additions to Esther, Wisdom of Solomon, Ecclesiasticus/Sirach, Baruch, Letter of Jeremiah, Additions to Daniel, 1 Maccabees, and 2 Maccabees; (2) books in the Greek and Slavonic Bibles but not in the Roman Catholic canon — 1 Esdras, Prayer of Manasseh, Psalm 151, and 3 Maccabees; (3) a book in the Slavonic Bible and in the Latin Vulgate appendix — 2 Esdras; and (4) a book in an appendix to the Greek Bible — 4 Maccabees. I have observed this order in the chapters that follow.

The early manuscripts of the Greek Bible indicate that there was some fluidity regarding the status of the Old Testament Apocrypha. The fourth-century Sinai manuscript contains Tobit, Judith, 1 Maccabees, 4 Maccabees, Wisdom, and Sirach. The fourth-century Vatican manuscript does not include the Books of Maccabees. The fifth-century Alexandrian manuscript contains the seven "Deuterocanonicals" but also suggests that *Psalms of Solomon* belongs with the Scriptures.

4

In the Latin West, the position of the Old Testament Apocrypha within the canon of Scripture seems to have been firm from Tertullian (late second and early third centuries) onward. In the East, the lists of Old Testament books drawn up by Origen and Athanasius correspond to the Hebrew canon, but both authors used the Apocrypha in their writings. It was Jerome who in the late fourth century urged the restriction of the Old Testament canon to the books in the Hebrew Bible. He was the first to call these books the "Apocrypha." Even though he quoted from them and praised their content, he did not regard them as part of the canon and argued that they should not to be used in establishing doctrines.

Augustine emerged in the early fifth century as the defender of the wider canon including the seven Apocrypha, and various local councils followed him. In fact, they were simply endorsing what had become the general consensus in the Christian West and in large parts of the Christian East. This remained the basic situation up to the time of the Protestant Reformation. The wider canon was accepted. But the additional books made little doctrinal or practical difference. Although there may have been some resistance to these books, it became customary in Latin Bibles to include them and other books not held to be canonical at all (Prayer of Manasseh and 1 and 2 Esdras).

When the Reformers embraced the principle of *sola scriptura,* "Scripture alone," they also raised the question about what constitutes Sacred Scripture. Martin Luther had a particular doctrinal objection to 2 Maccabees 12:45-46, which was used as the biblical justification for purgatory and prayers on behalf of the dead and was thus involved in the controversy over indulgences. Luther criticized 2 Maccabees (and Esther) as containing "too much Judaism and pagan vice," and he urged the adoption of Jerome's principle of "Hebrew truth," which meant an Old Testament consisting of the books in the Hebrew canon. However, Luther did include the Apocrypha as an appendix in his 1534 German translation of the Bible. Thus Luther set the pattern for many Protestant Bibles throughout the centuries according to which the Apocrypha have been included in a separate section but not interspersed among the uncontested books.

In response to Luther and other Reformers, the Council of Trent in 1546 rejected Luther's distinction between "Hebrew truth" and the Apocrypha. It followed the tradition of the Latin Vulgate and adopted the wider canon that included the seven contested books. It produced a definitive list of Old Testament books, and its decree is followed in Catholic Bibles until this day.

The seven additional books included in the Catholic and Orthodox Old Testament are not very controversial today. They are read in Catholic churches as Scripture but receive no special prominence. Protestant Bible publishers have been returning to the custom of including these books, though placing them in a special section. Whether readers wish to regard them as canonical depends largely on theological tradition and personal decision. Their presence within the Bible does make some difference. Just as the presence of the New Testament books makes the Christian Bible different from the Jewish Bible, so the inclusion of these books makes a Catholic or Orthodox Bible different from a Protestant Bible. These differences should be acknowledged. But they need not be exaggerated or developed into matter for polemics as they have been in the past. The goal of this introduction is to help people to read and understand the books, not to argue a theological position.

Reading the Texts

The Old Testament Apocrypha are best read as the books of the Old and New Testaments are read — on the literary, historical, and theological levels.

Reading the Apocrypha as *literature* involves asking and answering the basic questions of literary criticism: What words and images are used? How does the text develop its subject matter (plot or structure)? In what form(s) is the material presented? What is the point? Once these basic questions are raised, there is ample room for pursuing each question in more depth in light of the approaches that have been developed in biblical studies in recent years (form criticism, redaction criticism, semiotics, semantics, structuralism, feminist hermeneutics, and so forth). Since the Old Testament Apocrypha have received relatively little scholarly attention, they are excellent resources for testing the validity and value of the "new" literary methods.

The books treated in this volume fall into two main categories: narratives and discourses. The narratives include Tobit, Judith, Additions to Esther, Additions to Daniel, 1 and 2 Maccabees, 1 Esdras, and 3 Maccabees. The discourses are Wisdom of Solomon, Ecclesiasticus/Sirach, Baruch, Letter of Jeremiah, Prayer of Manasseh, Psalm 151, 2 Esdras/4-6 Ezra, and 4 Maccabees. The narratives range from the generally sober historical account in 1 Maccabees to the highly imaginative stories (historical novels) in Judith and 3 Maccabees. The discourses include a wisdom instruction (Ecclesiasticus/Sirach), prophecies (Baruch), apocalypses (2 Esdras), prayers (Prayer of Manasseh and Psalm 151), and sermons or orations (Wisdom of Solomon, Letter of Jeremiah, and 4 Maccabees). It should also be noted that the narratives use discourse forms (dialogues, prayers, etc.), and the discourses use narrative forms (e.g., the catalogue of heroes in Sirach 44–50).

Reading the Apocrypha as *history* involves attention to their literary-historical setting and to the actual historical setting in which they were composed. It also demands a critical assessment of the historical value of the information that these books provide. The books treated in this volume purport to cover Israel's history from David and Solomon to the destruction of the Second Temple in the late first century C.E. A reading of these books according to their literary-historical order might proceed as follows: Psalm 151, Wisdom of Solomon, Prayer of Manasseh, Tobit, Letter of Jeremiah, Additions to Daniel, Esther, Baruch, 1 Esdras, 3 Maccabees, Ecclesiasticus/Sirach, 2 Maccabees, 4 Maccabees, 1 Maccabees, and 2 Esdras.

Most of these books, however, have very different (and later) historical origins from the situations that they portray. For example, the Wisdom of Solomon was surely composed in Greek at Alexandria in Egypt in the first century B.C.E., not by the historical King Solomon. The materials attributed to Ezra in 2 Esdras originated both in a Jewish setting in the late first century C.E. (4 Ezra) and in Christian circles in the second and third centuries C.E. (5 and 6 Ezra). The Prayer of Manasseh represents what that king should have said in a prayer of repentance rather than what he actually said. In other words, many of these books are pseudepigraphic; that is, written under the name of an ancient and revered figure in Israel's past.

Many of these books fall into the category of imaginative literature. There is surely some good historical information in 1 and 2 Maccabees, but even there one finds a mixture of different literary forms and a narrow lens through which the events are described (dynastic history, or temple propaganda). Other books such as Tobit, Judith, Esther, Additions to Daniel, and 3 Maccabees are best viewed as historical novels. They are stories set in a biblical context but provide little or no reliable historical information. In fact, the most valuable contribution of the Old Testament Apocrypha comes in the uses that they make of biblical traditions. They show us how biblical data, motifs, and ideas were taken up and developed by later writers between the third century B.C.E. and the late first century C.E. They contribute greatly to the effective history or history of the interpretation of the Old Testament.

Reading the Apocrypha as *theology* in this introduction means focusing on the mystery of suffering. This theological focus touches upon a universal human experience, and it naturally raises broader questions about God, the human condition, the meaning of human life and history, ethics, and so forth. I am not suggesting that suffering is the only topic of every book, or that their authors were somehow obsessed by suffering. Indeed, for the most part these books are confident and hopeful statements in which the sufferings of God's people are ended or averted or relativized in light of the mercy of an all-powerful and just God.

All of these books in one way or another deal with suffering, either in the case of individuals (as in Tobit) or in the collective sufferings of Israel as God's people. They all agree that the God of Israel is omnipotent and just (though 4 Ezra raises some questions). They all admit that Israel has sinned, and that its sufferings are just punishments for its sins. Then, however, these books begin to approach the problem of suffering in different ways, ways that derive for the most part from the Hebrew Scriptures and appear in another theological context in the New Testament.

In some cases (as in 2 Maccabees), the present sufferings of Israel are viewed as a divine discipline by which the merciful God educates and purifies his people. In many instances (e.g., Tobit, Judith, Esther, Daniel, Judas Maccabeus), the fidelity of key figures among God's people moves God to act on behalf of the people and to rescue them from danger. In some cases (Letter of Jeremiah, Baruch, 1 and 2 Esdras) the present sufferings — especially the destruction of Jerusalem and the exile — serve as a warning for Israel to return to the way of the Torah.

Several books (Wisdom of Solomon, 2 and 4 Maccabees, 4 Ezra) present life after death or the full coming of God's kingdom as the time when God's sovereignty and justice will be fully manifested, and when the wicked will be punished and the righteous will be rewarded. Four Maccabees develops the idea (raised in Isaiah 53 and 2 Maccabees 7) of the expiatory or atoning value of the martyrs' deaths on behalf of God's people. Their sacrifice makes possible a renewed Israel in which God's sovereignty and justice are manifest and God's Torah can be observed.

The chapters that follow treat the Old Testament Apocrypha on the literary, historical, and theological levels. They pay particular attention to literary structure and form, to historical setting and origin, and to theological significance viewed through the lens of the mystery of suffering.

8

For Further Study

Beckwith, Roger. *The Old Testament Canon of the New Testament Church and Its Background in Early Judaism.* Grand Rapids: Eerdmans, 1986.

Bruce, E. F. *The Canon of Scripture.* Downers Grove, Ill.: Inter-Varsity, 1988.

Campenhausen, Hans von. *The Formation of the Christian Bible.* Philadelphia: Fortress, 1972.

McDonald, Lee M. *The Formation of the Christian Biblical Canon.* Rev. ed. Peabody, Mass.: Hendrickson, 1995.

Metzger, Bruce M. *An Introduction to the Apocrypha.* New York: Oxford University Press, 1957; rev. ed., 1977.

Meurer, Siegfried, ed. *The Apocrypha in Ecumenical Perspective.* Reading, UK and New York: United Bible Societies, 1991.

Pfeiffer, Robert H. *A History of New Testament Times with an Introduction to Apocrypha.* New York: Harper, 1949.

Sundberg, A. C. *The Old Testament in the Early Church.* Cambridge, Mass.: Harvard University Press, 1964.

For each part in each book of the Old Testament Apocrypha, the following volume presents the Greek (or Latin for 2 Esdras) text along with seven English translations:

Kohlenberger, J. R., ed. *The Parallel Apocrypha.* New York and Oxford: Oxford University Press, 1997.

Many English Bible editions come with introductions and notes for many of the books treated in this volume. Also, the following collections provide good expositions of all or some of the books:

Bergant, Diane, and Robert J. Karris, eds. *The Collegeville Bible Commentary.* Collegeville, Minn.: Liturgical Press, 1989.

Brown, Raymond E., Joseph A. Fitzmyer, and Roland E. Murphy, eds. *The New Jerome Biblical Commentary.* Englewood Cliffs, N.J.: Prentice-Hall, 1990.

Charles, Robert H., ed. *The Apocrypha and Pseudepigrapha of the Old Testament.* 2 vols. Oxford: Clarendon Press, 1913.

Charlesworth, James H., ed. *The Old Testament Pseudepigrapha.* 2 vols. Garden City, N.Y.: Doubleday, 1983-85.

Farmer, William R., ed. *The International Bible Commentary.* Collegeville, Minn.: Liturgical Press, 1998.

Mays, James L., ed. *Harper's Bible Commentary.* Rev. ed. San Francisco: HarperCollins, 1999.

The New Interpreter's Bible. Nashville: Abingdon, 1994-.

CHAPTER 2

Tobit: We Are Family

Basic Information

The book of Tobit is a good story with an edifying purpose. The plot of the story begins with the tribulations of two righteous persons — Tobit and Sarah (chaps. 1–3). Their stories come together through the journey of Tobias and Raphael (chaps. 4–6), which issues in the wedding of Sarah and Tobias (chaps. 6–9) and the healing of Tobit from his blindness (chaps. 10–11). The story ends with Raphael's revelation, Tobit's hymn, and his last testament (chaps. 12–14).

Central to the plot is the motif of a quest — the journey to a far country in search of Tobit's money, a bride for Tobias, and healing for both Sarah and Tobit — and the return home. The plot proceeds with a subtle shifting of scenes from one place to another (see 3:7; 3:16; 4:1; 10:1; 10:7b; 11:1).

The characters are well defined. Rather than focusing on a single hero, the author makes both Tobit and Tobias the centers of attention, while developing Tobit's wife Anna, Tobias's companion Azariah/Raphael, Sarah's parents Raguel and Edna, and Sarah (though her only words are "Amen, Amen" in 8:8). The trials and tribulations of these attractive characters elicit the reader's sympathy and concern.

The plight of Tobit is narrated in 1:3–3:6 in the first person singular ("I"), while the rest of the story proceeds from the third person ("he" or "she" or "they") perspective of a narrator. In almost every case the story moves forward by means of dialogues between the characters. There are prayers at decisive points (3:1-6; 3:11-15; 8:5-7; 8:15-17; 11:14-15; 13:1-17), along with instructions or testaments (4:1-21; 12:6-20; 14:3-11). The narrative is enhanced by several beautifully drawn and touching scenes: the quarrel between Tobit and Anna (2:11-14), Raguel's plan to bury Tobias in expectation of his death (8:9-14), the anxiety of Tobit and Anna as they await Tobias's return (10:1-7a), and the joyful surprise of Tobit and Tobias when they learn that Azariah is the angel Raphael (12:21-22).

There is ample use of irony — the device by which the narrator and the reader share information (for example, that Azariah is the angel Raphael) that the characters do not possess. And there are curious details that catch the reader's attention and contribute to the mystery: the bird droppings that lead to Tobit's blindness (2:10), the alleged medicinal properties of fish innards (6:5-9), the dog that accompanies Tobias and Raphael (6:2; 11:4), and the demon Asmodeus that kills Sarah's seven husbands (3:8; 6:14-15).

The edifying purpose is achieved in large part through the artistry of the plot, the characterization, and the literary forms. The book of Tobit tells the stories of two families of Diaspora Jews who suffer greatly on account of and despite their righteousness. In the end they all are fully vindicated and unite to form a single family. The plot and the characters make the religious values of the book of Deuteronomy come alive, and promote "family values" in the best sense.

The book presents itself as the memoir of Tobit and his son Tobias. According to 12:20 the angel Raphael instructed them to "write down all these things that have happened to you." The events narrated in the book are set in the late eighth and early seventh centuries B.C.E. Tobit and Tobias belong to the community of exiles from the northern kingdom of Israel then living in Nineveh, the capital of the Assyrian empire.

It is unlikely, however, that this literary scenario reflects the historical origin of the book. The end of the book (14:11b-15) narrates the deaths of both Tobit and Tobias. The sequence of Assyrian kings is incomplete and inaccurate (no mentions of Tiglath-pileser III and Sargon II), and the geographical information is sometimes confused. The book is best understood not as a memoir but rather as a historical novel set in the distant past. It was probably composed by a Jewish author in the third or second century B.C.E. It may have been written in the Land of Israel, in Egypt, or in the eastern Diaspora (Syria or Mesopotamia). In any case, it illustrates how Jews living in the Diaspora can

11

remain faithful (against all odds) to the ideals presented in the book of Deuteronomy.

The principal text of the book of Tobit throughout the centuries has been the Greek version. But there are two Greek versions. One is a short text represented by the Alexandrian and Vatican manuscripts, and the other is a longer text represented by the Sinai manuscript. Although the basic story is the same in both versions, there are so many differences in detail that it is difficult to speak about *the text* of Tobit. The NRSV has followed the lead of most scholars today in taking the longer version in the Sinai manuscript as its base text.

There had long been general agreement among scholars that Tobit was originally composed not in Greek but in a Semitic language, either Aramaic or Hebrew. The Qumran library has yielded five fragmentary manuscripts of the work, four in Aramaic and one in Hebrew. The Qumran discoveries are very important, though they do not solve all the problems. These discoveries affirm the integrity of the book, since there are texts from almost every chapter, including chapters 13 and 14 (which some suspected as having been added on later). They establish a date of composition before 100 B.C.E. and support the superiority of the longer Greek text found in the Sinai manuscript. They establish the likelihood of a Semitic original, more likely Aramaic than Hebrew. They show that there were versions in both Aramaic and Hebrew at an early date, and that the work was popular at Qumran (since it was preserved in five copies) even though there is nothing distinctively sectarian in it.

The story of Tobit and Tobias is set in the eastern Diaspora in the late eighth and early seventh centuries B.C.E. It is very much a biblical story in the sense that it reflects the theological program of the book of Deuteronomy, especially its emphases on reward for righteous actions and on the Jerusalem temple as the central shrine for all Israel. The setting reflects events narrated in the books of Kings, and there are references to Nahum and other prophets. The plight of Tobit echoes that of Job, especially in the portrayal of Tobit's wife. And there are many wisdom elements in the book. The Hebrew Bible is the book's principal source.

In addition to the Hebrew Bible, the author probably drew on the story or motif of "the grateful dead." What initially got Tobit into trouble was his zeal in seeing to the burial of fellow Israelites. He first loses all his property (see 1:20) and then is struck blind after having attended to a burial at Pentecost (see 2:7-10). When Tobit is healed and Raphael reveals himself as the angel of God sent to heal him, a major reason was to repay Tobit's willingness to bury the dead (see 12:13). The plan of Tobit and Tobias to give Raphael half of their possessions contributes to this motif. Another likely source or motif is "the dangerous bride." Sarah's seven husbands are killed by a demon before they can consummate their marriages with her. The demon is reserving Sarah for himself. But when Tobias follows Raphael's instructions, the demon loses all power and flees to the farthest reaches of Egypt where he is bound by Raphael (see 8:3). Also the readers are presumed to have some familiarity with the story of Ahikar and his wicked nephew Nadab (see 1:22; 14:10).

Content

Part One: The Tribulations of Tobit and Sarah (1–3)

A. The *Description of Tobit* (1:1-15) introduces one of the main characters and provides the situation in which the plot will unfold. From the heading of the book (1:1-2) we learn who Tobit is (an Israelite from the tribe of Naphtali), when he lived (in the time of the Assyrian king Shalmaneser V, in the late eighth century B.C.E.), and where he lived (first in Galilee, and then in exile in Assyria).

From 1:3 to 3:6 Tobit speaks for himself ("I, Tobit"). He first affirms his dedication to "truth and righteousness" and to acts of charity on behalf of his fellow exiles in Nineveh (1:3). Then in 1:4-9 he reviews his life while he was still in the land of Israel. He remained dedicated to Jerusalem and its temple even when members of his own tribe had deserted it, made all the sacrifices and paid all the tithes there, and lived in accord with the law of Moses. He also provides personal information: his father was dead; he learned the Torah from his grandmother Deborah; he married a wife from within his tribe; and he had a son named Tobias. On all counts Tobit appears to be the model of biblical piety — dedicated to good works, observant of the Torah, and part of a good family. He is Deuteronomy incarnate.

When he went into exile, Tobit continued to walk in the way of Torah observance by refusing to eat "the food of the Gentiles" (1:11-12). In other words, he observed the Jewish food laws. As a result, God blessed Tobit, and he even became a buyer for King Shalmaneser. On one of his business trips to Media, Tobit deposited a large sum of money with

Gabael (1:14). When Shalmaneser was succeeded by Sennacherib and political conditions deteriorated, Tobit was unable to go to Media and claim his money (1:15).

The entire opening section (1:1-15), then, tells us who Tobit is and what kind of person he is, and sets up the basic elements — exile to Nineveh, a change of rulers, and a sum of money rendered inaccessible — that serve to get the story started.

B. *Burying the Dead* (1:16–2:10) is one of Tobit's good works and one of the major themes in the book. But ironically this good work will cause Tobit great suffering. The beginning of Tobit's story stretches over the reigns of three kings: Shalmaneser (1:16-17), Sennacherib (1:18-20), and Esarhaddon (1:21-22). Because he found favor with Shalmaneser, Tobit could freely do good works for his fellow Israelites in exile, especially by burying their dead bodies. However, Sennacherib, frustrated at his inability to capture Jerusalem and angry at the great losses suffered by his army there (see 2 Kings 19 and Isaiah 37), began to kill Israelites at Nineveh and left them unburied as a sign of his hatred. Nevertheless, Tobit continued to bury the dead until someone informed on him. And so on account of his good work, Tobit had to flee Nineveh and lost all his property. Under Esarhaddon, Tobit's good fortune returned, especially through the intercession of his nephew Ahikar. The narrative thus far establishes Tobit's courage in burying the dead and the dangers associated with it.

These general themes are made concrete at the festival of Pentecost (2:1-10). Restored to his family and household, Tobit prepares to enjoy a holiday meal. Ever the model of biblical piety, he instructs his son Tobias to search for poor Israelites to share the banquet with him (2:2). When Tobias reports that he found the corpse of an Israelite thrown into the marketplace, Tobit arises and immediately tends to the dead body (2:3-4). This sad discovery serves as a reminder of the sufferings of God's people in exile, a mood captured by the quotation of Amos 8:10: "Your festivals shall be turned into mourning, and all your songs into lamentation."

When at sunset Tobit completes the burial, his neighbors express amazement at his fidelity to the task of burying the dead (2:7-8). Again Tobit's piety leads to personal suffering. After the burial, Tobit decides to sleep outside in the courtyard, perhaps to avoid waking the household, or perhaps to avoid imparting to it the ritual defilement incurred by contact with a corpse. When bird droppings come into his eyes, Tobit becomes blind and no medical solutions can be found to help him. And when his nephew Ahikar is transferred, Tobit is left alone with his son Tobias and his wife Anna (2:9-10).

C. The *Plight of Tobit* (2:11–3:6) is expressed in his angry confrontation with Anna (2:11-14) and his prayer to die (3:1-6). Anna had become the support of the family by doing "women's work" — probably weaving cloth at home. When her customers gave her a goat as a bonus, the blind Tobit assumed that it was stolen and demanded that she return it. She in turn lost patience with Tobit and asked: "Where are your acts of charity? Where are your righteous deeds?" (2:14). The model family is disintegrating, and the model of piety is reduced to making false accusations against a devoted wife.

Tobit's first-person narrative ends with a prayer that expresses the depth of his despair. He begins in 3:2 by praising the justice and mercy of God, despite his experience of suffering for having performed charitable deeds. Next in 3:3-5 he asks God to remember him and help him, and not to hold against him his sins and those of his people. Then in 3:6 he asks God to release him from his suffering by letting him die. In death he expects to become "dust" and to go to "the eternal home" (Sheol, the abode of the dead). Whatever hope for eternal life here is shadowy. For Tobit, death is preferable to his present life of misery. The pious Tobit had done all the right things and shown special courage in burying the dead. And yet he lost his property, lost his sight, and falsely accused his wife of stealing. From these experiences Tobit concludes that "it is better for me to die" (3:6).

D. The *Plight of Sarah* (3:7-15) parallels the plight of Tobit. She is righteous and innocent. She suffers greatly through the death of her seven husbands. She endures reproaches from her maid. And all she has left is prayer.

Sarah's plight is exactly contemporaneous with that of Tobit ("on the same day"). Tobit's first-person narration is dropped, and the narrator tells Sarah's story in the third person ("she"). In 3:7 we learn who Sarah is (the daughter of Raguel), when she lived (in Tobit's day), and where she lived (at Ecbatana in Media). Her plight is summarized in 3:8a: "She had been married to seven husbands, and the wicked demon Asmodeus had killed each of them before they had been with her as is customary for wives."

Sarah's sufferings are expressed in three forms of speech: conversation with a maid (3:8b-9), monologue (3:10), and prayer to God (3:11-15). In the conversation, the maid accuses Sarah of killing her husbands and of taking out her frustrations on the maids. In the monologue, Sarah contemplates suicide but decides against it because it would add to her father's sufferings. Like Tobit, she determines as a last resort to "pray the Lord that I may die" (3:10). In her prayer Sarah addresses God with respect (3:11b-12), asks to die (3:13), and proclaims her innocence and describes her sufferings (3:14-15). The final sentence in her prayer, however, offers God a choice: "But if it is not pleasing to you, O Lord, to take my life, hear me in my disgrace" (3:15). The prayer suggests that there may be a better way for Sarah (and Tobit) than to die. That better way is subject of the rest of the book.

E. The *Divine Decree* (3:16-17) brings together the two stories and indicates that God will solve the problems of both Tobit and Sarah. The instrument will be the angel Raphael, whose name means "God has healed." The human character who will link everyone together is Tobias, the son of Tobit. Through them Tobit will be healed from blindness and Sarah will get a loving husband. What joins the two plots is prayer offered by the two righteous sufferers "at the same time."

Part Two: The Journey (4–6)

A. The *First Testament of Tobit* (4:1-21) is occasioned by his prayer to die (see 3:6) and by his desire to provide for his family by having Tobias retrieve the money deposited with Gabael in Media (see 1:14). A testament is a farewell discourse delivered by someone who is about to die and wishes to impart guidance and advice to his family or followers (see Genesis 48–49, Joshua 22–24, and John 17 for some biblical examples). There is a second testament from Tobit in 14:3-11 and another testament from Raphael in 12:6-20. While much of the content here is general advice, it is directed to Tobias, who expects soon to bury his father and must first make the journey to retrieve the money.

The major topics in Tobit's first testament are burying one's parents and tending to their needs in their old age (4:3-4), living a righteous life before God and others (4:5-6a), practicing almsgiving toward the righteous poor (4:6b-11), marrying within the people of Israel and so avoiding "fornication" (4:12-13), practicing justice and temperance (4:14-15), giving alms to the righteous poor (4:16-17), and seeking advice from wise persons and from God (4:18-19). The testament concludes by defining true wealth as "fear(ing) God and flee(ing) from every sin and do(ing) what is good in the sight of the Lord your God" (4:21). One of the recurrent themes in Tobit's testament is that righteous behavior will enable one to prosper (4:6, 19) and serve as a protection in times of trouble (4:9). The emphasis on giving alms to the righteous poor and marrying within the people of Israel would be appropriate to those living outside the land of Israel. Perhaps the most famous sentence comes in 4:15: "And what you hate, do not do to anyone" — a negative version of what is commonly called the Golden Rule (see Matt. 7:12; Luke 6:31).

The first testament of Tobit functions as a pause or "time out." It has the effect of slowing the momentum of the plots developed in the first three chapters and placing the stories in a sapiential or ethical context.

B. The *Preparation for the Journey* (5:1–6:1) takes the form of a series of dialogues. Having heard Tobit's first testament, Tobias raises two questions in 5:1-2: How can he get the money from someone he does not know? and How can he journey to Rages in Media if he does not know the way? In 5:3 Tobit explains that he and Gabael each have two halves of two receipts which can be exchanged and matched, and that they will hire a guide ("a trustworthy man") for Tobias.

The guide turns out to be the angel Raphael (5:4) — something that the readers know from the narrator but the major characters learn only at the end of the story (chap. 12). When Tobias inquires of the guide, he is told that the guide is an Israelite who has traveled often to Rages in Media and stayed "with our kinsman Gabael." There are two problems here, one ethical and the other geographical. The ethical problem, of course, is that the guide is not an Israelite but an angel. The geographical problem is that Rages is a ten-days' journey from Ecbatana, and that Ecbatana is not in the mountains. When Tobias asks to check things out with Tobit, Raphael tells him to be quick about it (5:8), thereby suggesting a certain superiority to Tobias.

When Tobias brings Raphael to Tobit for an interview (5:9-17a), Raphael disturbs Tobit with his greeting ("joyous greetings to you!") and elicits from Tobit a complaint about his blindness. Raphael, however, assures him that "the time is near for God to heal you" (5:10). The mysterious stranger tells Tobit that his name is Azariah ("the Lord has helped") and that he is the son of Hananiah ("the Lord is merciful"). He comes from a family of Israelites who (like Tobit) worshiped at the Jerusalem temple. This information satisfies Tobit, and he agrees to hire Raphael as guide for his son Tobias.

The departure of Tobias and Raphael (5:17b–6:1) elicits different reactions from Tobit and his wife Anna. In 5:17b Tobit wishes them a safe journey and prays that God's angel may accompany them — a wonderful piece of irony, since God's angel Raphael will accompany Tobias. Anna, however, criticizes Tobit for sending Tobias after the money (5:18–6:1), since Tobias is "the staff of our hand" and she would rather lose the money than lose her only child. Tobit comforts her with the assurance that "a good angel will accompany him" (5:22) — another wonderful piece of irony.

C. The *Journey to Ecbatana* (6:1b-18) proceeds in three stages, and prepares for both the successful marriage of Sarah and the healing of Tobit's blindness. In the first stage (6:1b-6a) Tobias and Raphael reach the Tigris River. They are accompanied by a dog — a peculiar feature since in ancient Near Eastern cultures dogs were not pets ("man's best friend") but rather were regarded as scavengers. When at the Tigris a large fish jumps out and tries to swallow Tobias's foot, Raphael instructs Tobias to catch the fish and to cut out its gall, heart, and liver for medicine and to keep the rest for food. This providential event provides the means by which both Sarah and Tobit will find healing.

In the second stage (6:6b-9) the two travelers approach Media. Here Raphael explains the medicinal properties of the fish innards. The smoke from the burning heart and liver will chase away the demon (in the case of Sarah), and the gall will clear up blindness (in the case of Tobit). It is not clear that Tobias yet fully appreciates this information, but he will come to understand it as the story unfolds.

In the third stage (6:10-18) the travelers draw near to Ecbatana, and Raphael suggests that they spend the night with Raguel, the father of Sarah. He reminds Tobias that since he is the closest surviving male relative of Sarah, he has "a hereditary claim on her" to take her as his wife (see Deut. 25:5-10). The idea behind this law was to keep the widow and the property within the family. And so Raphael volunteers to arrange the marriage between Tobias and Sarah with her father Raguel. Tobias, however, knows what has happened to Sarah's seven previous husbands (6:14-15). He has heard that a demon kills anyone who approaches Sarah — presumably because the demon loves her and wants her for himself. Tobias's chief concern is not for himself but for his parents, since he is their only child and there would be no one to bury them if he were to die. In 6:16-18 Raphael reminds Tobias about his father's instructions to marry within the family (see 4:12-13) and assures him that the smoke given off by the burning liver and heart of the fish will drive away the demon. But Tobias and Sarah must pray for divine protection. Because it is God's will that Sarah be Tobias's wife ("she was set apart for you before the world was made"), all will turn out well. Reassured by the angel, Tobit falls in love with Sarah ("his heart was drawn to her").

Part Three: The Marriage of Sarah and Tobias (7–9)

A. The *Marriage* (7:1-17) takes place when Tobias and Raphael arrive at Raguel's house in Ecbatana. The story of the arrival (7:1-9a) takes the form of a recognition scene. Raguel immediately notices a strong resemblance between Tobias and his kinsman Tobit. When his wife Edna makes inquiries, she learns that the travelers are Israelites from Naphtali who live in Nineveh, that they know Tobit, and that Tobit is in good health. Then Tobias reveals that Tobit is his father (7:5), and they all weep over Tobit's blindness (thus foreshadowing his eventual healing). With this recognition scene the two plots, already linked in heaven (see 3:16-17), are now linked in the earthly realm.

The story of the marriage between Tobias and Sarah (7:9b-17) is told through a series of conversations. First Tobias asks Azariah/Raphael to ask Raguel to give him Sarah in marriage (7:9b). But Raguel tries to slow down the process ("eat and drink") and explains what has happened to the seven men who had already taken Sarah as a wife (7:10-11a). When Tobias insists that the marriage go forward, Raguel admits that Tobias has the only valid legal claim to Sarah (see Deut. 25:5-10), and declares them husband and wife: "from now on you are her brother and she is your sister. She is given to you from today and forever" (7:11). Next Raguel summons Sarah and gives her to Tobias ("take her to be your wife"), and draws up a marriage contract (7:12-13). Only then do they all eat and drink (7:14). Finally in 7:15-17 Raguel directs Edna to have the bridal chamber made ready, and Edna in turn weeps at the prospect of still another husband dying. All Edna can do is to encourage Sarah and to pray on her behalf. By developing the plot with the help of these conversations, the author makes vivid the personal involvement of the various characters.

B. The *Wedding Night* (8:1-21) justifies the faith shown by Tobias and Sarah. When they enter the bridal chamber (8:1-3), Tobias burns the fish's liver and heart, and the smoke drives the demon "to the remotest parts of Egypt" where Raphael goes and binds him, thus rendering the demon powerless. Through the power of God's angel the demon is easily defeated, and the way is clear for Tobias and Sarah to enjoy a safe and happy marriage.

Before consummating their marriage, Tobias and Sarah arise to offer a prayer (8:4-8). After blessing the God of Israel as the creator, Tobias recalls Adam and Eve as the first parents of us all (see Genesis 2) and proclaims the purity of his love for Sarah ("not because of lust but with sincerity"). His petition is, "Grant that she and I may find mercy and that we may grow old together." Both Tobias and Sarah seal the prayer with "Amen, Amen" — the only words that Sarah speaks in the entire book.

Meanwhile, Raguel expects the worst (8:9-14), and so he orders that a grave be dug for Tobias and that he be buried as quickly as possible lest the family experience even more shame. But when he sends a maid to ascertain what has happened to Tobias, she declares to everyone's surprise that Tobias is alive and that nothing is wrong. This happy and unexpected information elicits a benediction from Raguel in 8:15-17 in which he blesses God repeatedly for his mercy toward the newlyweds and prays that God continue to show mercy to them throughout their lives together.

So elated is Raguel that he has a huge wedding feast prepared (8:19-21). Whereas most weddings were celebrated for seven days, Raguel insists that Tobias stay with Sarah at his house for fourteen days. Whereas it was customary for the bride's father to provide a dowry for his daughter, Raguel promises to give to Tobias "half of what I own" now and the rest when he and Edna die. The two families have become one, and all of Raguel's possessions belong to Tobias. The successful marriage of the two only children has formed one happy family; as Raguel says to Tobias: "We belong to you as well as to your wife now and forever" (8:21).

C. The *Recovery of the Money* (9:1-6) is carried out by Azariah/Raphael. Since Tobias must stay at the wedding celebration for fourteen days and since he does not want to contribute further to his parents' anxiety by delaying his return home, he asks his guide/companion to go to Gabael in Rages and to bring the money and Gabael to the wedding feast at Ecbatana (9:1-4). Raphael carries out the mission successfully by giving Gabael the receipt and inviting him to the wedding feast (9:5). When Gabael meets Tobias (9:6), he too asks God's blessing on Tobias and Sarah, and declares: "Blessed be God, for I see in Tobias the very image of my cousin Tobit." The journey has achieved goals beyond what Tobit and Tobias imagined. Not only was the money retrieved, but Sarah has been rescued from the demon, Tobias has found a bride within the people of

Israel, and they have obtained the means by which Tobit's blindness will be healed.

Part Four: The Healing of Tobit's Blindness (10–11)

A. *Preparations for Tobias's Return* (10:1-13) are narrated in two scenes, one at Nineveh featuring Tobit and Anna (10:1-7a), and the other at Ecbatana featuring Tobias and Raguel with his family (10:7b-13). The scene in Nineveh consists of very realistic dialogue between parents worried about the delay in their only son's return home. Having counted the days that Tobias's trip should have taken, Tobit speculates that Tobias had been detained for some reason, or even that Gabael had died and so the money could not be retrieved (10:1-2). Anna, however, imagines an even more drastic fate ("my child has perished") and blames herself for allowing Tobias to go at all (10:3-5). When Tobit tries to reassure her that all will turn out well, Anna refuses his comfort and grows more fixed in her conviction that "my child has perished" (10:6-7a). The first scene ends with the touching picture of Anna going to the roadside every day to wait for her son, and coming back every evening to spend the night in tears of disappointment.

The second scene (10:7b-13) takes place in Ecbatana. Here as elsewhere in the book, the plot moves forward by means of dialogues. At the end of the fourteen days of wedding celebration, Tobias asks Raguel's permission to return home, and after some resistance ("stay with me") he receives it (10:7b-9). The departure scene in 10:10-13 is full of emotion. After giving Tobias half of his possessions as he promised, Raguel wishes him a safe journey, a prosperous life, and children from his wife Sarah. And he instructs Sarah to regard Tobit and Anna as if they were her own parents. Edna in turn wishes Tobias the same blessing as Raguel did, and asks him to take good care of her daughter. Finally Tobias blesses Raguel and Edna, and pledges that God has commanded him "to honor you all the days of my life" (10:13). The scene brings together the ideals of family piety and the intense human emotions involved in the departure of loved ones.

B. In immediate preparation for the *Healing of Tobit* (11:1-18) the scene shifts back to Nineveh. As the travelers draw near to Nineveh (11:1-4), Raphael suggests to Tobias that they go ahead of the party and tells him to have the fish gall ready. Again the mysterious dog makes an ap-

21

pearance (see 6:2). Meanwhile Anna continues her vigil by the roadside (11:5-6). When she finally sees Tobias, she calls out to Tobit: "Look, your son is coming, and the man who went with him!" The blind Tobit cannot see them and can learn about their return only from Anna. Again in 11:7-8 Raphael expresses full confidence that Tobit will see again ("I know that his eyes will be opened") and instructs Tobias on how to apply the fish gall to his father's eyes. There seems to be more emphasis on the medicinal properties of the fish gall than on whatever magical value it might have had. In 11:9-10 the family members come together. Anna embraces her son Tobias. When Tobit stumbles out of the house, Tobias runs up to him with the fish gall.

The healing (11:11-15a) is described as both a medical procedure and a miracle. Tobias blows into Tobit's eyes, applies the fish gall to them, and peals off the white films. The healing is instantaneous and complete ("I see you, my son, the light of my eyes"), and it elicits from Tobit a benediction ("Blessed be God") for the mercy shown to him in letting him see Tobias again.

When Tobit learns about the success of Tobias's journey and that his new daughter-in-law Sarah will soon arrive in Nineveh, he goes out to the city gate to meet her (11:15b-18). The people see Tobit walking without assistance and are amazed that he can see. Tobit ascribes the healing to God ("God has been merciful to me"), greets Sarah with great enthusiasm, and welcomes her into his home ("Come in, my daughter, and welcome"). Tobias's return with Sarah his bride and Tobit's healing provide the occasion for all the Jews of Nineveh to rejoice. Their number includes Ahikar and his nephew (see 1:22 and 14:10). They all celebrate Tobias's wedding for seven days.

Part Five: Conclusion (12–14)

A. *Raphael's Revelation* (12:1-22) takes place at the end of the wedding celebration in Nineveh. The occasion is the decision by Tobit and Tobias to pay Azariah/Raphael half of all that had been brought back from Gabael and Raguel — a most generous offer. The reason for their generosity is stated by Tobias: "For he has led me back to you safely, he cured my wife, he brought the money back with me, and he healed you" (12:3).

Rather than accepting a salary, Raphael in 12:6-15 offers a testament to Tobit and Tobias. He urges them to bless God and recount God's deeds to all peoples (12:6-7), and to practice almsgiving (12:8-10). Then he reveals himself as an angel: "I am Raphael, one of the seven angels who stand ready and enter before the glory of the Lord" (12:15). He explains that it was the prayers of Tobit and Sarah, as well as Tobit's fidelity in burying the dead, that prompted God to send Raphael among them and bring them healing.

Raphael's self-revelation as an angel leads to his departure (12:16-22). Tobit and Tobias are stunned by the revelation, but Raphael tells them not to be afraid and to bless God each day. Next he explains that "what you saw was a vision" and that as an angel Raphael really did not eat or drink anything. Then he announces that he is "ascending to him who sent me" and tells Tobit and Tobias to write down what happened to them. The ascension of Raphael inspires them to continue praising God, which sets the stage for Tobit's long thanksgiving in chapter 13.

B. *Tobit's Hymn* (13:1-17) consists of a call to praise God and an address to Jerusalem as the city of God. The call in 13:1-8 alternates between commands to praise God ("blessed be God . . . acknowledge him . . . exalt him . . . see what he has done . . . acknowledge . . . bless and exalt") and reasons for doing so ("because . . . for . . . for . . . because"). Tobit first celebrates the kingly rule of God and God's power over life and death, and finds even in Israel's exile a display of God's greatness. Then he develops the idea that, even though God punishes Israel for its sins, God will gather the people from exile provided it turns to God ("If you turn to him with all your heart and with all your soul"). Thus he expresses the classical theology of sin, exile, repentance, and return promoted in the book of Deuteronomy. In 13:6b-7 Tobit begins to speak in the first person singular: "In the land of my exile I acknowledge him. . . . As for me I exalt my God." Tobit becomes an example or paradigm for Israel's experience in exile and for its hopes regarding what God might do for it.

The *Address to Jerusalem* (13:9-17) applies the Deuteronomic pattern to the temple city. Afflicted for its sins, Jerusalem will return to glory if it acknowledges the Lord. Then it will witness the exiles returning to it (13:9-10). Two descriptions of the splendor of the New Jerusalem (13:11 and 13:16b-17) flank a series of curses and blessings (13:12-16a). The first picture (13:11) calls the New Jerusalem a "bright light" and focuses on all the nations converging on it and on the eternal existence of the restored city. The curses are directed at those who conquered and destroyed the Old Jerusalem, while the beatitudes are reserved for those who love the New Jerusalem and rejoice in its prosperity. The second picture

(13:16b-17) develops the theme of the splendor of the restored Jerusalem with reference to its precious stones and music in praise of God (see Isa. 54:11-12; 60:1-14). The idea of Jerusalem as Israel's central and only shrine is a major theme in Deuteronomy. After the first temple's destruction in 587 B.C.E. there were hopes for a new and even better temple and city.

C. The *Second Testament of Tobit* (14:1-11a) is given just before his death. This righteous man has fulfilled the Deuteronomic ideal by dying in peace and prosperity, at the very old age of 112, and surrounded by his sons and seven grandsons (14:2-3a). In his final testament he looks into the future and warns Tobias and his family to flee to Media because what the prophets said not only about Nineveh and Assyria but also about Samaria and Jerusalem will come to pass (14:3b-5). But God will bring the people back to Jerusalem where they will rebuild the temple, which will attract in turn all the nations (14:6-7; see the poetic version in 13:9-17).

In the second part of his testament (14:8-11) Tobit restates the ideal promoted throughout the book ("to do what is right and to give alms") and warns Tobias to leave Nineveh as soon as he buries his mother Anna. The problem is that there is much wickedness and deceit in Nineveh. Then in 14:10 Tobit cites the example of Ahikar to illustrate the value of almsgiving and righteous behavior. His nephew Nadab had arranged for Ahikar to be executed. But because Ahikar had previously helped out his prospective executioner, he managed to stay alive in hiding. When the king wished again for Ahikar's counsel, he came out of hiding and took his rightful place at the royal court while Nadab was executed for his evil deeds. The moral of this story and of the whole book is, "See what almsgiving accomplishes, and what injustice does — it brings death!" (14:11a).

D. *The End* (14:11b-15) recounts the happy deaths of the main characters in the story: Tobit and Anna (14:11b-12a), Raguel and Edna (14:12b-13), and Tobias (14:14). It also notes in 14:15 that Tobias lived to hear about Nineveh's destruction in 612 B.C.E. in accord with Nahum's prophecy (see 14:4).

Significance

The characters in the book of Tobit are attractive models of biblical piety. Their story is so skillfully told that readers enter into their tribulations and rejoice at their vindication, while knowing from 3:16-17 the divine decree that Tobit will see again and Sarah will find in Tobias a fine husband. The will of God works through the angel Raphael, good people, and even fish innards. The book affirms that the law of retribution — the righteous are rewarded, and the wicked are punished — applies in this life (despite trials and tribulations), not simply after death as in the book of Wisdom. It also affirms the Jerusalem temple as the central shrine for Israelites of the Northern Kingdom like Tobit (1:14) and for Jews living in the Diaspora (13:9-17). The book is in many respects the narrative embodiment of the values of Deuteronomy.

Issues. The recognition of the longer Greek text (the Sinai manuscript) as superior and the discovery of five fragmentary Semitic manuscripts (four in Aramaic, and one in Hebrew) at Qumran have greatly clarified textual issues, without solving all the problems. How the various texts agree and differ can be seen in Moore's commentary listed in the Suggestions for Further Study.

Attention to the artistry with which the story is told — plot, characters, and use of literary forms — has led to an appreciation of the author's literary sophistication (see also Judith and Esther). The author's skill in blending biblical materials (especially Deuteronomy) with the motifs of the grateful dead and the poisonous bride as well as the story of Ahikar provides evidence for Jewish openness to, and self-confidence about, the world beyond Judaism.

The chief theological problem raised by the book of Tobit is the affirmation that the law of retribution applies in this life. It does, of course, for Tobit and Sarah. But it is not always the case that righteous people are vindicated and rewarded in their lifetimes (as Wisdom 1–5 makes clear). And there is also the prior question why Tobit suffers blindness after performing good deeds and why Sarah lost seven husbands to the demon Asmodeus. The book of Tobit provides a "happy ending." But the reasons for the sufferings of the righteous and the nature of their vindication remain problematic.

Influence. The five copies at Qumran (in two different Semitic languages), the different editions of the Greek text, and the translations into other languages indicate the popularity of the work in antiquity. The *Testament of Solomon* contains a dialogue between Solomon and the demon Asmodeus (5:1-13) that depends on the stories of Sarah and Raphael in the book of Tobit. The emphasis on charity and burial of the dead in the *Testament of Job* (39–40; 53:5-7) may reflect the influence of the book.

25

There are also imaginative medieval Jewish adaptations and expansions of the Tobit story in Aramaic and Hebrew.

The most famous parallel to the New Testament comes in Tobit's first testament: "And what you hate, do not do to anyone" (4:15) — a negative version of the Golden Rule (see Matt. 7:12; Luke 6:31). The case brought to Jesus by the Sadducees about resurrection (Mark 12:18-27; Matt. 22:23-33; Luke 20:27-38) concerns a woman who had seven husbands and kept marrying on the basis of Deuteronomy 25:5-10 — a situation very like that of Sarah. The frequent use of "brother" and "sister" for persons not belonging to the same immediate family but rather to an extended family is often cited in the discussions about the family of Jesus (see Mark 3:20-21, 31-35; 6:1-6). And the scene of Raphael's self-revelation and departure ("I am ascending to him who sent me") in chapter 12 contains features found in the New Testament accounts of Jesus' transfiguration and of his post-resurrection appearances and ascension.

The book of Tobit is part of the Roman Catholic, Orthodox, and Slavonic canons of Holy Scripture.

Suggestions for Further Study

Moore, Carey A. *Tobit: A New Translation with Introduction and Commentary.* Anchor Bible 40A. New York: Doubleday, 1996.

Wills, Lawrence M. *The Jewish Novel in the Ancient World.* Ithaca, N.Y.: Cornell University Press, 1995.

Zimmermann, Frank. *The Book of Tobit.* New York: Harper, 1958.

For comprehensive bibliographies on Tobit and the other books treated in this volume, see

Lehnardt, Andreas. *Bibliographie zu den Jüdischen Schriften aus hellenistisch-römischer Zeit.* Gütersloh: Gütersloher Verlagshaus, 1999.

CHAPTER 3

Judith: By the Hand of a Woman

Basic Information

The book of Judith is another good story with an edifying purpose. It tells how Judith — whose name means "Jewish woman" — defeated the enemies of Israel by her beauty and by her hand. The recurrent motif in the book is "by the hand of a woman." Of course, the credit for Israel's victory belongs to God. But the hand of Judith was the instrument that God chose to save the people from destruction and the Jerusalem temple from defilement.

The plot begins in 1:1–2:13 with successful campaigns by Nebuchadnezzar (the Babylonian king who is erroneously identified as an Assyrian residing in Nineveh) and his commission to the general Holofernes (probably a Persian name). Holofernes is ordered to conquer those nations — including Israel — that refused to become allies of Nebuchadnezzar. Next the description of the threat posed by Holofernes' army to the city of Bethulia (otherwise unknown) and to the Jerusalem temple (2:14–7:32) proceeds according to a chiastic outline: A — the campaign of Holofernes against Israel's neighbors (2:14–3:10), B — the response of Israel (4:1-15), C — Achior's report to Holofernes (5:1–6:11), C′ — Achior's report to Israel (6:12-21), B′ — the response of Israel (7:1-5), and A′ — the campaign of Holofernes against Israel (7:6-32). Then the story of how God saved Israel through the hand of Judith (8:1–16:25) is told with another chiastic outline: A — Judith (8:1-8), B — Judith's plan to save Israel (8:9–10:8), C —

Judith's victory over Holofernes (10:9–13;11), B′ — Judith's plan to save Israel (13:12–16:20), and A′ — Judith (16:21-25). In Parts II and III the plot moves with the help of shifts in place between the Assyrian camp and Bethulia.

Central to the plot are theological questions. Who is the Lord? Is it Nebuchadnezzar, as Holofernes proclaims? Or is it the God of Israel, as Judith eventually proves? And how does the Lord work? Is it through the gigantic armies of Nebuchadnezzar and Holofernes? Or is it "by the hand of woman"?

Judith, of course, is the main character. She is a pious widow whom God uses to save Israel through her piety, beauty, and cleverness (which includes flattery and lies, as well as the beheading of Holofernes). But Judith does not appear until chapter 8. Before that, Nebuchadnezzar and Holofernes play the role of the arrogant enemies of Israel. Uzziah is the timid and ineffectual leader in Bethulia. Achior the Ammonite tells the truth about Israel, and is eventually rewarded by being saved from harm and becoming part of God's people.

The narrator makes ample use of speeches and dialogues to give liveliness to the plot. A final hymn (16:1-17) summarizes in poetic form what has been told at length in prose. The key to the book is appreciating its use of irony. For example, when Holofernes and Judith converse about "my lord," he refers to Nebuchadnezzar while she means the God of Israel. And the greatest irony is that the instrument chosen by the Lord to save Israel is not a huge army but "the hand of woman."

The basic theological message of the book is that as long as Israel does not sin, it cannot be conquered by another nation (see 5:17-18; 11:10). The true Lord will protect Israel and defeat its enemies by whatever means God sees fit.

The story is set in the early sixth century B.C.E. The events described from chapter 2 onward take place in the eighteenth year of King Nebuchadnezzar (see 2:1), which was 587 B.C.E., the year in which Jerusalem was captured and the first temple was destroyed. However, much of what is presented as historical data is incorrect or confused. For example, Nebuchadnezzar ruled over the Babylonian empire, not the Assyrian empire and not in the Assyrian capital of Nineveh (which was already destroyed). At several points (see 4:3; 5:18-19) the exile and the return are said to have already occurred. And there is no record of a city named Bethulia, of anything like the crisis described in the book, or of a woman named Judith who saved her people. The book is best understood as historical fiction, a work of literary imagination based on biblical precedents and perhaps commenting on events in Jewish history in the second century B.C.E.

The most obvious biblical source is the story of Jael, the woman who killed the general Sisera by hammering a tent peg into his temple (see Judges 4–5). Also central to the book is the Deuteronomic principle that when Israel sins it is punished, and when Israel avoids sin it prospers. Judith's confidence in God is due in large part to her observation that in "our generation" there was no idolatry — the greatest sin — in Israel. The final hymn (16:1-17) and much in the prose narrative are influenced by the language and ideas of the Song of Moses in Exodus 15 in which God the warrior is celebrated.

If the book of Judith can be linked to any event in Second Temple Judaism, the most likely candidate is the threat posed to Jerusalem and its temple by Antiochus IV Epiphanes around 167 B.C.E. The best evidence for this link is the claim in 3:8 that Holofernes was commissioned to promote the cult of Nebuchadnezzar as the only god, and the persistent concern that Bethulia's fall would mean easy access for the enemy army to Jerusalem. But of course, it was the Maccabean warriors, and not "the hand of a woman," who regained the temple and restored the traditional worship there.

The basic text is in Greek. No fragments of Judith have been found among the Dead Sea Scrolls. But the Semitic-biblical style of its language and certain peculiar expressions regarded as translation errors have led many scholars to assume a Hebrew or Aramaic original. Jerome reported that when he made the Latin Vulgate translation, he used a "Chaldean" (Aramaic) version. This fact may explain many of the differences between the Greek and Latin versions. Yet that Aramaic version has not survived, and the extant Hebrew versions appear to be translations from the Latin Vulgate.

It is tempting to place the book's composition in the land of Israel in the second or first century B.C.E., though the evidence for this or any other hypothesis is not strong. Rather than being overly concerned with questions of factual reliability and historical origin, it is better to enjoy the book as an entertaining work of religious imagination. It combines war, sex, and violence with religion. Since irony is the key to the book, the reader needs to be attentive to the double meanings that run through it and to the central claim that God can save Israel through the most unlikely instrument, the hand of a woman.

Content

Part One: Nebuchadnezzar's Campaigns and Plan (1:1–2:13)

A. *Nebuchadnezzar's Campaigns* (1:1-16) provide the context for Judith's action. The book tells the story of an arrogant and powerful king whose forces are no match for the God of Israel working by the hand of a woman. The campaign in the East (1:1-16) shows how powerful Nebuchadnezzar is. The twelfth year of his reign was 593 B.C.E. The way in which he is introduced in 1:1, however, indicates that the book is not intended as accurate history. Nebuchadnezzar was king of the Babylonians, not the Assyrians; he never ruled in Nineveh; and there was no Median king named Arphaxad.

The huge and apparently invulnerable city of Ecbatana that Arphaxad was building (1:2-4) will be no protection against Nebuchadnezzar (see 1:14). As Nebuchadnezzar plans his attack, he enlists many allies from among Arphaxad's neighbors in the East (1:5-6). But when he seeks help from the Persians and the peoples of the West including those in the land of Israel (1:7-11), he meets rejection because they "regarded him as only one man" — as just another warrior king and not "the lord of the whole earth" as he claims to be (see 2:5).

Swearing to take revenge against the peoples of the West (1:12), Nebuchadnezzar in 588 B.C.E. first leads his forces against Arphaxad, captures the "invulnerable" Ecbatana, kills Arphaxad in the mountains, and returns to Nineveh for a victory celebration that lasts 120 days (1:13-16).

B. *Nebuchadnezzar's Plan* (2:1-13) concerns Israel and the other peoples who refused to become his allies. Having proven himself a mighty warrior in the East, Nebuchadnezzar then proceeds to carry out his threat of vengeance against the peoples of the West who failed to show him proper respect. The campaign against the West (and the actions described in the rest of the book) takes place in the eighteenth year of Nebuchadnezzar's reign (2:1) — which is 587 B.C.E., the year in which Jerusalem was captured and its temple was destroyed. In 2:1-3 the king proposes to his chief ministers "a secret plan" to destroy all those peoples who had refused to become his allies against Arphaxad. This includes Israel.

The agent of the secret plan is to be the general Holofernes (2:4), and in 2:5-13 Nebuchadnezzar gives him instructions about the campaign against the West. The speech begins and ends with references to Nebuchadnezzar's greatness: "Thus says the great King, the lord of the whole earth . . . take care not to transgress any of your lord's commands." Holofernes is to bring a large army against the West, demand tokens of submission from them ("earth and water"), and prepare the way for Nebuchadnezzar to take full possession of these lands. The key claim made by Nebuchadnezzar appears in 2:12: "What I have spoken I will accomplish by my own hand." As the story proceeds, the plan of "the Great King, the lord of the whole earth" will be undone by the God of Israel working through the hand of a Jewish woman named Judith (see 8:33; 9:9; 12:4). The central question of the book of Judith is this: Whose hand will prevail — the hand of the Great King, or the hand of the Jewish woman?

Part Two: Holofernes' Campaigns (2:14–7:32)

A. The *Campaign of Holofernes Against Israel's Neighbors* (2:14–3:10) brings destruction and fear. In response to Nebuchadnezzar's instruction, Holofernes musters a huge army and assembles the supplies necessary for its move westward (2:14-18). The army is so massive that it covers the earth like locusts or dust (2:19-20). While the itinerary of the campaign is confusing in its geographical details (2:21-27), the most important feature is the impression of total destruction given by the verbs of violence ("ravaged," "plundered," "seized," "killed," "burned," "destroyed," "sacked").

As Holofernes' army gets closer to the land of Israel, "fear and dread of him" come upon the seacoast towns (2:28). So desperate are those peoples that they proclaim themselves "the servants of Nebuchadnezzar" and beg, "Do with us whatever you will" (3:1-4). Despite their surrender, Holofernes forces their soldiers into his army and decrees a change in religion by demolishing the shrines and cutting down the sacred groves (3:5-8). We are told that Holofernes had been "commissioned to destroy all the gods of the land, so that all nations should worship Nebuchadnezzar alone" (3:8). (This program evokes the stories in Daniel 3 and 6, where Jewish courtiers are placed in a crisis of conscience when they are commanded to worship the king as God. The books of Daniel and Judith may reflect claims about the divinity of the Seleucid King Antiochus IV, whose title was "god made manifest.") As Holofernes' army draws near, Israel knows that it can expect military conquest and the abolition of its ancestral religion.

31

Before attacking Israel (3:9-10), Holofernes encamps near Dothan and Beth-shean/Scythopolis where he rests and resupplies his army. The stage is set for an attack on Israel as the climax of the campaign. The question is this, Who is God? Is it King Nebuchadnezzar or the ancestral God of Israel?

B. The *Response of Israel* (4:1-15) is fear. The people in Judea (4:1-3) hear about Holofernes' success, especially how "he had plundered and destroyed all their temples." They naturally fear for their own temple in Jerusalem. (In another case of historical confusion we are told in 4:3 that the Judeans had recently returned from exile, while according to 2:1 the exile had not yet begun.)

Israel's response to the crisis is both military (4:4-7) and religious (4:8-15). The military response consists in taking to the hills and fortifying the mountain villages. Then the high priest Joakim asks the people of Bethulia and Betomesthaim to seize the mountain passes to prevent Holofernes' army from attacking Jerusalem. (Again there are factual problems. The cities of Bethulia and Betomesthaim are otherwise unknown, and there is no mountain pass in the area so narrow that only two soldiers could go through at once.) Joakim's advice highlights the perilous state of Jerusalem and its temple in the face of Holofernes' campaign.

The religious response (4:8-15) involves prayers and acts of penance. At the urging of Joakim and the elders at Jerusalem, the people cry out to God for protection, put sackcloth on themselves and even their cattle, engage in fasting, and offer sacrifices. When the priests offer sacrifices, they place ashes on their headgear ("turbans") as a sign of the people's penance. The religious response will prove to be more effective than the military response does: "The Lord heard their prayers and had regard for their distress" (4:13). This is so because the struggle is ultimately theological (Who is God?) rather than military. By proclaiming Nebuchadnezzar as the only God deserving worship and by threatening to destroy the temple in Jerusalem, Holofernes has transformed his campaign into a religious contest.

C. *Achior's Report to Holofernes About Israel* (5:1–6:11) continues the theme of a religious contest. The occasion (5:1-4) for the report is Holofernes' puzzlement over Israel's resistance and his search for information about Israel from its neighbors and traditional enemies. Although at first sight his question seems to be military, it is really theological at the level on which the book of Judith operates: "Who rules over them as king and leads their army?" As the story proceeds, Holofernes will discover that God rules over Israel and leads its army.

The Ammonite Achior speaks up in 5:5-21 and gives a quick and reliable survey of Israel's history from Abraham, through the settlement in Canaan, the sojourn in Egypt and the exodus, the conquest of Canaan, and the exile, to the return from exile. But the theological analysis is more important than the historical details are. In keeping with the theology of Deuteronomy, Achior says that as long as Israel "did not sin against their God they prospered" (5:17). The exile, according to Achior again expressing the biblical tradition, was a just punishment for Israel's turning from God's way. And the return from exile was a reward for turning back to God. This theological analysis of Israel's history forms the basis for Achior's advice to Holofernes. He will conquer Israel only if Israel has sinned against God; otherwise, the God of Israel will defend his people.

Achior's report draws an arrogant response from the other native leaders ("We are not afraid of the Israelites") in 5:22-24. Then in 6:1-9 Holofernes responds directly to Achior in the presence of other leaders. His address is full of ironies. He asks, "What god is there except Nebuchadnezzar?" and denies that Israel's God can save his people (6:2). In fact, Israel will be saved by its God, and Nebuchadnezzar will be exposed as no god at all and hardly "lord of the whole earth" (6:4). To punish Achior for telling what turns out to be the truth, Holofernes proposes to hand him over to the Israelites in the expectation that he will surely be killed along with them (6:8). He promises Achior that "you shall not see my face again" (6:5) — a boast that does come true, but not in the way that Holofernes imagines. His claim that "none of my words shall fail to come true" (6:9) captures the irony of the entire response.

And so in 6:10-11, in what Holofernes plans as a clever punishment for Achior's report but what turns out to be a reward for his telling the truth to Holofernes, Achior is brought out of the camp to the outskirts of Bethulia. By passing out of the Assyrian camp and into the city of God's people, Achior will experience "salvation."

C'. *Achior's Report to Israel About Holofernes* (6:12-21) is occasioned by Achior's being left bound outside Bethulia (6:12-13). When the Israelites take Achior into their town, the leaders call an assembly to question him. When Achior tells them "all that Holofernes had boasted he would do against the house of Israel" (6:17), Israel's response is prayer to God and praise for Achior (6:18-21). The people pray that God will see the arrogance of Israel's enemies Nebuchadnezzar and Holofernes, and show mercy to his people. In what is a contest about "Who is God?" Israel's reliance on prayer will be vindicated and Achior, who had been handed over to what Holofernes regarded as certain death, will be saved.

B'. The *Response of Israel* (7:1-5) is fear. Why the people are afraid is explained by the advance of Holofernes's army toward Bethulia (7:1-3). All of Holofernes' vast forces are focused on one small outpost in Israel, the last defense for Jerusalem and its temple against the Assyrians. When the Israelites see this army, they are "greatly terrified." The narrative in chapter 7 is moved forward at several points by direct discourse (7:4, 9-15, 24-28, 30-31). Here in 7:4 the people say that Holofernes' army will "strip clean the whole land" and acknowledge that the power of his forces is so great that the earth will not support them. As before, there is also a military response (7:5) when the people get their weapons and stand on guard for the attack. The irony is that the attack will never come, and that Israel will be saved not by military might but by the hand of the woman Judith.

A'. *Holofernes' Campaign Against Bethulia* (7:6-32) takes a surprising turn. Instead of a direct attack, Holofernes accepts the advice of Israel's neighbors to cut off the water supply to Bethulia. The neighbors present this strategy as a way of avoiding casualties, destroying Bethulia completely, and avenging Israel's insult to Holofernes. Having "seized the water supply and the springs," Holofernes and his huge army only have to wait Israel out (7:16-18).

Meanwhile (7:19-22) the Israelites realize the Assyrian strategy and begin to experience the effects of the water shortage. They rise up and tell Uzziah to surrender and interpret their plight as just punishment for their sins (7:23-28). In response (7:29-31) Uzziah asks for five more days of holding out and promises that if nothing changes he will surrender then. In 7:32 he sends home the "women and children" — even though Israel will be saved by the woman Judith.

Part Three: By the Hand of a Woman (8–16)

A. *Judith* (8:1-8) is finally introduced by a genealogy, a report about her husband and how she came to be a widow, and a description of her exemplary religious conduct. Her genealogy (8:1), the longest given for any woman in the Bible, encompasses sixteen generations. Her husband

Manasseh (8:2-3) died of a heatstroke during the barley harvest (April-May) and was buried near Bethulia. The widow Judith (8:4-8) devotes herself to prayer (presumably the purpose of the tent on the roof), penance (sackcloth), and regular fasting (except on the Jewish festivals). She is rich and beautiful (8:7) and fully capable of maintaining her husband's estate. The final sentence captures the essence of Judith's person: "No one spoke ill of her, for she feared God with great devotion" (8:8). The instrument for delivering God's people will be a widow (apparently childless) whose weapons are fear of God, beauty, and wisdom.

B. *Judith's Plan to Save Israel* (8:9–10:8) is first proposed indirectly in her meeting with the elders of Bethulia (8:9-36). When Judith hears about the crisis caused by the lack of water, she sends her maid to summon the elders (8:9-10). In her speech ("Listen to me") she first (8:11-17) rebukes them for putting God to the test by giving God five more days before they surrender to the Assyrians. In 8:18-23 she holds out hope because this generation has not engaged in idolatry, and reminds them that if Bethulia falls, "all Judea will be captured and our sanctuary will be plundered." (Again this passage treats the exile of 587 B.C.E. as a past event.) Finally in 8:24-27 Judith gives her theological interpretation of the sufferings of God's people: they are a test from God (8:25) and a discipline (8:27). Rather than taking the crisis as an occasion to test God, the people of Bethulia should view it as a test from God and respond accordingly.

Uzziah's response in 8:28-31 is polite but self-serving and patronizing. After praising Judith as a good and wise woman, he excuses his putting God to the test on the grounds that the people pressured him and "made us take an oath that we cannot break." And so his advice to Judith is that she should pray for rain — the most he apparently could imagine that this pious widow could do.

Judith's answer in 8:32-34 ("Listen to me") is bold: "I am about to do something that will go down though all generations of our descendants." She asks only that the elders allow her and her maid to leave the city. She promises that "the Lord will deliver Israel by my hand." Uzziah and the elders grant her request (8:35) and pray that "the Lord will go before you, to take vengeance on our enemies." It is God working through the hand of Judith who will save the people of Bethulia and the Jerusalem temple.

In her prayer (9:1-14) Judith adopts the posture of a suppliant (prostration, ashes on her head, sackcloth) and times it to coincide with the offering of incense in the Jerusalem temple (9:1). Her prayer alternates between reflections on the threat to Israel (9:2-4, 7-10) and professions of faith in God's power (9:5-6, 11-14).

Judith's first reflection (9:2-4) recalls the rape of Dinah by Shechem son of Hamor (see Genesis 34) and the revenge taken by her ancestor Simeon. Although Judith will run the risk of rape by Holofernes, she prays that she ("a widow") may play the role of Simeon in avenging Israel's enemies. Her first confession (9:5-6) appeals to God's sovereignty over the past, present, and future, and to God's foreknowledge.

Her second reflection (9:7-10) focuses on the present Assyrian threat and gives special attention to the plan to defile God's sanctuary in Jerusalem. She first alludes to God as a mighty warrior (see Exod. 15:3): "You are the Lord who crushes wars; the Lord is your name." Then she prays that God will give her ("a widow") a strong hand and crush the arrogance of Israel's enemies "by the hand of a woman." Her second confession (9:11-14) addresses God with a wonderful litany ("God of the lowly, helper of the oppressed . . .") and prays that God will let her be the instrument by which the covenant and the Jerusalem temple are protected against Israel's enemies.

As Judith prepares for her mission (10:1-5) she removes her sackcloth and widow's garments, and dresses herself in an attractive way to seduce Holofernes, perhaps also symbolizing the joy that her victory will bring to God's people. She takes along her own food and dishes (10:5), presumably to enable her to observe the Jewish food laws in the Assyrian camp. When the elders see her at the city gate (10:6-8), they are amazed at her beauty and wish God's blessing on her mission. For her part Judith places all her trust in God: "She bowed down to God."

C. *Judith's Victory Over Holofernes* (10:9–13:11) takes place in the Assyrian camp. Judith's entrance into the camp of Holofernes is narrated by a series of four meetings. At the city gate of Bethulia (10:9-10) Judith receives permission from the elders to depart, and she and her maid pass through the gate, descend the mountain, and pass through the valley. The scene switches from Bethulia to the Assyrian camp.

To the Assyrian patrol (10:11-16) Judith volunteers that she is "a daughter of the Hebrews" and has a plan by which Holofernes can capture the hill country without losing a man (a lie). Then in the Assyrian camp (10:17-19) the men marvel at Judith and comment: "Who can despise these people, who have women like this among them?" As Judith approaches the tent of Holofernes (10:20-23), he and his servants also marvel at her beauty. At each point the Assyrians are so taken by Judith's beauty (see

10:14, 19, 23) that she gains immediate access to Holofernes and so to the opportunity to carry out her plan in a way that Holofernes will be slain.

Holofernes begins his first meeting with Judith (11:1-4) by proclaiming his personal integrity (but see 12:16 for his real intentions) and assuring her safety inside the Assyrian camp. But Judith has no real need for his assurances. In fact, it is his safety that is at risk.

Judith's speech to Holofernes in 11:5-19 is a breathtaking mixture of irony, flattery, and lies. Her principle seems to be, "All's fair in war." After promising to say "nothing false," she first (11:5-8) says with perfect irony: "God will accomplish something through you, and my lord will not fail to achieve his purposes." Whereas Holofernes imagines that "my lord" refers to him, Judith really means it as a reference to God. She flatters Nebuchadnezzar as "king of the whole earth" and Holofernes as "the most informed and the most understanding in military strategy." As the story proceeds, we will see how these pretentious human leaders are to be humbled by "my lord" working through the hand of a woman.

Next in 11:9-15 Judith confirms the truth of Achior's statement in 5:17-19 that Israel can be defeated only if it sins against God. She concocts the story that the people of Bethulia are about to eat unclean and even consecrated food as soon as they get permission from the Jerusalem council. Once they do so, "they will be handed over to you."

Finally in 11:16-19 Judith explains that her people's willingness to sin had led her to flee Bethulia (another lie!), and she volunteers to tell Holofernes as soon as she learns from God in her prayer when Israel has sinned. With delicious irony she promises Holofernes: "Then I will lead you through Judea until you come to Jerusalem" — something that she will do with his effects but not in the way that Holofernes imagines (see 16:19).

According to 11:20-23 Holofernes is totally taken in by Judith's beauty and wisdom, and fails to understand that destruction awaits those who have despised "my lord," who is really the God of Israel and not Nebuchadnezzar. The irony underlying the whole conversation revolves around the identity of "my lord."

Judith has five days to act before the people of Bethulia surrender (see 7:30-31). In her first three days in the Assyrian camp (12:1-9), she establishes a pattern. Refusing to eat Holofernes' food, she eats and drinks from her own ritually pure supply stored in her food bag. When Holofernes inquires what she plans to do when her supply runs out, Judith assures him with perfect irony that by then God will have carried out "by my hand what he has determined" (12:4). She requests permission to

37

leave the camp each night to bathe near Bethulia and to pray that the God of Israel will direct her "for the triumph of his people." Then she eats her food. By following this regime over three days, Judith has set the stage for her "getaway."

On the fourth day (12:10-20) Holofernes tries to carry out the plan that he had from the first moment he saw Judith — to seduce her (12:16). At a banquet for his attendants, he directs the eunuch Bagoas to summon Judith on the grounds that it would be shameful to let her go without having had intercourse with her. He reasons that, if he does not seduce her, she will laugh at him (as impotent or a eunuch or homosexual?). In fact, Judith will have the last laugh on him. When summoned by Bagoas, Judith responds with apparent politeness: "Who am I to refuse my lord?" — another irony based on the double meaning of "my lord," since Judith is cooperating with the God of Israel. She prepares herself so as to seduce the seducer. She agrees to join the banquet on the grounds that "today is the greatest day in my whole life" (12:18) — which indeed it will be, but not for the reasons that Holofernes imagines. So smitten is he with Judith that he gets very drunk — thus making it possible for Judith to smite him.

The second part of the evening (13:1-10a) does not go as Holofernes planned. Whereas he wanted privacy with Judith and so dismissed his servants, he was thus left alone with her and "dead drunk" — an easy prey. On her part Judith arranged with her maid and Bagoas that she would be going out to pray according to her usual schedule that she had established over the three preceding days. The schedule would facilitate her "getaway." Inside the tent Judith prays at the decisive moments in her action. While standing beside Holofernes' bed, Judith prays that God may regard her deed as undertaken for "the exaltation of Jerusalem" and for the destruction of Israel's enemies (13:4-5). While taking Holofernes' sword, she prays: "Give me strength today, O Lord God of Israel!" Her cutting off his head is narrated in one short sentence (that, according to John Ruskin, has inspired "a million bad pictures"): "Then she struck his neck twice with all her might, and cut off his head" (13:8). Thus by the hand of a woman the arrogant enemies of Israel are defeated. Leaving his body in the tent, she gives the head to her maid to place in the (now almost empty) food bag — another part of the "getaway" plan.

Reversing their movements in 10:9-10, Judith and her maid go out of the Assyrian camp, ascend the mountain to Bethulia, and ask that the city gate be opened. With these movements the scene shifts from the Assyrian camp back to Bethulia.

B'. *Judith's Plan to Save Israel* (13:12–16:20) after the beheading of Holofernes is a mixture of praise to God and military strategy, conveyed by narratives, speeches, dialogues, prayers, and a long hymn (16:1-17).

In her return to Bethulia (13:12–14:10) Judith gives all the credit to God ("Praise God") for having destroyed Israel's enemies "by my hand." When she pulls the head of Holofernes out of her food bag, she proclaims that "the Lord has struck him down by the hand of a woman" and preserved her from defilement and shame ("no sin"). The people respond with a benediction praising God for humiliating their enemies. As the leader of Bethulia, Uzziah joins the chorus of praise for Judith and for God. He celebrates Judith's "walking in the straight path before our God" (13:20). For Uzziah (and for the author) Judith remains a model of piety, devoted to prayer and the Torah, and undefiled by her seduction of Holofernes. That she lied to him and beheaded him do not count as sins or moral faults.

Judith's plan (14:1-5) to defeat the Assyrian army involves hanging the head of Holofernes on the highest point of the city wall and having the Israelite army appear to prepare for attack. The strategy is that when the Assyrian army discovers that Holofernes has been killed, they will panic and flee before the pursuing Israelite forces. But first it is necessary to verify that the severed head did indeed belong to Holofernes. And only Achior could do that.

When Achior the Ammonite (14:6-10) is summoned into the assembly at Bethulia, he sees the head and faints away (what some might expect a woman to do). On his recovery, Achior declares Judith "blessed . . . in every tent of Judah" and gives her the opportunity to tell her story once more before the assembly. So impressed by Judith and her actions is Achior that he professes his faith in the God of Israel and joins the house of Israel by having himself circumcised.

In 14:11–15:7 Judith's plan works perfectly. First the head of Holofernes is raised on the city wall. When the people of Bethulia take up arms, the Assyrian army expects that this will mean their utter destruction and so they turn to the leader Holofernes. But Bagoas finds Holofernes dead. Fear and trembling come upon the Assyrian army, and they and their allies flee in disarray. Bagoas aptly summarizes what has happened: "One Hebrew woman has brought disgrace on the house of King Nebuchadnezzar" (14:18). The flight of the Assyrian army and their allies gives the people of Bethulia the opportunity to attack and conquer. They are joined by other Israelites in routing the enemies of God's people. The focus of their attention is the booty left by the Assyrian army. Acting on the principle "All's fair in war," they become rich on the spoils from the Assyrian camp.

The celebration of Israel's victory by the hand of the woman Judith takes place in five acts. First (15:8-10), the high priest Joakim and the elders of Jerusalem bear witness to what "the Lord has done for Israel" and describe Judith as "the glory of Jerusalem . . . the great boast of Israel."

Second (15:11), the people plunder the Assyrian camp for a whole month (there was so much!) and present Holofernes' personal effects to Judith (see 16:19).

Third (15:12-13), Judith leads the women of Israel in a celebratory dance, after the example of Miriam (see Exod. 15:20-21).

Fourth (15:14–16:17), Judith leads the people in a choral thanksgiving hymn reminiscent of the Song of Moses at the sea (see Exod. 15:1-19). After a call to worship God in music and song (16:1), Judith assumes the role of "Mother Israel" and describes the threat posed by the Assyrian army to "my" territory, young men, infants, children, and virgins, and how God foiled them "by the hand of a woman" (16:2-5). Then in 16:6-10 the people proclaim that God has indeed acted not through warriors or giants but through the beauty of Judith. After giving the details of Judith's beauty, they announce that "the sword severed his neck." Judith takes up the song again in 16:11-12 and describes how Israel routed the Assyrians. She ends in 16:13-17 with a call to praise God as "wonderful in strength invincible," proclaims "fear of the Lord" as greater than sacrifice, and warns "the nations that rise up against my people" of their eternal punishment.

Fifth (16:18-20), Judith and the people journey to Jerusalem where they undergo ritual purification (which was necessary because of their contact with the Assyrian dead), offer sacrifices to God, dedicate Holofernes' effects as votive offerings, and celebrate their victory for three months. The goal of Judith's action was both to save her city of Bethulia and to protect Jerusalem and its temple from defilement and destruction by Israel's enemies. And so it is fitting that the celebration of Judith's victory should take place in Jerusalem.

A'. Judith (16:21-25) returns to her estate in Bethulia to resume her life as a pious and exemplary widow. She is honored by her people, refuses proposals to marry again, and lives a long life (105 years). Before her death she sets free her faithful maid and divides her property among Manasseh's and her relatives. She is interred in the burial cave of her husband. A seven-day period of national mourning marks her death. She is rightly celebrated as the protector of God's people: "No one ever again spread terror among the Israelites during the lifetime of Judith, or for a long time after her death" (16:25).

Significance

The situation described in the book of Judith involves suffering for the people of Bethulia as well as the threat of the defilement of the Jerusalem temple (and so suffering for all Israel). For its refusal to become an ally of Nebuchadnezzar, Israel is forced to deal with Holofernes' decree that Nebuchadnezzar be worshiped as a god. For its fidelity to the God of Israel, the people of Bethulia find themselves in a crisis. After more than a month without access to the city's water supply, they exact from Uzziah a promise to surrender in five days' time. They attribute their present sufferings to past sins, and call upon "God the Lord of our ancestors, who punishes us for our sins and the sins of our ancestors" (7:28).

Judith proposes a different interpretation of Israel's sufferings. She tells the people that the threat posed by Holofernes and his army is a test from God ("who is putting us to the test as he did our ancestors," 8:25). And so she advises the people not to turn their sufferings into a test of God ("You are putting the Lord Almighty to the test," 8:13) by imposing a five-day time period for God to save them before they surrender. She also interprets the present crisis as a discipline from God who "scourges those who are close to him in order to admonish them" (8:27).

Judith trusts in the sovereignty and justice of God. She accepts the principle that if Israel avoids sin, no nation can conquer it. She is convinced of her people's innocence at this time because there is no worship of "gods made with hands" (8:18). Therefore, convinced that God can save Israel even "by the hand of a woman," she moves into action against Holofernes.

As "Jewish woman," Judith is a symbol for Israel. In the final hymn she adopts the persona of the Mother of Israel and speaks about "my" territory, young men, infants, children, and virgins. She makes Israel's cause her own task and brings about Israel's rescue singlehandedly. She takes the initiative when everyone else wants to surrender, and her courage contrasts sharply with the fear and cowardice displayed by Uzziah and the elders of Bethulia.

Nevertheless, Judith is very much part of a patriarchal society and lives as a pious widow before and after her grand deed. What gives her the opportunity to do that deed are her physical beauty and Holofernes' desire to have sexual relations with her. She leads on Holofernes by flattery, tells him lies, and uses his own sword to behead him when he is in a drunken stupor. Her success in conquering the enemy of Israel is due to the cultural expectations of a male-centered society. By exploiting Holofernes' lust and his assumption that this beautiful Jewish widow was surely no threat to him and his army, Judith was able to kill by her own hand the great general and put his army to flight.

Issues. What are we to make of the many historical inaccuracies in the book? Some scholars dismiss the author as hopelessly ignorant about Jewish history and as reflecting the general Jewish ignorance about the distant past. Others are anxious to preserve the "historicity" of the story and so attribute the "mistakes" to copyists' errors in transmitting the text. Still others detect a literary purpose — a warning from the start that the book should be taken as fiction and not as a historical account. There is probably some truth in each of these explanations, but none of them is entirely satisfactory.

What are we to make of the moral insensitivity displayed by Judith and so by the author? Judith flirts with Holofernes and leads him on by flattery. She lies to him about Israel's plan to eat forbidden foods and so commit sin in God's eyes, thus insuring its defeat by the Assyrians. And she cuts off Holofernes' head when he is too drunk to know what is happening. Two obvious responses are, "It's only a story" and "All's fair in war." Nevertheless, Judith is celebrated in the story as the Mother of Israel and as the model for pious widowhood. And while desperate wartime conditions often force good people to take desperate measures and do bad things, there is a particularly gruesome dimension to beheading Holofernes, putting his head into the food bag, and then displaying it at the highest point on the city wall. Moreover, the author has the people revel in plundering the Assyrian camp, where there was so much spoil that the process took thirty days. The book of Judith is "only a story," but it does raise disturbing moral questions (especially when it is regarded as canonical Scripture).

Influence. Evidence for the impact of the book of Judith on Judaism and early Christianity in the early centuries of the Common Era is hard to find. There are no clear references to it in the New Testament, and whatever allusions to it have been proposed are either vague or reflect the common use of earlier biblical material.

Its inclusion in the Christian Bible eventually led Jews and Christians to use the book as a starting point for their own literary and artistic creations. The colorful medieval Jewish midrashim on Judith link the story to the celebration of Hanukkah, thus anticipating the modern scholarly hypothesis of its Maccabean origin. There are many depictions of the Judith story in illustrated Christian Bible manuscripts, and it has been the subject of epic poems and operas. Her slaying of Holofernes has attracted the attention of portrait artists for whom the combination of war, sex, violence, and religion has proved irresistible.

Christians have traditionally found in Judith a symbol of the church and/or Mary the Mother of Jesus. Insofar as Mary is regarded as the Daughter of Zion and a symbol of the people of God, this interpretation is appropriate. In both cases a lone Jewish woman — one a childless widow and the other a virgin — plays a pivotal role in the salvation of God's people. However, in recent years it appears that recognition of the book's fictional character and its moral insensitivity has prompted liturgists and exegetes to play down the Marian interpretation of Judith.

The book of Judith is part of the Roman Catholic, Orthodox, and Slavonic canon of Holy Scripture. For Jews (and so also for Protestants) it is not canonical. This may be due simply to the fact that it was preserved in Greek and so could not be part of the Hebrew canon. But if it was composed in Hebrew or Aramaic, modern scholars suggest that it may have been excluded from the Jewish canon because of the story's setting in Samaritan territory, the "easy" conversion of the Ammonite Achior, and/or the portrayal of Judith as a "radical feminist."

For Further Study

Craven, Toni. *Artistry and Faith in the Book of Judith.* Chico, Calif.: Scholars Press, 1983. (I have followed her outline in broad strokes, especially for the divisions and the concentric patterns in Parts II and III.)

Enslin, Morton S. *The Book of Judith.* Leiden: Brill, 1972.

Moore, Carey A. *Judith.* Anchor Bible 40. Garden City, N.Y.: Doubleday, 1985.

Stocker, Margarita. *Judith — Sexual Warrior: Women and Power in Western Culture.* New Haven and London: Yale University Press, 1998.

VanderKam, James C., ed. *"No One Spoke Ill of Her": Essays on Judith.* Atlanta: Scholars Press, 1992.

CHAPTER 4

The Additions to Esther: These Things Have Come from God

Basic Information

The book of Esther is unique in the Hebrew Bible because it contains no explicit mention of God. Rather, it develops an implicit theology in which God works indirectly to save Israel from the danger of annihilation. The main characters are Mordecai and Esther (the human instruments of Israel's salvation), Haman (the villain), and the Persian king (who has the power to destroy or save Israel).

In the Hebrew version Queen Vashti's refusal to participate in the king's banquet makes it possible for the Jewish woman Esther to become his queen (1:1–2:18). When Mordecai uncovers the plot against the king, he informs Esther, who tells the king (2:19-23). Haman conceives a fierce hatred for Mordecai and for the Jews, and he gets the king to issue a decree by which all Jews in the Persian empire are to be killed on the thirteenth day of Adar (chap. 3). At Mordecai's urging, Esther agrees to help the Jews in their danger, and invites Haman and the king to a banquet (chaps. 4–5).

The turning point in the plot comes in 6:1 when the king happens to have read to him the report about how Mordecai saved him. The king wants to honor Mordecai, and he asks advice from Haman, who imagines that he is the one who is to be honored (chap. 6). Then Esther points to Haman as the enemy of Israel and of the king, and Haman is hanged on the same gallows that he built for Mordecai (chap. 7). Finally the king rescinds the earlier decree and guarantees the safety of the Jews (chaps. 8–9). What was intended as the day of Israel's destruction is turned into the festival of Purim. The book ends with brief notices about the good fortunes of the king and Mordecai (chap. 10).

In some respects the Hebrew version of Esther is a literary masterpiece. It is full of apparent coincidences. Vashti loses royal power and Esther gains it just in time to save Israel from crisis. Mordecai happens to overhear the plot and so saves the king. The king happens to be awake one night and hears about Mordecai. Haman happens on the scene when the king wants advice about honoring someone, and so on. Of course, behind all the "coincidences" is the hand of the God of Israel. These reversals are not due to chance. The story is told with some dark humor or irony. For example, the wicked Haman ends up promoting the cause of his hated rival Mordecai and is hanged on the very gallows that he had prepared for Mordecai.

The story of Esther is set in the Persian court at Susa in the fifth century B.C.E. The author knows Persian customs and is respectful of the Persian king as long as he does not persecute the Jews. The book was composed in Hebrew, probably in the mid- or late-fourth century B.C.E. It is historical fiction — a short story or novella — like Tobit and Judith. It tells how the God of Israel saved Israel from annihilation by means of Mordecai and Esther. It also explains why the Jews celebrate the feast of Purim (meaning "Lots") in the middle of the month of Adar — about a month before Passover.

Despite its literary merits and subtle theology, the Hebrew book of Esther presented problems in Judaism. Not only does it not mention God, but also it is silent about circumcision, food laws, and Sabbath observance — which were major concerns for Jews in the Diaspora. Moreover, Esther becomes queen by first having become part of the royal harem and is involved in a mixed marriage with the Gentile Persian king.

The Greek translation of the book of Esther turns the implicit theology of the Hebrew version into an explicit theology by introducing mention of God into various points in the main narrative (see 2:20; 4:8; 6:13). The Greek version also contains six additions. In his Latin translation Jerome gathered all the additions into an appendix and made them into what became known as chapters 11–16. The Greek Esther in the

NRSV Apocrypha follows the order in the Greek manuscripts but retains the chapter and verse numbers in the Latin tradition.

The six additions serve to heighten the role of God and to give greater prominence to Esther. Addition A recounts Mordecai's dream and tells how he uncovered the plot against the king. Addition B purports to present the decree condemning the Jews to destruction. Addition C gives the prayers of Mordecai and Esther in the midst of the crisis. Addition D provides a highly emotional account of Esther's entrance into the royal court. Addition E purports to present the second decree which rescinds the first decree. Addition F explains Mordecai's dream and provides a colophon.

Additions B and E were composed in Greek and served to satisfy curiosity about what the two decrees might have said. The other additions were probably composed in Hebrew or Aramaic and then translated into Greek. The dream and its interpretation (A and F) and parts of Esther's prayer (C = 14:8-10) suggest some connection with the crisis under Antiochus IV Epiphanes. None of the additions appears to have been part of the original Hebrew version.

The survey that follows gives special attention to the Additions A through F, but it also summarizes in square brackets the main text as it appears in the Greek version and highlights its references to God and to issues associated with the Torah.

Content

A. Addition A concerns *A Dream and a Conspiracy* (11:1–12:6). It first (11:1-4) provides basic information about Mordecai: he was a Benjaminite exile serving the court of the Persian king Artaxerxes in Susa (see 2:5-6).

Mordecai's dream in 11:5-12 places the story of Esther in a cosmic and even apocalyptic framework. At the sound of thunder and earthquakes, two dragons emerge and all the nations prepare to wage war against "the righteous nation." In their plight the righteous people cry out to God. The answer to their prayer takes the form of a tiny spring that becomes a great river. Its appearance is accompanied by abundant light and a great reversal: "the lowly were exalted and devoured those held in honor" (11:11). The interpretation given the dream in Addition F equates the two dragons with Mordecai and Haman, and the spring becoming a river with Esther. Since the dream reveals "what God had determined to do" (11:12), it provides a framework for interpreting the story that follows.

The second part (12:1-6) explains how Mordecai became influential at the royal court and why Haman hated him. There are, however, tensions between this account and what appears in the main text. On overhearing the conspiracy against the king between two eunuchs named Gabatha and Tharra, Mordecai reports the plot to the king, who interrogates the plotters and has them executed. (In 2:21-23 it is Esther rather than Mordecai who reports to the king.) The king has a written record made of Mordecai's benefaction and orders him to serve in his court and rewards him (12:4-5).

Mordecai's success and rise to prominence are balanced by the introduction of Haman, who is to be his rival and the enemy of Israel (12:6). Addition A ascribes Haman's hostility to his support of the eunuchs' conspiracy. (In 3:2 Haman seems to be especially upset by Mordecai's refusal to bow down to him.)

[The *Banquet* (1:1-22) given by King Artaxerxes is interrupted when Queen Vashti refuses his command to "display her beauty to all the governors" (1:11). The king and his counselors decide that Vashti must be replaced lest the other women follow her example of disobedience. The *Search for a New Queen* (2:1-18) brings Esther into the plot. Having been introduced into the king's harem, she finds favor with the king and is given the queen's diadem. Though Esther has kept secret her Jewish identity, her guardian Mordecai instructs her "to fear God and keep his laws" (2:20). The *Plot* (2:21-23) is foiled when Mordecai uncovers the conspiracy and has Esther reveal it to the king (see 12:1-2). *Haman's Hostility* (3:1-13) arises from Mordecai's unwillingness to do obeisance to him. On learning that Mordecai is a Jew, Haman determines to destroy the entire Jewish people. Their destruction is to take place on the day determined by casting lots, which turns out to be the thirteenth (or fourteenth) of Adar. The king gives Haman permission to issue such a decree under his name.]

B. Addition B (13:1-7) provides the "full text" of the *Decree Against the Jews,* which is only described in the Hebrew version. This text was clearly composed in Greek and was not part of the original Hebrew version. It uses some of the rhetoric and formulas of official decrees, and so contributes to the "realism" of the Greek version by highlighting the degree to which Haman went to destroy the Jewish people.

The decree is addressed by the king (though we are to imagine that Haman wrote it in his name) to the governors of the 127 provinces in his kingdom (13:1). The alleged reason for the decree is to secure the peace of the entire Persian empire, and the text is presented as an expression of the king's rational and kindly manner (13:2).

The text praises Haman (and so is self-praise) for his constant good-will and fidelity, and in particular for his pointing out the threat posed by the Jews to the unity and peace of the empire. It describes the Jews as "a certain hostile people" who perversely follow "a strange manner of life and laws" (13:3-5). Because of their contrary laws, the Jews are said to present an obstacle to the king's program for a unified and peaceful kingdom.

The action proposed by the decree (13:6-7) is that all Jews — men, women, and children — are to be destroyed on the fourteenth day of the twelfth month (Adar). The goal is that in a single day this hostile people will "go down in violence to Hades" and that the peace and unity of the empire will be secured.

[The *Consternation of the Jews* (3:14–4:17) begins with the posting of the decree throughout the empire. At Susa the panic of the Jews contrasts with the carousing of Haman and the king (3:14-15). Mordecai adopts the manner of the penitent petitioner and runs through the city warning that "an innocent nation is being destroyed" (4:1). When Esther through her eunuch tries to comfort Mordecai, he urges her to plead Israel's case before the king. He tells her to "call upon the Lord; then speak to the king in our behalf, and save us from death" (4:8). When Esther objects that no one can approach the king without being summoned by him (4:9-11), Mordecai warns her that as a Jew she too will be killed and suggests that she has become the queen for this very crisis. Convinced by Mordecai's reasoning, Esther proposes a three-day fast among all the Jews of Susa (to win God's favor) and determines to approach the king on their behalf.]

C. Addition C (13:8–14:19) presents the *Prayers of Mordecai and Esther*. Since fasting is generally accompanied by prayer, this Addition tells us how and for what these representatives of Israel in Susa were praying.

Addition C is biblical in form and content, and it may well have been composed in Hebrew. Its effect is to transform an implicitly religious book into an explicitly religious one. The two main characters pray for their people's deliverance to the only Lord, the God of Israel. The ap-

48

parent irregularities associated with Esther's lifestyle — marriage to a Persian king, and eating "common" food — are confronted and subordinated to her role as the intercessor for God's people.

Mordecai (13:9-17) addresses the God of Israel as "the Lord of all" whom no one can resist (13:9-11). Then he explains why he refused to do obeisance to Haman (13:12-14). It was not out of personal pride but out of reverence for the sovereignty of the God of Israel: "so that I might not set human glory above the glory of God, and I will not bow down to anyone but you" (13:14). Finally Mordecai's petition (13:15-17) recalls God's love for the patriarchs ("God of Abraham") and rescue of the people from Egypt, and asks that God "spare your people" and show "mercy upon your inheritance."

The prayer of Esther (14:1-19) is made in a spirit of "distress and mourning" (14:1-3a). She addresses God as "my Lord" and as the only real king, and calls upon God to help her while reminding God that God promised to Israel "an everlasting inheritance" (14:3b-5). Esther goes on in 14:6-10 to attribute Israel's sufferings to its sins ("we have sinned before you"), especially the sin of idolatry ("we glorified their gods"). But she complains that Israel's enemies have gone too far by trying to abrogate the Torah ("what your mouth has ordained") and to turn the Jerusalem temple into a place of idolatry.

In 14:11-14 Esther analyzes the present crisis as a contest over kingship between the God of Israel ("do not surrender your scepter") and the enemies of Israel. She pleads that God will "make yourself known in the time of our affliction" and save Israel through Esther who has no helper except God. In 14:15-18 Esther defends herself against the possible charges that she has married a non-Jew, that she takes pleasure in wearing the queen's diadem, and that she eats impure food. Instead, she says that her only real joy has been the God of Abraham. Therefore in 14:19 Esther implores God to save Israel "from the hands of evildoers" and to save her from being overwhelmed by fear in approaching the king.

D. Addition D (15:1-16) describes *Esther's Entrance* before the king — which the Hebrew version recounts in two verses (5:1-2). The effect of Addition D is to highlight the figure of Esther and the emotional struggle that she endured to save her people. It also explains why the king was willing to receive her and grant her requests: "God changed the spirit of the king to gentleness" (15:8).

At the end of Esther's three days of fasting and prayer, she arrays herself in "splendid attire" and sets out for the royal court (15:1-5). Although she invokes "the aid of the all-seeing God and Savior," her heart is nonetheless "frozen with fear." On entering the royal throne room, Esther is overwhelmed and terrified both by the king's splendid appearance and by his angry glance, and so she faints away (15:6-7). But then "God changed the spirit of the king to gentleness," and the king explains that the prohibition against approaching the king without being summoned applies "only to our subjects" but not to Queen Esther (15:8-10). Though reassured by the king, as soon as Esther begins describing the king's glorious appearance, she faints again, thus worrying the king and his servants (15:11-16).

[When the king promises to grant Esther's request "even to half of my kingdom" (5:3), she asks that the king and Haman come to a banquet. Haman's delight at being singled out to dine with the king and the queen is spoiled for him by the sight of Mordecai the Jew. And so on the advice of his wife and friends, he constructs a gallows for Mordecai to be hanged.

Because "the Lord took sleep from the king" (6:1), he happened to read how Mordecai had saved him from the conspiracy of the eunuchs. Determined to honor Mordecai publicly, he asks Haman's advice on how to do so without telling him who is to be honored. Haman provides the advice since he imagines that he will receive the honors. When he is told to "do as you have said for Mordecai the Jew" (16:10), he is deeply frustrated. His friends and wife add to his displeasure regarding Mordecai the Jew by reminding him that "the living God is with him" (6:13).

On the second day of the banquet, the king once more asks Esther what she wants. She asks for her own life and for the life of her people (7:3), pointing out "this evil man Haman" as the enemy of God's people. When the king sees Haman pleading with Esther, he imagines that he is attacking her and orders that Haman be hanged on the gallows that he had prepared for Mordecai.

In a *Great Reversal* (8:1-12) the king grants Haman's property to Esther, who turns it over to Mordecai. Then Esther requests that the decree sent by Haman to destroy all the Jews in the empire be rescinded. The king gives Esther permission to have another decree published that will rescind Haman's decree. He also allows the Jews to keep their own laws and to defend themselves, and even to attack their enemies on the very day on which they were to be destroyed.]

E. Addition E (16:1-24) is a *Second Decree*. It provides the "full text" not in the Hebrew version and rescinds the first decree of Haman in Addition B. It is written in the same "official" Greek style as Addition B is and likewise is intended to fill in what was perceived as lacking in the Hebrew text. Again the decree is officially addressed by the king to the governors of the 127 provinces in his empire (16:1). He begins in general terms (16:2-9) by complaining about people (like Haman) who scheme against their benefactors (like Artaxerxes) and imagine that they will escape "the evil-hating justice of God" (16:4). Next in 16:10-14 he assigns blame to Haman and even claims that he was really a Macedonian who was plotting against the Persian empire. He praises Mordecai as "our savior and perpetual benefactor" (16:13).

Then in 16:15-18 the king describes the Jews as "children of the living God" and praises their laws as "most righteous" while calling Haman "thrice accursed." He rescinds the first decree and interprets Haman's death as a just punishment inflicted by God. Therefore in 16:19-24 the king allows the Jews to live under their own laws and to defend themselves against attacks. He also decrees that the thirteenth day of Adar — which had been designated as the day of destruction for the Jews — should be turned into a day of joy. And he threatens that any city or country that fails to respect the second decree will be destroyed.

[With the promulgation of the second decree (8:13), the *Great Reversal Becomes a Reality.* Mordecai appears in public in the glorious attire that Haman had unwittingly prescribed for him and impresses both Jews and Gentiles (8:14-17). On the thirteenth day of Adar (9:1-19) the pagan rulers honor Mordecai, and the Jews get revenge and plunder from their enemies. Esther joins in the vengeance by asking the king that the bodies of Haman's ten sons be hung up for all to see (9:13). Both in Susa and elsewhere in the empire, this day and the following days are celebrated with "joy and gladness." The records of these events (9:20-32) provided by Mordecai and Esther serve as the foundational documents for celebrating the feast of Purim (meaning "Lots") every year. The main narrative ends in 10:1-3 with descriptions of the king's glorious achievements and of Mordecai's great reputation among both Jews and Gentiles.]

F. Addition F (10:4–10:13) contains an *Interpretation of Mordecai's Dream.* In light of what has happened, Mordecai concludes that "these things have come from God" (10:4). Then in 10:6-9a he equates figures in the dream with characters in the narrative: the spring that became a river is Esther; the two dragons are Haman and Esther; and the nations are those Gentiles who sought to destroy Israel, whereas the righteous nation is Israel. Mordecai attributes Israel's rescue to God, and in particular to God's providence in making two lots — one for Israel and the other for the nations — and in guiding events so as to rescue Israel "from all these evils." Therefore the fourteenth (and fifteenth) day of Adar is to be observed forever in Israel as the feast of Purim (or "Lots").

G. The *Colophon* (11:1) explains when and how the Greek translation of the book of Esther was made and came to Egypt. Since there were several Egyptian rulers named Ptolemy and Cleopatra, their fourth year could have been 114 B.C.E. (most likely), 77 B.C.E., or 48 B.C.E. The Greek Esther was translated by Lysimachus of Jerusalem and brought to Egypt by Dositheus and Ptolemy. The writer of the colophon seems to express some doubts about Dositheus ("who said that he was a priest and a Levite" — one cannot be both) and about the text itself ("which they said was authentic"). Thus the colophon is a witness to ancient suspicions surrounding the book of Esther.

Significance

With its occasional references to God in the main text and the many references to God in the six additions, the Greek version makes explicit the implicit theology of the Hebrew text. The thrust of the Greek version is well summarized by Mordecai's statement in Additions F: "These things have come from God."

The Greek version also takes account of possible objections to Esther's conduct. Mordecai instructs her "to fear God and keep his laws, just as she had done when she was with him" (2:20). In her prayer in Addition C, Esther claims to "abhor the bed of the uncircumcised and of any alien" and denies having eaten at Haman's table or drinking the wine of libations at the king's feast (14:15, 17).

With the opening dream (Addition A) and the closing interpretation (Addition F), the Greek version places the sufferings of Israel in a cosmic and apocalyptic framework. In her prayer in Addition C, Esther attributes the present sufferings of Israel to its sins (especially idolatry). But she goes on to complain that Israel's enemies are going too far in abrogating the Law and temple worship (14:6-10). And the emotional description of her entry into the royal throne room in Addition D shows that trust in God and fear can coexist in the midst of suffering. And, of course, the entire book of Esther recounts how God rescued Israel from suffering and death through Mordecai and Esther.

The text of the first decree in Addition B is an important document in the history of anti-Semitism. It accuses the Jews of being a "hostile people" and of "perversely following a strange manner of life and laws" (13:4-5). These statements echo charges made against Jews in antiquity. The second decree in Addition E takes back the charges and claims that Jews "are governed by the most righteous laws and are children of the living God" (16:15-16). These statements reflect how Jews viewed themselves and wanted others to see them.

Issues. What is the effect of the six additions? On a purely literary level they can seem to destroy the careful structure of the Hebrew narrative and to make explicit what for the sophisticated reader is better left implicit. Do we really need to be told that God is behind all the coincidences?

And yet there is some value to reading Esther with the additions. By addressing some of the peculiar omissions in the Hebrew text, the additions establish Esther as a religious book. The cosmic-eschatological framework gives added importance to the crisis that the book recounts. The prayers are appropriate to the story and add to the evidence for Jewish prayer in the Second Temple period.

What about Esther's morality? Many problems remain. The Greek version does at least address some of these issues, though it hardly provides satisfactory answers to all the questions. Moreover, the vengeance taken on the sons of Haman as well as the other enemies of Israel seems excessive.

Influence. The Hebrew Esther is canonical for Jews and Protestants. In the Roman Catholic and Greek and Russian Orthodox churches, the expanded Greek version with the additions is the canonical form. The canonical status of Esther was debated in antiquity among both Jews and Christians. It is the only book in the Hebrew Bible not represented among the Dead Sea Scrolls. Indeed, the revised and expanded Greek version of Esther was most likely produced to make the book more acceptable.

Among Jews, the Hebrew book of Esther is the foundational document for the feast of Purim. Though a minor feast and surrounded by humor and parody, Purim does commemorate the miraculous (however indirect) deliverance of Israel in the face of an evil tyrant (Haman) and his plan to annihilate God's people. Thus Purim has particular relevance in the post-Holocaust era.

For Further Study

Berg, Sandra Beth. *The Book of Esther: Motifs, Themes, and Structure*. Missoula, Mont.: Scholars Press, 1978.

Laniak, Timothy S. *Shame and Honor in the Book of Esther*. Atlanta: Scholars Press, 1998.

Levenson, Jon D. *Esther: A Commentary*. The Old Testament Library. Louisville: Westminster John Knox, 1997.

Moore, Carey A. *Daniel, Esther and Jeremiah: The Additions*. Anchor Bible 44. Garden City, N.Y.: Doubleday, 1977.

———. *Esther*. Anchor Bible 7b. Garden City, N.Y.: Doubleday, 1971.

CHAPTER 5

The Wisdom of Solomon: Immortality, Wisdom, and History

Basic Information

In the ancient manuscripts this work is entitled the "Wisdom of Solomon" (Greek) or the "Book of Wisdom" (Latin). It is more a book about wisdom — its benefits, nature, and role in history — than a wisdom book giving practical advice (like Proverbs and Sirach). It is an exhortation to seek wisdom and to live by it.

Though never explicitly named, the one giving the exhortation is intended to be Solomon (see chaps. 6–9), the sage-king of ancient Israel. He addresses the "rulers of the earth" (1:1; see 6:1). However, the actual author cannot be Solomon (since he writes in Greek and uses Stoic and Platonic philosophical ideas), and the primary audience is more likely to have been Jews rather than Gentile kings. The writer exhorts and encourages Diaspora Jews to remain faithful to the Jewish tradition. The work is an apology or defense of Judaism (as the author understood Judaism) as superior to other religions.

Several factors point to Alexandria in Egypt as the place of composition: the use of Greek, the philosophical concepts, the focus on the exodus, the polemic against Egyptian animal-worship, and so on. A date in the first century B.C.E. seems most likely, though any time from the second century B.C.E. to the first century C.E. is possible. Efforts to link it with a specific crisis in the history of the Jewish community at Alexandria such as the threat posed by the cult of the Roman emperor Caligula (37-41 C.E.; see 14:17) have not won much support.

Alexandria was one of the great intellectual centers of the Greco-Roman world, and also had a very large Jewish community. Philo represents the full flowering of Alexandrian Judaism in the first century C.E. In his many writings one can discern a serious attempt to bring together the Jewish Scriptures, Greek philosophical concepts (chiefly Stoic and Platonic), and allegorical interpretation. The Wisdom of Solomon is best viewed as representing an early stage in this intellectual development.

The book was composed in Greek. When dealing with biblical matters, the author shows a knowledge of the Septuagint (whose home was Alexandria). His chief biblical sources include the Servant Song of Isaiah 53 and perhaps Ecclesiastes in chapter 2, the description of Wisdom as personal figure from Proverbs 8 in chapter 7, Solomon's prayer for wisdom from 1 Kings 3:3-9 in chapters 6–9, the relevant parts of Genesis in chapter 10 and elsewhere, the biblical accounts of the exodus and Israel's wandering in the wilderness in chapters 11 and 16–19, and the polemics against idolatry in Isaiah 40–55. He also uses many words and concepts not found elsewhere in the Greek Bible. He adapts basic tenets of Stoicism (the world soul) and Platonism (the preexistence and immortality of the soul) to enhance biblical ideas and to bolster his criticisms of non-Jewish religious practices. His real passion, however, is the superiority of Jewish wisdom.

The three main parts in the book concern righteousness and immortality (chaps. 1–5), wisdom (chaps. 6–9), and wisdom's role in the early history of Israel (chaps. 10–19). The language and style indicate that all three parts were written by the same author, though not necessarily at the same time. The parts are linked together so that it is possible to take chapter 6 as the end of Part 1 or the beginning of Part 2, and chapter 10 as the end of Part 2 and the beginning of Part 3. The third part consists of seven comparisons designed to show that in the exodus God used the same elements to help the Israelites and to harm the Egyptians. However, between the first and second comparisons there are excurses on God's justice and mercy (11:15–12:27), and on the folly of idolatry (chaps. 13–15).

The book of Wisdom is important for its theological method. The author's chief source is the Bible. He drew on many passages, most obviously from the book of Exodus but also from other texts. Not satisfied with repeating the words of Scripture, he often provides symbolic interpretations and sometimes even "scientific" explanations of biblical narratives.

The author also knew and used basic concepts of Stoic and Platonic philosophy, and in chapter 2 he seems to criticize tenets of Epicurean philosophy. How did he come to know Greek philosophy, and how much did he know? More a rhetorician than a philosopher, he probably learned his philosophical concepts through the rhetorical tradition rather than directly at a philosophical school. He did not know nearly as much philosophy as Philo did. But he did know enough to make these concepts contribute to his arguments.

From his rhetorical education, the author drew on various techniques and figures of speech that other Greek and Latin orators and writers used: inclusion, or beginning and ending a unit in similar ways (1:1, 15); the sorites, or chain of elements (6:17-20); comparison (especially in chaps. 11–19, but elsewhere too); and so on.

This effort at using Greek philosophy and rhetoric in the service of biblical religion makes the author to some extent also a pioneer in inculturation, or adapting the religious message to different thought patterns and modes of expression. Nevertheless, he remained absolutely convinced of the superiority of Judaism and used his philosophical and rhetorical training to criticize the idolatry of other religions and the materialism of Epicureanism.

Content

Part One: Righteousness and Immortality (1–5)

A. The *Opening Exhortation* (1:1-15) begins with a call to "love righteousness" (1:1) and ends by giving the reason for doing so: "For righteousness is immortal" (1:15). While ostensibly directed to "you rulers of the earth" (literally, "you who judge the earth"), the exhortation (and the entire book) seems more properly aimed at young Jewish intellectuals who were in danger of turning aside from their religious and cultural traditions and adopting pagan ways of thinking and acting.

The opening exhortation consists of imperatives and declarative statements along with reasons and explanations ("because" . . . "for"). Thus it adopts the form of the wisdom instruction familiar from Proverbs 1–9 and 22–24, Ecclesiastes, and Sirach. It usually communicates by parallel clauses in which the same point is made in slightly different ways. Thus it follows the style that is typical of Hebrew poetry in general and of biblical wisdom books in particular.

The term "righteousness" or "justice" that brackets the exhortation (1:1, 15) is used in its comprehensive biblical sense of right relationship with God and the right behavior toward others that flows that relationship. The meaning is clarified by two parallel clauses in 1:1: "think of the Lord in goodness, and seek him with sincerity of heart." Those who sin and put God to the test and fail to trust in God (1:2) will find neither righteousness nor God. There can be no coexistence between God's wisdom and sin. On the one hand, wisdom refuses to "enter a deceitful soul" or to "dwell in a body enslaved to sin" (1:4). On the other hand, "a holy and disciplined spirit" will have nothing to do with unrighteousness (1:5). Here the Greek philosophical terms "soul . . . body . . . spirit" appear in their popular ethical usage of designating the whole person rather than in their technical philosophical senses.

The wisdom that comes from God is a "kindly" or "philanthropic" spirit — in the sense that it displays God's love for human beings (1:6a). Again there can be no kinship between wisdom and blasphemers (1:6b), the first of several references to sins of the tongue in this passage (see 1:8-11). But there is much more to the kindly spirit which is wisdom. Wisdom is in fact "the spirit of the Lord" and functions like the world soul of Greek (Stoic) philosophy in that it "fills the world and holds all thing together" (1:7). Instead of dwelling on the cosmic dimensions of wisdom, however, the author quickly returns to ethical warnings against "those who utter unrighteous things" and "the counsels of the ungodly" (1:8-9), and to reminders that God knows all things ("a jealous ear hears all things," 1:10) and that a "lying mouth destroys the soul" (1:11). The references to "grumbling" in 1:10-11 evoke ancient Israel's murmuring in the wilderness and specify the kind of speech that is criticized throughout 1:6-11 as irreligious in content.

In 1:12-15 the exhortation moves to death and immortality. Whereas "righteousness is immortal" (1:15) in the sense that it leads to eternal life with God, it is possible to "invite death" by taking the wrong path in life ("the error of your life") and "by the work of your hands" (1:12), probably the first reference to idol making and idolatry, which are the major concerns of chapters 13–15. Though death is a possibility, the author is quick to note in 1:13-14 that "God did not make death," thus alluding to Genesis 3 with its claim that death is the result of the sin of Adam and Eve.

The opening exhortation introduces important features of the book of Wisdom: the instructional format, parallel clauses, motive clauses ("because" . . . "for"), the presence of Greek philosophical terms and concepts in a Jewish context, an emphasis on ethics that links theology and right actions, and the connection between righteousness and immortality. This last theme is developed in what follows with reference to the opposite ideas: unrighteouness and death.

B. The *Reflection on the Errors of the Wicked* (1:16–2:24) is presented mainly in "we" language with comments at the beginning (1:16–2:1a) and the end (2:21-24). The introductory comment accuses the ungodly of making a covenant with death and of unsound reasoning. The ungodly themselves affirm that life is short and death marks its end (2:1b). According to them, birth is a matter of chance, and death means annihilation, since the human spirit and reason are entirely material: "the body will turn to ashes and the spirit will dissolve like empty air" (2:3). Even the immortality that might come from a good reputation and from good deeds is transitory (2:4). Life is like "the passing of a shadow," and there is no return from death (2:5). The fundamental error of the ungodly concerns the nature and goal of the human person (immortality). Their philosophy is materialistic and pleasure-seeking. While often identified as Epicurean, it has echoes in other systems and indeed in much modern thinking.

This basic error shapes the way in which the ungodly live (2:6-9). They describe their lifestyle in seven wishes ("let us . . .") that equate human existence with the pursuit of various pleasures, ranging from costly wines and perfumes to "revelry" and enjoyment. The reason for their choice of this lifestyle comes at the end of the series: "because this is our portion, and this is our lot" (2:9b). And yet the ungodly cannot be satisfied only with the pursuit of their own pleasure. They must also demonstrate their superiority over weaker members of society — the righteous poor, widows, and old people (2:10). The justification for such oppressive behavior is a principle that has often been invoked throughout human history: "But let our might be our law of right, for what is weak proves itself to be useless" (2:11).

The presence of righteous persons (2:12-16) is especially distasteful to the ungodly. Because the righteous regard themselves as children of God, believe in immortality for the righteous, and act accordingly, they become living reproaches to the wicked. Depending on whether the meaning attributed to "the law" in 2:12 ("he reproaches us for sins against

59

the law") is law in general or the Jewish law in particular (Torah), it is possible that the "ungodly" include Jews who adopt a philosophy and way of life foreign to the Judaism promoted by the book of Wisdom. Indeed, there are so many parallels between the speech of the ungodly in 2:16-20 and the Ecclesiastes/Qoheleth that some scholars argue that the target of the author's criticisms was "the Preacher" rather than the Epicureans.

According to the reasoning of the ungodly, the real test of the righteous will take place at death: "let us test what will happen at the end of his life" (2:17). And so they plan to subject the righteous person to suffering, a trial, and execution. Their own language is reminiscent of Isaiah 53 (the Suffering Servant Song), an impression heightened by the fact that the Greek word *pais* can mean both "servant" and "son." They imagine that if the righteous person is really God's *pais,* God will have to help in a miraculous rescue. In this way they show a failure to understand the ways of God and immortality.

The final comment in 2:21-24 underlines both the importance of immortality and the erroneous reasoning of the ungodly. God's goal or purpose for humankind in creation was incorruption (2:23), whereas death entered only through the Devil's envy (see Genesis 3). Immortality or eternal life with God remains "the wages of holiness" and the "prize for blameless souls" (2:22) — a gift from God to the faithful righteous. The ungodly fail to understand any of this.

C. The *Contrast between the Destinies of the Righteous and the Wicked* (3:1-12) is based on the conviction that, even though the ungodly imagine that death is the end of human existence, "the souls of the righteous are in the hand of God" (3:1). Instead of torment, death and departure, destruction, and punishment, which are all that the wicked materialists can discern, the hope of the righteous is "full of immortality" (3:4). Whatever suffering the righteous endured was a discipline (3:5-6). Their existence after death (3:7-9) is glorious ("they shine forth . . . like sparks"); they share in the realm over which God presides; and they participate in God's truth, love, and merciful care. This description (see Dan. 12:1-3) highlights the gift-character of immortality and suggests that it is not sharply distinguished from resurrection. Likewise, the term "visitation" evokes the last judgment or at least God's decisive intervention on behalf of the righteous.

The hope of immortality put forward in the book of Wisdom has enormous ethical and theological significance. It gives purpose and direction to human ethical activity, since eternal life with God is the reward for righteous living. It also provides a solution to the problem of innocent suffering. God's justice is deferred until the time of death and/or the last judgment. The sufferings that the righteous undergo in the present serve as a test of their virtue and/or as a source of discipline by which they are brought back to the way of righteousness.

The description of the fate of the ungodly (3:10-12) is based on the principle that evil carries its own punishment. The sin of the ungodly consists in disregarding what is right (or the righteous) and in rebelling against God, which in turn consists in despising wisdom and instruction. Therefore the ungodly are miserable, their activities are useless, and their hope is vain. Their foolishness affects not only the ungodly themselves but also their families — their wives, children, and descendants. These final comments prepare for the reflection on childlessness that follows, since one way in which humans try to insure their immortality is through their offspring.

D. The *Reflection on Childlessness* (3:13b–4:15) consists of three contrasts (3:13b-19; 4:1-5; 4:6-9) and a biblical example (4:10-15). At issue in the entire section are the conventional (in the Bible and other ancient writings) approaches to immortality through children and a good reputation. In the Wisdom of Solomon, however, immortality is God's gift of eternal life to those who embrace wisdom and act righteously.

The first contrast (3:13b-19) concerns two figures — the barren wife and the eunuch — who were despised in a society in which having children was regarded as a blessing from God and a way to immortality. The sexual imagery in this and the following contrasts most likely refers to idolatry on the basis of the familiar biblical equation between adultery/fornication and idolatry. The barren wife who has avoided adultery will be vindicated in God's judgment, and the eunuch who has avoided unrighteousness before God and other people will be the recipient of divine favor (3:13-14). Genuine immortality is a divine gift based on wisdom and good deeds, not on having children (3:15). By contrast, the "children of adulterers" (idolators?) do not live long; and even if they do, they live without effect and honor in their old age (3:16-19).

The second contrast (4:1-5) concerns "childlessness with virtue" and "the prolific brood of the ungodly." On the one hand (4:1-2), genuine immortality is based on a virtuous life, since virtue is known to God and other humans, and will be celebrated and prized by generations to come. On the other hand (4:3-5), the "illegitimate seedlings" have no

61

depth, fail to take root, are shaken by the wind, produce no fruit, and are good for nothing.

The third contrast (4:6-9) deals with "children born of unlawful unions" (idolatry) and the righteous who may die young. The former will serve as witnesses against their parents in the divine judgment, whereas the latter will be "at rest" because the real signs of fulfillment in human life are understanding and a blameless life (that is, wisdom and righteousness).

The biblical example (4:10-15) explains the mysterious fate of Enoch ("Enoch walked with God; then he was no more, because God took him," Gen. 5:24) in terms of wisdom, righteousness, and immortality. This is the first instance of the author's frequent practice of referring to famous biblical characters without naming them. He interprets the transfer of Enoch from earth to heaven in moral terms. God took Enoch "from the midst of wickedness" as a sign of love and care for the righteous "so that evil might not change their understanding or guile deceive their souls" (4:11). This section ends in 4:15b in almost the same way it began (see 3:9). All this happens so that we may recognize "that God's grace and mercy are with his elect, and that he watches over his holy ones."

E. The *Contrast between the Righteous and the Ungodly* (4:16–5:14) emerges most sharply with regard to death and the final judgment. The contrast is developed in a brief description (4:16–5:3), in the words of the ungodly themselves (5:4-13), and with a few comparisons (5:14).

The description (4:16–5:3) affirms that the righteous dead will judge the ungodly, while the ungodly fail to understand God's purpose in keeping the wise and righteous for eternal life. The wicked will suffer disgrace in death, and even the memory of them will disappear. Only at the last judgment will they recognize their own sins and "the unexpected salvation of the righteous" (5:2). Then they will want to repent, but it will be too late.

The words of the unrighteous in 5:4-13 parallel those in their earlier speech in 2:1a-20. But now they take back what they had said before. At the judgment they regret their foolish assessment of the just as mad and undergoing dishonorable death, when in fact the latter will be vindicated as "children of God" whose lot is among the saints (5:4-5). The ungodly finally admit their error: "So it was we who strayed from the way of truth, and the light of righteousness did not shine on us" (5:6). Their neglect of the Lord's way as well as their arrogance and pursuit of wealth have proved fruitless (5:7-8). This idea is developed with the help of several similes in which what the ungodly imagined to be important is compared to a shadow, a rumor, a ship sailing in the sea, a bird flying in the air, and an arrow shot at a target (5:9-12). The final self-assessment of the ungodly is that "we had no sign of virtue to show, but were consumed in our wickedness" (5:13).

Four more comparisons in 5:14 round off this section. The wicked and what they stand for are insubstantial and evanescent — like chaff, a light frost, smoke, and a guest who stays only one day.

F. That the *Immortality of the Righteous* is a gift from God rather than a natural endowment (the immortal soul) is affirmed in 5:15-23a. This passage with its emphasis on the divine warrior and the role of creation in the battle against evil places immortality in an eschatological or at least conflictual framework. The key sentence is 5:17: "The Lord will take his zeal as his whole armor, and will arm all creation to repel his enemies." Evoking the ancient image of the divine warrior, the passage lists the spiritual weapons (see Eph. 6:10-20) used by God in the struggle: zeal as the panoply or whole armor, righteousness as the breastplate, impartial justice as the helmet, holiness as the shield, and stern wrath as the sword. Creation itself joins in the fight on the side of God, with its various forces — lightning, hailstones, seas, rivers, winds, and tempests — serving to punish the wicked. Because God shows a special care for the righteous, they are immortal.

Part Two: Wisdom (6–9)

A. The *Opening Exhortation* (6:1-11) to the kings of the earth rounds off the first part of the book (see 1:1-15) and prepares for the instruction on wisdom that follows. After calling the kings to listen attentively lest they be overcome by lawlessness and evildoing (6:1-2; see 5:23b), the speaker reminds them that the God who gave them power will demand a strict accounting (6:3-8). Since rulers have an effect on all those ruled by them and since God has no fear of human rulers, they can expect a strict inquiry. The threat of divine judgment leads into an invitation to learn wisdom in 6:9-11. As always, the wisdom taught in this book is associated with righteous living and holiness. What follows is a full-scale instruction about the nature of wisdom.

B. The *Search for Wisdom* (6:12-25) takes its starting point from the portrayal of wisdom as a female personal figure in Proverbs 8. Because wisdom is glorious ("radiant and unfading"), she can be found easily by those who seek her out (6:12). In fact, wisdom finds people on her own initiative: "she goes about seeking those worthy of her" (6:16). Whoever rises early to seek wisdom will discover her already sitting at the gate of the house.

In 6:17-20 the search for wisdom is further described with the help of a sorites — a figure of speech that traces the quest for wisdom with seven links in a chain: the beginning of wisdom, desire for instruction, love of wisdom, keeping wisdom's laws, assurance of immortality, nearness to God, and a kingdom. Although the final element ("a kingdom") may appear anticlimactic in view of the two preceding items, it does allow the speaker to evoke the rhetorical situation in which he is offering an exhortation to kings (see 6:1-11).

The speaker, who will identify himself as Solomon in chapter 7, promises that kings who honor wisdom will reign forever. He proposes to tell these rulers "what wisdom is and how she came to be" (6:22), and professes that he has no desire to keep wisdom for himself out of "sickly envy" (6:23). Rather, he is convinced that "the multitude of the wise is the salvation of the world, and a sensible king is the stability of any people" (6:24).

C. *How to Obtain Wisdom* (7:1-22) is illustrated by an appeal to the example of "Solomon," the wise king. In 7:1-6 Solomon presents himself as much like any other human. A descendant of Adam ("the first-formed child of earth") and conceived through sexual relations, Solomon was an ordinary infant and mortal like everyone else. He summarizes his kinship with other humans in terms of life and death: "there is for all one entrance into life, and one way out" (7:6).

Solomon obtained wisdom by asking for it in prayer (7:7-14; see 1 Kings 3:3-9): "I called on God, and the spirit of wisdom came to me." Solomon found wisdom to be superior to everything that other people regard as precious such as royal symbols, gold and silver, health and beauty, and light. He has discovered that wisdom leads to all these things because she is their mother, and he is willing to share his gift of wisdom with others because it is "an unfailing treasure for mortals" (7:13-14).

As he draws closer to explaining what wisdom is, Solomon asks God's help insofar as God is "the guide even of wisdom and the corrector of the wise" (7:15). The scope of Solomon's wisdom is encyclopedic, embracing even the natural sciences (see the list in 7:17-21). He acknowledges, however, that he has come to know all these things because "wisdom, the fashioner of all things, taught me" (7:22). Note that God in 7:15 and "wisdom" in 7:22 are described in very similar ways.

D. The *Nature of Wisdom* (7:22b–8:1) is described in several ways. First, in 7:22b-24 there is a list of twenty-one attributes ("intelligent, holy, unique, manifold, subtle," etc.), followed by another identification of wisdom as the world soul (see 1:7): "more mobile than any motion . . . she pervades and penetrates all things." Next in 7:25-26, wisdom's close relationship with God is expressed in terms such as "breath," "emanation," "reflection," "mirror," and "image." Then in 7:27-28, wisdom's close relationship to humans is described: "she passes into holy souls and makes them friends of God and prophets." In 7:29–8:1 there is a return to the cosmic dimensions of wisdom; she is superior to the sun, stars, and light, and "orders all things well." And there is also a moral dimension: "against wisdom evil does not prevail."

This description takes wisdom beyond the realm of practical advice for happy and successful living, and makes her into a personal figure with cosmic, theological, historical, and moral significance. Wisdom is surely not a goddess beside the God of Israel. The author is a Jewish monotheist. For him, the God of Israel is the creator and lord of all, and the only true God. Wisdom is at least an attribute of God — like justice and mercy. But there seems to be more to it than that. The female characteristics may be due simply to the feminine gender of the Hebrew (*ḥokma*) and Greek (*sophia*) nouns for "wisdom," though it is possible that Wisdom is the Jewish equivalent of the goddess Isis (see 7:22-24, which many regard as the equivalent of an Isis aretalogy) or of other goddess figures. At any rate, early Christians had little problem in transferring the attributes of wisdom personified to Jesus (see Col. 1:15-20; John 1:1-18; Heb. 1:1-4).

E. The *Search for Wisdom* and for the benefits she brings (8:2-16) is described again in terms of Solomon's seeking a spouse: "I desired to take her for my bride." Because wisdom has lived with God and been loved by God, and because she is "an initiate in the knowledge of God and an associate in his works" (8:4), what she can give is superior to all human possessions and understanding.

Wisdom is the source of all virtues (8:7). Note that first on the list of virtues is "righteousness," which is used here in its biblical sense of right relationship with God and with humans. Then comes the list of cardinal virtues familiar from Greek philosophy: self-control, prudence, justice, and courage.

Wisdom is also the repository of all human experience (8:8), not only of the past but also of the future, since she "infers the things to come." Because Solomon took wisdom as his "wife," he has become successful and famous. In 8:9-12 Solomon claims that the good counsel and encouragement that he received from wisdom have won him great respect ("glory among the multitudes"). And in 8:13-16 Solomon attributes the "immortality" that he has gained as a famous king to his association with wisdom ("because of her") and to the peaceful life that he has enjoyed with her as his spouse.

F. The *Prayer for Wisdom* (8:17–9:18) is one of the elements in the biblical tradition that made Solomon famous (see 1 Kings 3:3-9). Solomon first explains that, having recognized that immortality and happiness reside with wisdom, he resolved to obtain wisdom (8:17-18). Though naturally well disposed to receive wisdom ("a good soul fell to my lot"), he affirms in 8:21 that she is a gift from God and can therefore be obtained only through prayer.

The prayer for wisdom consists of an address (9:1-3), two petitions (9:4-9, 10-12), and a concluding reflection (9:13-18). The address, which is a paraphrase of Genesis 1–2, praises God for creating the world and for giving humankind dominion over the earth. Especially significant here is the equation between God's creative word and wisdom: "who have made all things by your word, and by your wisdom have formed humankind."

The first petition (9:4-9) is "Give me the wisdom that sits by your throne." Solomon needs the gift of wisdom because he is "weak and short-lived" (9:5-6), and because without it he could not build the temple in Jerusalem (9:7-8). He needs wisdom because she was with God at creation and has perfect knowledge of God's will (9:9). The second petition (9:10-12) is "Send her forth from the holy heavens." With wisdom guiding and guarding him, Solomon can accomplish his works as king. Wisdom serves as an intermediary between God and Solomon.

The concluding reflection (9:13-18) explains why wisdom's mediatorship is necessary. No human can fully understand the ways of God, in part because the "perishable body weighs down the soul, and this earthly tent burdens the thoughtful mind" (9:15). What enables humans to grasp the plans of God is the gift of wisdom: "you have given wisdom and sent your holy spirit from on high" (9:17). Note the equation between wisdom and the "holy spirit." Solomon concludes in 9:18 that wisdom has been active throughout the history of God's people. This in turn announces the theme for the next major part of the book.

Part Three: Wisdom's Role in Israel's Early History (10–19)

A. The survey of *Wisdom's Role in Israel's Early History* from Adam to Moses (10:1-21) provides a transition from the description of wisdom in chapters 6–9 to the focus on events surrounding the exodus in the rest of the book. The basic theme is that even in the early history of God's people wisdom was at work and was, indeed, the means by which God directed the course of history. The passage refers to several biblical heroes (and a few villains) without giving their names. This rhetorical device presumes that readers can identify the figures and may promote their active involvement.

Wisdom protected "the first-formed father of the world" (Adam) and allowed him to exercise the dominion that God granted despite his sin (10:1-2). While Adam's original sin of Genesis is overcome by the power of wisdom, the sin committed by Cain in killing Abel (10:3) is the result of his turning away from wisdom. It was wisdom who saved humankind and the whole earth from the flood in Noah's time through "steering the righteous man by a paltry piece of wood" (10:4). Out of the confusion that arose from building the Tower of Babel, wisdom chose Abraham and helped him pass through the trial associated with the sacrifice of Isaac (10:5).

In the destruction of Sodom and Gomorrah and the surrounding cities, wisdom was active in rescuing Lot and punishing the ungodly "who passed wisdom by" (10:6-8). The pillar of salt which Lot's wife became and the smoldering wasteland near the Dead Sea serve as "a monument to an unbelieving soul." That wisdom rescues "from troubles those who served her" is illustrated by Jacob's struggles with Esau and other enemies (10:9-12). Particular attention is given to Jacob's wrestling with the angel and the vision he received — again through the agency of wisdom: "she showed him the kingdom of God and gave him knowledge of holy things." Jacob's career is put forward as teaching the lesson that "godliness is more powerful than anything else" (10:12). And in the amazing career of Joseph (10:13-14), wisdom was at work in delivering him from danger and false accusation, and in leading him to "everlasting honor."

In the exodus from Egypt (10:15-21) it was wisdom who delivered Israel from bondage, raised up Moses ("a servant of the Lord"), and worked "wonders and signs" through him. Wisdom guided the people by pillars of cloud and fire, brought Israel through the Red Sea, drowned its enemies, and inspired the victory song in Exodus 15: "for wisdom opened the mouths of those who were mute, and made the tongues of infants speak clearly" (10:21; see Isa. 35:6). From Adam to Moses, wisdom directed the fortunes of God's people.

B-1. The *First Contrast* (11:1-14) begins a series of seven contrasts associated with the exodus. The basic principle underlying all seven contrasts is stated first in 11:5: "For through the very things by which their enemies were punished, they themselves (Israel) received benefit in their need." At the end of the first contrast, the series is interrupted by a theological reflection (11:15–12:27) and an excursus on idolatry (13–15).

The initial contrast begins and ends with references to Moses: "by the hand of a holy prophet . . . who long before had been cast out and exposed." The primary agent in the exodus, however, is wisdom, though here and in the rest of the book wisdom and God tend to merge and it is often hard to know who is being addressed as "you."

The contrast takes its point of departure from the account of the water given to Israel from the rock in the wilderness (11:2-4; see Exod. 17:1-7). The gift of abundant water contrasts with the first plague visited upon Egypt before the exodus, when the waters of the Nile turning to blood resulted in great thirst among the Egyptians (11:6-8; see Exod. 7:14-25). In both cases the instrument was water and the problem was thirst. Whereas the thirst of the Israelites in the wilderness was a merciful discipline from God, the thirst of the Egyptians was a punishment visited upon them by God's wrath (11:9). Whereas God treated the Israelites "as a parent does in warning," God dealt with the ungodly Egyptians "as a stern king does in condemnation" (11:10). The Egyptians endured a double punishment in that they not only suffered thirst but also finally recognized that "through their own punishments the righteous had received benefit" and that "it was the Lord's doing" (11:12-13). The Egyptians, who once rejected Moses, came to marvel at him (11:14).

C. The *Excursus on God's Justice and Mercy* (11:15–12:27) first affirms the principle that "one is punished by the very things by which one sins" (11:16). Since the Egyptians worshiped "irrational serpents and worthless animals," God sent upon them "a multitude of irrational creatures to punish them" (11:15-16), which is presumably a reference to the plagues of frogs, gnats, and flies described in Exodus 8. Even though the Creator could have punished the Egyptians in other ways (by bears, lions, dragons, and so on), God customarily acts according to a certain proportionality and harmony: "You have arranged all things by measure and number and weight" (11:20).

The proportionality and harmony manifest in creation, however, do not negate God's sovereignty and mercy (11:21–12:2). In comparison with God, the whole world is "like a speck that tips the scales and like a drop of morning dew." God has created all things and loves all things, because God's "immortal spirit is in all things" (12:1). God punishes people by the very things in which they sin in order to correct them and bring them to repentance and trust in God.

This pattern can be discerned not only in the exodus but also in the conquest of Canaan (12:3-11). The Canaanites were punished because of their idolatry, which is described in gruesome detail in 12:3-6. It was God's plan to settle the Holy Land with "a worthy colony of the servants of God" (12:7). But instead of destroying the Canaanites all at once, God first sent wasps or hornets (see Exod. 23:28) to give them "an opportunity to repent," even though it was unlikely that they would repent.

The warning given to the Canaanites shows the sovereignty and mercy of God (12:12-18). No one can accuse God of injustice since God made these nations and cares for all peoples. Unlike those humans who proclaim that their might makes right (see 2:11), God's strength is "the source of righteousness" (12:16), and God judges with mildness and governs with forbearance (12:18).

God's way of acting holds important lessons for Israel (12:19-22). It teaches that the righteous must be kind, that God gives an opportunity to repent, and that we can rely on the goodness and mercy of God. At the same time, it helps to explain the sufferings that Israel endures. They are a temporary discipline or "chastening" as opposed to the more severe punishments visited upon the enemies of Israel (12:22; see 2 Macc. 6:12-16).

The reflection returns in 12:23-27 to the case of the Egyptians. As 11:1-14 shows, God "tormented them through their own abominations." Having rejected relatively mild rebukes from God, they experienced God's just judgment in that the creatures that they regarded as gods became the means by which they were punished.

D. In the *Excursus on Idolatry* (chapters 13–15), the first form of idolatry that is condemned in 13:1-9 is nature worship. This involves mistaking creatures (however beautiful and powerful they may seem to be) for the Creator. The fault of those who engage in nature worship is that they render themselves "unable from the good things that are seen to know the one who exists" (13:1). Although the speaker appears tolerant at first in judging nature worshipers ("these people are little to be blamed"), he then grows impatient with their failure to "find sooner the Lord of these things."

The next form of idolatry involves worshiping wooden images (13:10-19). After a survey of the works of human hands that some people call gods, the passage traces the process by which a woodworker carves and paints an idol, mounts it securely lest it fall and be unable to get up, and prays to it for all the most important things in life: possessions, family, health, and so on. Another illustration of the folly of idolatry is provided by the case of one who on setting out on a sea voyage prays to a wooden idol "more fragile than the ship that carries him" (14:1). The ship was planned as a business venture to make money, and it was built by human craftsmen as the instruments of wisdom. But it is "your providence, O Father, that steers its course" and brings it safely to land — as was the case with Noah's ark when "the hope of the world took refuge on a raft." Both the idol and the idol maker are accursed (14:8-11), and there will be a visitation upon them because they have made part of God's creation into "snares for souls."

Idolatry had its origin in human invention (14:12-21). It was not in God's plan for creation and will not last forever. Meanwhile, it is the source of sinfulness and corruption. Two examples suggest how idolatry may have begun. First (14:15), a father who lost a child through sudden death made an image of the child, which in turn became an object of worship. Second (14:16-21), people who wanted the image of a king began to worship the image, which in turn encouraged the king to make it into a cult and ambitious artisans to produce even more beautiful (and less realistic) images of the king. Because people regarded as gods the images of a dead child and a king, this became "a hidden trap for humankind" (14:21).

The theme of idolatry as the root of all sins and vices is developed in 14:22-31: "For the worship of idols not to be named is the beginning and cause and end of every evil" (14:27). A mistake about God inevitably leads to murder, theft, sexual perversions, and so on (see Rom. 1:18-32). Particularly wicked are vices associated with pagan religious rituals ("secret mysteries") and with false oaths sworn in the name of idols (which are not gods at all).

The excursus on idolatry closes with a contrast between the worship of the true God and the worship of clay idols and of animals (15:1-19). The true God is addressed as "our God" and celebrated as the source of righteousness and immortality. The claim that "even if we sin we are yours" is a tribute to God's fidelity, and is immediately balanced by the promise that "we will not sin" (15:2). The true God has nothing to do with idolatry.

The folly of worshiping clay idols (15:7-13) is treated with reference to the process of idol making and the guilt of those who manufacture the idols. The potter creates idols out of the same clay as other vessels but will die even before the clay idol disintegrates. The idol makers refuse to know "the one who formed them," and cynically regard their work as only a business and see life as "a festival held for profit" (15:12).

The Egyptians (15:14-19) are declared foolish and miserable on two counts. First (15:15-17), they thought that their idols were gods, even though they were powerless and manufactured by humans. Second (15:18-19), they went so far as to worship "hateful animals" and did not even have the good taste to choose intelligent and beautiful animals to worship. Their idolatry is the most wretched of all the forms treated in the excursus.

B-2. Returning to the series begun in 11:1-14, the *Second Contrast* (16:1-4) concerns the different ways that God treated the Egyptians and the Israelites. Because of the Egyptians' worship of "hateful animals" (15:18), God sent upon them "a multitude of animals" to torment them — most likely a reference to the plague of frogs (see Exod. 8:1-15). This plague had the effect of making the Egyptians lose their appetites and so suffer from hunger ("inescapable want"). For the Israelites enduring hunger in the wilderness, however, God provided "quails to eat, a delicacy to satisfy the desire of appetite" (16:2; see Exod. 16:13). The Israelites were not only fed luxurious food but also had the satisfaction of knowing that their enemies were being punished (in contrast to their own short-time suffering).

B-3. The *Third Contrast* (16:5-14) compares what happened to the Egyptians in the plagues of locusts (see Exod. 10:1-20) and flies (see Exod. 8:20-32) with what happened to Israel in the wilderness during the episode of the bronze serpent (see Num. 21:5-9). Little attention is given to the Egyptians, beyond saying that they were killed "because they deserved to be punished by such things" (16:9) — presumably on account of their animal worship (as in 16:1-4). Since the Israelites were healed from the bites of poisonous serpents only by looking at the bronze image of a serpent, the biblical episode could be taken as an instance of idol worship on Israel's part. To correct this impression, the speaker first (16:6-8) interprets the sufferings of the Israelites as a warning and the bronze serpent as "a symbol of deliverance" (16:16), insisting that they were healed by "the Savior of all" in order to show Israel's enemies that God delivers from every evil. Then in a second attempt at explanation (16:10-14) the speaker attributes Israel's sufferings to God's mercy (as God's way of reminding Israel of the commandments) and Israel's healing to the power of God's word: "it was your word, O Lord, that heals all people" (16:12). The entire episode proves that only God has "power over life and death."

B-4. The *Fourth Contrast* (16:15-29) concerns what came from the heavens upon the Egyptians (hail and lightning) and upon the Israelites (manna), respectively. The combination of hail and lightning described in the series of plagues in the book of Exodus (see Exod. 9:23-25) is identified in 16:15-19 with water and fire — two of the essential elements of the universe. By using these elements to punish the Egyptians, God showed that "the universe defends the righteous" (16:17). In destroying the Egyptians and their crops, God used the water and the fire in a kind of harmonious mixture to maximum effect (16:18-19).

What came down from the heavens upon the Israelites was manna (see Exod. 16:1-21), which is here called the "food of angels" (16:20). Whereas the biblical account emphasized that there was enough manna to satisfy the needs of the Israelites, the speaker emphasizes its sweetness and good taste ("to suit everyone's liking"), as well as its miraculous ability to withstand the fire and rain (16:21-23). Two lessons or "morals" are drawn from the manna episode. The first lesson (16:24-26) is that God uses the elements of creation such as water and fire to punish the unrighteous (such as the Egyptians) and to satisfy the needs of the righteous — in order that Israel might learn that "your word sustains those who trust in you." The second lesson (16:27-29) is drawn from the biblical idea that the manna appeared only in the morning and concerns the value of morning prayer: "one must rise before the sun to give you thanks."

B-5. The *Fifth Contrast* (17:1–18:4) concerns the darkness visited upon the land of Egypt and the light that Israel experienced in its exodus. The description of the plague of darkness in the book of Exodus takes up only three verses (10:21-23), whereas in Wisdom 17:1-21 it is described in great detail. The emphasis is on both the total character of the darkness (objective dimension) and the fear that it inspired among the Egyptians (subjective or psychological dimension). These themes are developed in two parallel descriptions (17:1-10 and 17:14-21) that are interrupted by a moral commentary (17:11-13). Whereas the Egyptians imagined that the Israelites were their slaves, in fact they were "captives of darkness and prisoners of long night" (17:2). Whereas darkness had once served as a cloak to hide the Egyptians' sinfulness, it became a punishment for them. The darkness, which was described enigmatically as "a darkness that can be felt" in Exodus 10:21, was so absolute that no fire or heavenly body or magical art could penetrate it. The complete darkness made all the more terrifying the specters or phantoms that the Egyptians imagined as well as the sounds made by passing wild animals or hissing snakes. The result was that the Egyptians became sick with "ridiculous fear" and perished in "trembling fear."

The moral commentary (17:11-13) associates wickedness and fear ("wickedness is a cowardly thing"), offers a definition of fear ("a giving up of the helps that come from reason"), and suggests that fearful people prefer ignorance to finding out what is causing their torment. While this commentary is intended to sound abstract and philosophical, in the context of the book of Wisdom it also evokes the connection between righteousness and wisdom that was stressed in chapters 1–5.

The second description (17:14-21) again refers to the "monstrous specters" and the terrifying sounds (which are described with great detail in 17:18-19). It also emphasizes the paralysis that the fear of the darkness caused ("paralyzed by their souls' surrender . . . paralyzed then with terror," 17:15, 19) and the universality of the experience among the Egyptians ("with one chain of darkness they all were bound"). But the darkness affected only the Egyptians, and in fact their fear was even worse punishment than the darkness (17:20-21).

By contrast (18:1-4), for Israel there was "very great light" — a pillar of fire to lead them on their journey out of Egypt by night (see Exod. 13:17-22) and a "harmless sun" by day (note the omission of the pillar of cloud). The Egyptians in their darkness heard the voices of the Israelites and were so thankful that they did not take vengeance on them and begged their forgiveness. The light that was given to the Israelites in their exodus from Egypt was an anticipation of the law that would be given to them on Mount Sinai and that through them would be transmitted to the whole world: "through whom the imperishable light of the law was to be given to the world" (18:4).

B-6. The *Sixth Contrast* (18:5-25) deals with the deaths of Egyptians and of Israelites. At Passover the firstborn male children of the Egyptians were slain (see Exod. 12:29-30), and at the crossing of the Red Sea members of the Egyptian army were drowned (see Exod. 14:26-31). The death of the firstborn and the flood are explained (18:5) in light of the plot to kill the Israelite children and the rescue of the child Moses (see Exod. 1:1–2:10). The basic principle of interpretation is restated in 18:8: "For by the same means by which you punished our enemies you called us to yourself and glorified us." The salvation of Israel was supposedly promoted by the sacrifices of the "holy children of good people" and their agreement to the divine law (18:9), while the death of the Egyptian children was linked to their practice of the "magic arts" (18:13). The agent in destroying the enemies of God and God's people was "your all powerful word" (18:15) — a combination of wisdom as the word of God active in history, the divine warrior figure familiar from ancient Near Eastern literature and the Hebrew Bible, and a gigantic angel "who touched heaven while standing on earth" (18:16). There is an attempt throughout to exculpate God and Israel, and to blame the Egyptians for their own misfortunes: they killed Israelite children (18:5); they indulged in magic arts (18:13); they were forewarned by "dreadful dreams" (18:17); and they knew why they were suffering (18:19). Children and water meant liberation for Israel but destruction for Egypt.

But Israelites died too. The case presented for comparison in 18:20-25 came in the aftermath of the revolt of Korah, Dathan, and Abiram (see Numbers 16) when 14,700 Israelites died from a plague (Num. 16:49). Rather than dwelling on their deaths, however, the speaker observes that "the wrath did not long continue" (17:20) and focuses on how Aaron the high priest put a quick end to the plague "by his word" (18:22). This passage is noteworthy for its personifications of death as "the avenger" (18:22) and "the destroyer" (18:25), and for its interpretation of the priestly robe of Aaron as a depiction of the whole world and the "glories of the ancestors" (18:24). Even in the death of Israelites the speaker discerns the power of God's word spoken by the priest Aaron.

B-7. The *Seventh Contrast* (19:1-22) presents an interpretation of the events at the Red Sea (see Exodus 14). God's purpose in these events was "that your people might experience an incredible journey, but they themselves [the Egyptians] might meet a strange death" (19:5). In 19:1-4 the speaker balances both the foreknowledge of God ("God knew in advance") and the culpability of the Egyptians because they decided to pursue the fleeing Israelites: "for the fate they deserved drew them on to this end" (19:4).

In 19:6-12 he provides a surprisingly positive picture (compare Numbers 11) of Israel's journey in the wilderness. To make Israel's way smooth, God used various elements in creation to the extent that one can say that "the whole creation in its nature was fashioned anew" (19:6). For its part, Israel rejoiced and praised God for delivering them, and recalled how God supplied them with animals, fish, and quail while punishing the Egyptians with gnats and frogs.

74

Once more and for the last time in 19:13-17, the speaker insists on the justice of God in punishing the Egyptians: "they justly suffered because of their wicked acts" (19:13). The Egyptians not only refused to receive the Israelites as guests but even went so far as to enslave them. The fact that at first they welcomed (in Joseph's time) and then afflicted Israel makes it all the more understandable why they should have been punished.

Finally in 19:18-21 the speaker returns to his theme of God's fashioning creation anew (see 19:6) and provides a "scientific" explanation for how God did it: "the elements changed places with one another" (19:18). After using the analogy of notes on harp, he develops his "atomic" theory of transformations with reference to humans (Israel) crossing through the sea and sea creatures invading the land (frogs), to fire and water, and even to the manna. The book ends with an apt summary of the author's interpretation of the exodus and his perspective on (and hope for) Israel: "For in everything, O Lord, you have exalted and glorified your people, and you have not neglected to help them at all times and in all places" (19:22).

Significance

The author of the book of Wisdom used Greek rhetorical techniques and philosophical concepts to convey biblical teachings about the power and justice of God, the human condition, the nature of wisdom, the folly of idolatry, and God's action in history.

The emphasis on immortality is the writer's most original and influential contribution to biblical theology. This idea, which was common in some Greek philosophies but barely present in the Hebrew Bible, allowed him to acknowledge the reality of innocent suffering in the present, while defending the omnipotence and justice of God. In this way he deferred the vindication of the righteous to their life after death or to the Last Judgment. He interpreted the present sufferings of faithful Jews as a test or temporary discipline, while holding to the conviction that the ancient Egyptians and Canaanites got what they deserved (because they were idolators and sinners).

Another important contribution to biblical theology comes in the treatment of wisdom. For the writer, wisdom is not simply proverbs and instructions about conduct. Rather, wisdom has a cosmic dimension (as the world soul), a personal dimension (as a female figure), and a historical dimension (as God's agent in Israel's history).

Issues. The basic three-part structure of the Wisdom of Solomon is clear. But within this outline there are many connections, excursuses, anticipations, and other rhetorical devices indicating an even more complex and sophisticated structure that has resisted unanimity among scholars. Also the logic of some of the comparisons in the third part is hard to grasp, leading some scholars to suppose that the author grew tired or failed to revise what he wrote.

Another area of debate has been the occasion of the book's composition. Was it a response to a particular crisis in the history of the Alexandrian Jewish community? Or should it be taken as a general essay applicable to Diaspora Jews at almost any time from the second century B.C.E. through the first century C.E.?

The precise nature of the immortality envisioned in the book is also a matter of controversy. The author appears to believe in the preexistence of souls (see 8:19-20) and to view the soul as weighed down by the body (see 8:15). But he insists that immortality is a gift from God (see 8:13) and not simply part of the human condition. In the same passage, he first presents immortality as granted immediately after death (see 3:1-6) and goes on to place immortality in the context of the Last Judgment and other end-time events (see 3:7-9).

Influence. The book of Wisdom is a very important document in the history of Diaspora Judaism. Using the language of Greek philosophy, it represents an early attempt by a Jewish writer to present biblical teachings with a new vocabulary and conceptuality. At the same time, he leaves the biblical teachings open to change by trying to express them with new terms and ideas. The effort at uniting the Bible and Greek philosophy reaches its mature development in the writings of Philo of Alexandria; it can also be seen in 4 Maccabees. The author's polemic against idolatry finds resonances in the Letter of Jeremiah and in Bel and the Dragon, and most dramatically in Paul's meditation on idolatry as the origin of ignorance and sin (see Rom. 1:18-32).

The personification of wisdom has special relevance for the early Christian understanding of Jesus as the Wisdom of God. Several hymns preserved in the New Testament celebrate Jesus in terms reminiscent of the book of Wisdom: the "image of God" (see Col. 1:15-20), the "Word" of God (see John 1:1-18), and the "reflection of God's glory" (see Heb. 1:3). Moreover, the plot of the wicked against "the righteous man" (see

2:12-20) with its echoes of the Suffering Servant of Isaiah 53 fits nicely into early Christian efforts to explain the mystery of the cross. Finally, the idea of wisdom as a "spirit" with cosmic, personal, and historical dimensions contributed greatly to the early Christian doctrine of the Holy Spirit.

Suggestions for Further Study

Cheon, Samuel. *The Exodus Story in the Wisdom of Solomon.* Sheffield: Sheffield Academic Press, 1997.

Collins, John J. *Jewish Wisdom in the Hellenistic Age.* Louisville: Westminster John Knox, 1997.

Grabbe, Lester L. *Wisdom of Solomon.* Sheffield: Sheffield Academic Press, 1997.

Kolarcik, Michael. *The Ambiguity of Death in the Book of Wisdom 1–6.* Rome: Biblical Institute Press, 1991.

———. "The Book of Wisdom." In *The New Interpreter's Bible,* vol. 5, 435-600. Nashville: Abingdon, 1997.

Reese, James M. *The Book of Wisdom, Song of Songs.* Old Testament Message 20. Wilmington, Del.: Glazier, 1983.

———. *Hellenistic Influence on the Book of Wisdom and Its Consequences.* Rome: Biblical Institute Press, 1970.

Winston, David. *The Wisdom of Solomon.* Anchor Bible 43. Garden City, N.Y.: Doubleday, 1979.

CHAPTER 6

Ecclesiasticus/Sirach:
Fear of the Lord

Basic Information

The title "Sirach" derives from the author's name "Jesus son of Eleazar son of Sirach" (50:27). It is customary to refer to the author as "Ben Sira" ("son of Sirach"). In the Latin tradition the book is known as "Ecclesiasticus" ("church book").

Sirach is a wisdom book. It assumes a situation in which Ben Sira, the experienced sage and teacher, is instructing a younger man ("my child") who wishes to become wise. The prospective sage is male, someone who has financial resources and will become head of a household. The young man is being trained to become a scribe — someone not only able to read and write but also prepared to exercise public leadership (see 38:24–39:11). Ben Sira conducted a school in Jerusalem, perhaps near the temple, for such young men (see 51:23-30). There he showed his students how to join the wisdom traditions of the ancient Near East with their Jewish religious traditions.

Ben Sira's favorite mode of communication is short sayings of two members in synonymous (same ideas) or antithetical (opposite ideas) parallelism. His major contribution to the Hebrew wisdom tradition consisted in joining individual sayings by common words or themes, and using small units to develop logically a theme or an argument in paragraph form. Within this general literary framework he used the devices typical of the wisdom literature: numerical sayings ("I take pleasure in three things . . ."), beatitudes ("happy are those who . . ."), warnings ("do not . . ."), questions, comparisons, and so forth. He also employed poetic devices (assonance, alliteration, rhyme), inclusions (beginning and ending a unit in the same way), chiasms, and acrostics (51:13-30). The book reaches its climax with a hymn about God's glory made manifest in nature (42:15–43:33) and a poetic retelling of Israel's history (chaps. 44–50).

More is known about the historical circumstances of Sirach than most other ancient books. It was written in Jerusalem by a teacher named Jesus (50:27) around 180 B.C.E. This date places Ben Sira in Jerusalem, when Palestine was under Egyptian Ptolemaic rule and then from 198 onward under Syrian/Seleucid rule. Yet Ben Sira does not refer directly to these turbulent times, preferring instead to dispense timeless wisdom apparently applicable in all times and places. Though often described as a traditionalist or conservative, Ben Sira was a pioneer in integrating biblical and secular wisdom. The striking parallels with the Greek poet Theognis and the demotic Egyptian Instruction in Papyrus Insinger suggest some literary dependence on or at least participation in the international wisdom movement.

Sirach was composed about 180 B.C.E. in Hebrew. It was translated into Greek by the author's grandson in Egypt about 117 B.C.E. (see the Prologue). The Greek version became the primary text and the source of the Latin and most other texts. In 1896 and thereafter substantial parts of the Hebrew text were recovered from the Cairo Genizah, and in 1964 several chapters of the Hebrew text were found at Masada. Both the Greek and the Hebrew textual traditions have long and short recensions, thus creating many textual complexities. The Hebrew fragments are regarded as generally authentic, though there is some evidence of retranslation from the Syriac version.

According to the grandson there is "no small difference" between the Hebrew and the Greek texts. Most modern translations take the Greek version as the base text (since it is the most complete and has functioned as the church's book through the centuries) and distinguish between the short and long Greek recensions by different sizes of type and or by footnotes. Some translations use the Hebrew fragments to correct corruptions in the Greek tradition or to represent more accurately what Ben Sira meant.

It is not easy to discern a clear outline in Sirach, especially in the material up to chapters 44–50. Most of the book consists of short blocks or essays on various topics, with the same topic being taken up at several different places. To work through each unit would make our treatment in this introduction too long and too tedious. So, by way of compromise, I will first present both a structural outline and a topical outline of the entire book, and then treat seven topics in some detail as an illustration of how to read Sirach and of what one can expect from it.

Content

Part One: Structural and Topical Outlines

A. *Structural Outline:* One way to approach Sirach is to read it straight through. This is the way that Ben Sira wrote it and the way it has come down to us. Many commentators take the series of wisdom poems as structurally significant, and so they divide the book into parts on that basis (1:1-10; 4:11-19; 6:18-37; 14:20–15:10; 24:1-33; 38:24–39:11). For the most part the book gives the impression of being an anthology of wisdom teachings with a loose general structure. Nevertheless, the wisdom poems do at least offer some principle for dividing this huge book into manageable parts. And so the following outline is divided into seven main sections.

1. The origin and nature of wisdom (1:1-30); fear of the Lord (2:1-18); parents and children (3:1-16); humility (3:17-29); and almsgiving (3:30–4:10).
2. The benefits of wisdom (4:11-19); honor and shame (4:20–6:4); and friendship (6:5-17).
3. Discipline as the way to wisdom (6:18-37); avoiding evil (7:1-17); social relations (7:18-36); caution in social relations (8:1-19); relations with women (9:1-9); friendships (9:10-16); wise rulers (9:16–10:5); pride (10:6-18); honor and shame (10:19–11:6); true wealth (11:7-28); caution in social relations (11:29–12:18); rich and poor (13:1-24); and using money (13:25–14:19).
4. Seeking and finding wisdom (14:20–15:10); free will and sin (15:11-20); human responsibility and effects (16:1-23); creation and responsibility (16:24–17:24); call to repentance (17:25-32); God's majesty and mercy (18:1-14); words and gifts (18:15-18); reflection and action (18:19-29); self-control (18:30–19:3); gossip

80

(19:4-17); wisdom and cleverness (19:20-30); speech (20:1-31); the destructive power of sin (21:1-10); the sage and the fool (21:11-28); dealing with fools (22:1-18); friendship (22:19-26); prayer and sin (22:27–23:6); sins of speech (23:7-15); and sins of the flesh (23:16-27).

5. Praise of wisdom (24:1-34); happiness (25:1-11); the bad wife and the good wife (25:13–26:27); sin and related topics (26:28–27:29); forgiveness of sins (27:30–28:7); destructive speech (28:8-26); money matters (29:1-20); depending on others (29:21-29); fathers and sons (30:1-13); happiness (30:14-25); riches (31:1-11); manners and moderation (31:12–32:13); wisdom, Torah, and fear of the Lord (32:14–33:6); the pairs (33:7-15); autobiographical note (33:16-19); master of the household (33:20-33); sources of wisdom and happiness (34:1-20); true religion and social justice (34:21–35:26); prayer for God's people (36:1-22); friends and associates (36:23–37:15); wisdom and moderation (37:16-31); sickness and doctors (38:1-15); and mourning (38:16-23).

6. Tradesmen and the scribe (38:24–39:11); God's creation and evil (39:12-35); misery and joy (40:1-30); death and reputation (41:1-13); shame (41:14–42:8); father and daughters (42:9-14); and God's glory in creation (42:15–43:33).

7. God's glory in Israel (44:1-15); the patriarchs (44:16-23); Moses, Aaron, and Phinehas (45:1-26); Joshua and Caleb, the Judges, and Samuel (46:1-20); early kings (47:1-25); prophets and kings (48:1–49:16); Simon the high priest (50:1-24); postscript and epilogue (50:25-29); and three appendixes (51:1-30).

B. *Topical Outline:* Another approach to reading the Sirach is to focus on topics that are treated in several places in the text. The following list may facilitate a topical reading and also indicates the most important subjects in the book.

Autobiography: 24:30-34; 33:16-19; 34:9-13; 39:12-13; 50:27; 51:13-30.
Creation: 16:24–17:24; 18:1-14; 33:7-15; 39:12-35; 42:15–43:33.
Death: 38:16-23; 41:1-13.
Fear of the Lord: 1:11-20; 2:1-18; 34:14-20.
Friendship: 6:5-17; 9:10-16; 19:13-17; 22:19-26; 27:16-21; 36:23–37:15.

Happiness: 25:1-11; 30:14-25; 40:1-30.

Honor and Shame: 4:20–6:4; 10:9–11:6; 41:14–42:8.

Humility and Pride: 3:17-29; 10:6-18.

Manners and Moderation: 31:12–32:13; 37:27-31.

Money Matters: 3:30–4:10; 29:1-20; 29:21-28.

Parents and Children: 3:1-16; 7:23-25; 16:1-4; 30:1-13; 41:5-10; 42:9-14.

People of God: 36:1-22; 44:1–50:24.

Prayers: 22:26–23:6; 36:1-22; 39:12-35; 50:22-24; 51:1-12; 51:12ff.

Rulers: 9:16–10:5.

Sacrifice: 34:21–35:26; 50:5-21.

Sickness and Doctors: 38:1-15.

Sin: 7:1-17; 15:11-20; 16:1-23; 16:24–17:24; 17:25-31; 18:30–19:3; 21:1-10; 22:26–23:6; 23:7-15; 23:16-27; 26:28–27:29; 27:30–28:7.

Social Justice: 4:1-10; 34:21-27; 35:14-26.

Social Relations: 7:18-36; 8:1-19; 11:29–12:18; 33:20-33.

Speech: 5:9-15; 18:15-18; 18:19-29; 19:4-17; 20:1-31; 23:7-15; 27:4-7; 27:11-15; 28:8-26.

Wealth: 11:7-28; 13:1-24; 13:25–14:19; 31:1-11.

Wisdom: 1:1-10; 4:11-19; 6:18-37; 14:20–15:10; 19:20-30; 21:11-28; 22:1-18; 24:1-34; 32:14–33:6; 34:1-20; 37:16-31; 38:24–39:11; 51:13-30.

Women: 9:1-9; 23:22-26; 25:13–26:27; 36:26-31; 42:9-14.

Part Two: Seven Topics

A. *Fear of the Lord* is the proper response to God's gift of wisdom. It refers to the respect, gratitude, and conduct that are owed to God. It is Ben Sira's integrating theme and provides the theological framework for the entire book.

The poem celebrating the fear of the Lord in 1:11-20 first reflects on the happiness that it brings in all phases of life (1:11-13). Then it praises fear of the Lord as the beginning, fullness, crown, and root of wisdom (1:14-20).

The instruction about fear of the Lord in 2:1-18 begins (2:1-6) by warning the prospective sage to expect testing and to persevere in trusting

God. Ben Sira explains the suffering of the righteous as a test or discipline with the help of the common biblical analogy of gold tested in fire. He contrasts those who fear the Lord (2:7-9, 15-17) with the fainthearted (2:12-14) and asks, "Has anyone trusted in the Lord and been disappointed?" (2:10). Those who fear and love the Lord are said to be filled with God's law (2:16) — a characteristic emphasis of Ben Sira, who equates wisdom and the Torah elsewhere (see 24:23). In the final verse (2:18) he commends the lordship of God as superior to that of humans because God is the merciful one.

In 34:14-20 Ben Sira reflects on fear of the Lord as a positive ideal: "Happy is the soul who fears the Lord." With a series of striking images ("a shelter from scorching wind and a shade from noonday sun . . . he lifts up the soul and makes the eyes sparkle"), he describes the blessings that accompany those who fear the Lord. Because fear of the Lord involves the proper perceptions about who God is and who we are before God, it can be said that fear of the Lord is the beginning of wisdom.

B. *Friendship* receives more attention from Ben Sira than from any other biblical writer. His positive ideal is "friends in the Lord." His approach is not theoretical, nor is he much concerned with defining friendship or giving reasons why people need friends.

In 6:5-17 he offers practical advice about making friends and warns against fair-weather friends. He urges caution in making close friends ("let your advisers be one in a thousand") and describes faithful friends as "a sturdy shelter . . . a treasure . . . life-saving medicine." The best friends are "those who fear the Lord" because they share common values and can be trusted.

After comparing old and new friends, Ben Sira in 9:10-16 lists three kinds of persons to be avoided as friends — sinners, the ungodly, and those who have the power to kill — along with the reasons why they should be avoided (9:11-13). Those who are to be sought out as friends — the wise, intelligent, and righteous — share the sage's concern for the law of the Most High and fear of the Lord. True friendship is best found "in the Lord," where friends share common spiritual ideals.

For times when a friend or neighbor is the topic of gossip, Ben Sira in 19:13-17 recommends a direct approach. A personal confrontation can enable one to discover either that the story is false or that the friend's indiscretion is real and so can serve as the occasion for correction and reform.

According to 22:19-26 friendships are destroyed especially by "reviling, arrogance, disclosure of secrets, or a treacherous blow" (22:22). A faithful friend stands by especially in hard times, whether that means sharing in the friend's subsequent prosperity or suffering harm because of the friend (22:23, 25-26). Avoiding harsh words and keeping confidences are the best ways to keep a friendship.

In choosing a friend (37:1-6) one should be aware of "friends only in name," friends who become enemies, and fair-weather friends. Failures in friendship are traced to the "inclination to evil" (37:3), an important concept in Ben Sira's approach to sin. But friends who prove faithful in times of testing ("during the battle") should be rewarded.

C. *Honor and Shame* are part of the cultural context in which Ben Sira gives his advice about social relations. In Ben Sira's world, honor and shame derived from what other people thought of you and your social standing in the community. Those who had power, prestige, and wealth were generally regarded as honorable, while those who did not were despised. Ben Sira accepts some aspects of this worldview, while modifying it in accord with his Jewish religious approach to wisdom.

In 4:20–6:4 Ben Sira distinguishes between "a shame that leads to sins" and "a shame that is glory and honor" (4:21). In his examples he gives particular attention to the need for truthful speech (4:22-31; 5:9–6:1) and proper attitudes toward God (5:1-8). Whereas giving in to passion (6:2-4) makes one a laughingstock, those who follow the course of wisdom will bring honor upon themselves.

From his religious perspective Ben Sira in 10:19–11:6 redefines honor and shame. Those who fear the Lord are worthy of honor, and those who transgress the Lord's commandments deserve dishonor (10:19). Various aspects of this principle are developed in the short units in 10:20–11:6 that treat fear of the Lord and wisdom as the sources of true glory, avoiding boasting, humility, honor for the wise and the rich, wisdom as a source of honor, not judging by appearances, not boasting about fine clothes, and the reversals that befall kings. Instead of power, prestige, and riches, the sources of genuine honor are knowledge, wisdom, fear of the Lord, and keeping God's commandments.

In light of his redefinition of honor, Ben Sira presents lists of things of which one ought to be ashamed and not be ashamed in 41:14–42:8. The shameful things range from committing sexual immorality before one's parents to leaning on your elbow at meals. The first and most important thing on the list of things not to be ashamed of is "the law of the Most High and his covenant."

D. *Women* constitute a major topic for Ben Sira. What he says must be set in the literary and historical context according to which the principal addressee is a young man who wants to become a sage. In 9:1-9 Ben Sira the experienced sage/teacher gives advice about the kinds of women who can bring harm and disgrace to the prospective sage: a jealous wife, a dominating woman, a loose woman, a singer, a virgin, a prostitute, a beauty, and another man's wife.

Ben Sira and his first readers lived in a patriarchal society in which the husband exercised authority over his wife and the rest of the household. He introduces his advice about the bad wife and the good wife (25:13–26:27) by saying, "I would rather live with a lion and a dragon" (25:16) than with an ill-tempered wife. His patriarchal approach is reflected in his statements that it is shameful for a husband to live off his wife's money (25:22), that woman is the origin of sin (25:24), and that the husband has the prerogative in divorce (25:26). The good wife, however, is the source of long life, joy, and peace for her husband (26:1-4). The second description of the evil wife (26:5-12) consists of a numerical proverb culminating in the heartache caused by a jealous wife (26:5-6), three sayings on bad wives (26:7-9), and advice to keep strict sexual control over a rebellious daughter (25:10-12). The contrasting section on the good wife (26:13-18) praises her virtues (charm, silence, modesty) and physical beauty. Ben Sira's ideal woman is pious and modest, shows honor to her husband, and is quiet (26:19-27).

The instruction on choosing a wife (36:26-31) contrasts the happiness of a man married to a beautiful and modest woman (36:27-29) with the rootlessness and aimlessness of an unmarried man (36:30-31). Ben Sira's cultural assumptions emerge in his comment that "a woman will accept any man as a husband" (marriages were arranged, and the woman had little or no choice), and in his remark that one who acquires a wife gets "his best possession."

The major concern in the instruction about fathers and daughters (42:9-14) is the father's honor and shame before other men. The assumption is that daughters in "good" families live sheltered lives as they are prepared for arranged marriages with men from other "good" families. The passage consists of a list of the father's worries about his daughter (42:9-10) and a stern warning to supervise her closely (42:11-13). If not, the father runs the risk of becoming a "laughingstock . . . byword . . . shame." The low point in Ben Sira's attitude toward women comes in 42:14a: "Better is the wickedness of a man than a woman who does good."

E. The *Doctrine of the Pairs* in 33:7-15 is Ben Sira's way of explaining how an all-good and all-powerful God can allow the existence of evil (the question of theodicy). He proposes by way of explanation a modified dualism according to which God remains sovereign over both good and evil (see Isa. 45:7) and appeals to the divine plan working itself out in the nature of things.

Ben Sira leads up to this teaching by reflecting on the fact that some days are important (Passover, Sabbaths, etc.) and other days only get a number (Day One, Day Two, etc.). Next in 33:10-13 he discerns this duality in God's creation of human beings and dealings with them ("like clay in the hand of a potter"). Then in 33:14 he discerns in God's plan for creation a dualism of good versus evil, life versus death, and the godly versus sinners. Finally he articulates his doctrine of the pairs: "Look at all the works of the Most High; they come in pairs, one the opposite of the other" (33:15).

Rather than appealing to a Satan figure who leads the children of darkness to do the deeds of darkness, Ben Sira traces the duality to God's plan for creation. Nevertheless, human beings are not doomed to sin, however strong the power of the "evil inclination" (the disposition internal to persons that inclines them toward evil). Free will can overcome all moral obstacles: "If you choose, you can keep all the commandments" (15:15).

In explaining the existence of evil and suffering (39:12-35), Ben Sira affirms that God created all things as good, but for evil people these good things can have evil effects (39:25). So even necessities of life such as water and fire can have bad effects that serve to punish the wicked.

F. *Death* according to 38:16-23 is inevitable and irrevocable for human beings. When a loved one dies, the grief should be intense but circumscribed. The rituals associated with mourning for the dead should be observed "for a day or two." But excessive grief can be harmful: "Do not forget, there is no coming back; you do the dead no good, and you injure yourself" (38:21). Although there is no explicit denial of life after death, neither is there much affirmation of it ("the dead is at rest"). Ben Sira's real interests are in getting the prospective sage to face the fact of death and to put grief over the death of a loved one in proper perspective.

For Ben Sira, the "name" (the reputation and memory that one leaves behind) is the most important mode of immortality (44:1-13). Death is unwelcome to the prosperous and welcome to the wretched. Death is nonetheless "the Lord's decree for all flesh." Through their "abominable children" (41:5-10) the wicked — those who have forsaken the law of the Most High — suffer perpetual disgrace, for their children not only endure their parents' shame but also replicate their behavior. But a good and virtuous "name" lasts forever (41:11-13). It outlives the human body, lasts longer than a thousand hoards of gold, and has no limit (as even the days of a good life have).

G. *Wisdom* is the major topic in Sirach and serves as the thread that holds the book together. Where wisdom comes from, how one gets it, and what it is, are the topics of the opening verses (1:1-10). Ben Sira explains that God is the origin of wisdom, that God gives wisdom to those who love God, and that wisdom has been created by God. Ben Sira portrays wisdom as a female figure (as in Prov. 8:22-31) and later identifies wisdom with the Torah (24:23). The proper response to God's gift of wisdom is fear of the Lord.

The benefits of seeking wisdom according to 4:11-19 include instruction and help, life, joy, glory, and blessing from God (4:11-14). Despite its many benefits, the way of wisdom involves testing and discipline (4:17-19). Those who persevere on wisdom's way will find joy and knowledge, whereas those who fail to do so will end in destruction.

The theme of discipline as the way to wisdom is developed in 6:18-37. The three units begin with "my child" and advise the young sage to accept "discipline," the kind of intellectual and moral formation that produces wisdom and its rewards. The first unit (6:18-22) contrasts those who accept discipline and those who reject it. The second unit (6:23-31) develops the image of discipline as a "yoke" that binds the whole body. The third unit (6:32-37) directs the young sage to spend time with wise elders and to listen to their discourse as a way of becoming wise.

The search for wisdom is described in 14:20-27 in terms of images of the hunt, the house, and the shady tree. The reflection on the rewards of wisdom in 15:1-10 begins by linking fear of the Lord, the Torah, and wisdom — the essential elements in Ben Sira's theology (15:1). Wisdom, portrayed as a female figure (15:2-6), will shower benefits on the wise, including the "bread of learning" and the "water of wisdom" as well as "an everlasting name" (the immortality of memory).

The praise of wisdom in 24:1-34 is most significant for Ben Sira's assertion that wisdom dwells in the Jerusalem temple and for his identification of wisdom and the Torah. After describing herself as a creature of God (24:3-7), lady wisdom in 24:8-12 recounts how God assigned her a dwelling place in Israel at the Jerusalem temple. Then the comparisons of wisdom to various trees and bushes (24:13-17) emphasize her attractiveness and life-giving power. Finally wisdom issues an invitation (24:19-22) to eat from her fruits, with the observation that those who eat and drink from them will seek even more.

Ben Sira's own comments in 24:23-34 begin by equating wisdom and the Torah: "All this is the book of the covenant of the Most High God, the law that Moses commanded us as an inheritance for the congregations of Jacob" (24:23). Then he compares wisdom to six mighty rivers (24:25-27) and describes himself (a wisdom teacher) as being "like a canal . . . a water channel" (24:30).

At Ben Sira's school young men learned not only to read and write but also to become public figures, intellectuals, and leaders. In 38:24-34 he contrasts the leisure available to the scribe with the preoccupations of the farmer, artisan, smith, and potter. The tradesmen make contributions that are necessary for society, but they cannot exercise the political and legal leadership that the scribes do. The proper scribal education (38:34b–39:11) includes training in the law of the Most High and other elements of Israel's religious tradition, in the ancient secular wisdom traditions expressed in proverbs and parables, in service among the great, and in travel. This training must be accompanied by prayer and the wisdom of the Torah, since God is the ultimate source of wisdom (39:5-8). The reward of such scribal training is public recognition and fame, as well as a "name" that lives on after the scribe's death.

The third and final appendix at the end of the book (51:13-30) is an autobiographical poem on the search for wisdom. It first describes Ben Sira's quest for and discovery of wisdom (51:13-17) and his effort at living by wisdom (51:18-22). The search involves prayer and temple worship, and ends with the praise of God. The second part (51:23-30) is Ben Sira's invitation for students to come to his school. Though there is no set fee (51:25), the kind of schooling will result in acquiring silver and gold (51:28). Ben Sira's call to "put your neck under her yoke" (51:26) and his testimony "I have labored but little and found for myself much serenity" (51:27) are parallel to, if not the sources of, Jesus' invitation to discipleship in Matthew 11:28-30.

Significance

In its own right Sirach is an entertaining and (mostly) edifying book. Much of it is solid advice on the level of practical human experience. The variety of literary devices gives it a freshness lacking in other wisdom books. Moreover, the breadth of its subject matter offers a window into the agenda of Jewish religious life and thought in the early second century B.C.E. Its beautiful reflections on the search for wisdom and the personification of wisdom continue to provide inspiration for serious religious thinkers. The texts on the value of the "name" and the catalogue of Israel's heroes can teach people today what it means to stand in a religious tradition.

Ben Sira's approach to the mystery of suffering and theodicy can be discerned from the seven topics treated above. For him suffering is part of life, and the sage should therefore look upon suffering as both a test and a discipline. But fools bring most of their sufferings upon themselves. If you wish to avoid unnecessary suffering, follow the way of wisdom marked out by the Torah and fear of the Lord.

According to Ben Sira, God is the Lord of all, and by his word all creatures have been made. All creatures do his will and are good by nature. But there is also a duality in creation (the doctrine of the pairs), and so God's good creations can be used to punish wicked persons. Despite these constraints, Ben Sira is a strong advocate of free will: "If you choose, you can keep all the commandments" (15:15). The rewards for leading a life guided by wisdom and the Torah are happiness in the present and a "good name" after death. There is no clear doctrine of the afterlife in Sirach.

Issues. One set of issues concerns the text. By rendering his grandfather's Hebrew composition into Greek, the translator made it available to a new audience (Diaspora Jews) in a different language and with a different conceptuality. Where the Hebrew fragments are available, it is possible to see that, in comparison with most books of the Septuagint, the grandson's version is relatively free with regard to word order, vocabulary, and quantity of words. Furthermore, the complexity of the textual transmission has resulted in confusion regarding the numbering of chapters and verses. All the Greek manuscripts show a textual displacement whereby 30:25–33:13a and 33:13b–36:16a changed places.

Another set of issues concerns the content. Ben Sira's statements about women, however understandable they have been in their original literary and historical contexts, are offensive to most readers today. Equally outrageous today are his sayings on how to treat slaves (33:25-30), which not only assume the existence of slavery as an institution but recommend very harsh discipline for slaves. Less obvious but nonetheless troublesome are his obsession with honor and shame (despite efforts at re-interpreting them), his excessive caution in social relations, and his quickness to dismiss many other persons as "fools."

Influence. The book of Sirach is regarded as canonical Scripture by Roman Catholic and Orthodox Christians but not by Jews and Protestants (though it is used in the latter traditions).

The Hebrew text of Ben Sira's book was not entirely lost after the Greek translation. It continued to be used at Qumran and Masada, served as the basis for the Syriac version, and was copied at least up to the time of the medieval manuscripts from the Cairo Genizah. But probably because it was regarded as having been composed too late, it did not become part of the Hebrew canon of Scripture, which served as the basis for the Protestant Old Testament. Nevertheless, Sirach was frequently quoted in the Talmud and other Rabbinic works.

The grandson's Greek version became part of the larger canon followed by the Roman Catholic and Orthodox churches today. It was part of the Septuagint and the Christian Old Testament from earliest times. Its presence in the larger Christian canon along with the Wisdom of Solomon greatly expands the corpus of biblical wisdom literature.

Ben Sira's appropriation of Old Testament texts makes it a good example of intrabiblical dialogue. His style is often called "anthological" in the sense that he used the Old Testament books as sources for his vocabulary and phrases but in new combinations and fresh ways. His book is thoroughly biblical in thought and expression.

The book of Sirach is not quoted directly in the New Testament. The strongest parallel is Matthew 11:28-30 (see Sirach 6:24-25; 51:26-27). But even there it may be a matter of common terminology and conceptuality. Yet Sirach is a precious resource for understanding the presuppositions of Judaism in the late Second Temple period and for discerning what was or was not innovative about Jesus and early Christianity.

The earliest patristic evidence for Sirach occurs in *Didache* 4:5 and *Barnabas* 19:9, which appear to cite Sirach 4:31. The book was translated into Latin, Coptic, Syriac, Ethiopic, Armenian, and Arabic, thus insuring a wide circulation. Many Greek church fathers (Clement of Alexandria, Origen, John Chrysostom, Cyril of Jerusalem) and Latin fathers (Tertullian, Cyprian, Jerome, Augustine) quoted or incorporated material from Sirach in their own works. Throughout the late patristic and medieval periods, Sirach generated a rich commentary tradition.

For Further Study

Beentjes, Pancratius C., ed. *The Book of Ben Sira in Modern Research.* Berlin and New York: de Gruyter, 1997.

Coggins, Richard J. *Sirach.* Sheffield: Sheffield Academic Press, 1998.

Collins, John J. *Jewish Wisdom in the Hellenistic Age.* Louisville: Westminster John Knox, 1997.

Crenshaw, James L. "The Book of Sirach." In *The New Interpreter's Bible,* vol. 5, 601-867. Nashville: Abingdon, 1997.

Mack, Burton. *Wisdom and the Hebrew Epic: Ben Sira's Hymn in Praise of the Fathers.* Chicago and London: University of Chicago Press, 1985.

Skehan, Patrick W., and Alexander A. Di Lella. *The Wisdom of Ben Sira.* Anchor Bible 39. New York: Doubleday, 1987.

Trenchard, Warren C. *Ben Sira's View of Women: A Literary Analysis.* Chico, Calif.: Scholars Press, 1982.

Wright, Benjamin C. *No Small Difference: Sirach's Relationship to Its Hebrew Parent.* Atlanta: Scholars Press, 1989.

CHAPTER 7

Baruch: Sin, Exile, Repentance, and Return

Basic Information

The exile of the political and religious leaders of Judah and the destruction of the Jerusalem temple in the early sixth century B.C.E. constituted an enormous challenge to Israel's faith. How could the powerful and just God of Israel have allowed these events to happen? What about the validity of the promises to Abraham and to David that God would make Israel a great people and be with this people forever?

One classic response (see Deuteronomy 28–33; Jeremiah 26–33) to these questions involved the combination of four themes: sin, exile, repentance, and return. The exile was the consequence of Israel's sin. Because Israel failed to heed the voice of God and did not walk according to the Torah, God used the Babylonians as the instruments of his anger and punished the people by the exile. Now what is needed from the exiled people is their repentance and their dedication to live according to the Torah. Then God will restore the renewed Israel to its great city and its temple. The assumption is that God is powerful and just. The problem is Israel's sinfulness and spiritual obtuseness. But there is still hope for Israel if it repents. Then God will make good on the promises and bring about the people's return and make it flourish.

This theological interpretation of the exile permeates and unifies the different parts of the book of Baruch. The narrative framework (1:1-

14) introduces Baruch and the exile community in Babylon, and presents what follows as their letter to those who still remained in Jerusalem. A prayer placed in the mouth of the exiles (1:15–3:8) admits that the exile was God's punishment for the people's sins and nonetheless appeals to God's goodness and mercy and to the glory of God's name as reasons why God should forgive Israel in exile and allow the return to Jerusalem. A poem about wisdom (3:9–4:4) reflects the elusiveness of real (divine) wisdom, holds out the possibility of discovering God's wisdom in the Torah, and suggests how Israel might repent and live in such a way as to make return a possibility. A poem of consolation (4:5–5:9) acknowledges that the exile was a just punishment for Israel's sins but also (and more importantly) offers encouragement about the return from exile. Thus the body of the book moves from confession of sin and sadness over the exile, through a meditation on the mysterious ways of God and on the identification of wisdom and Torah, to a confident hope of return from exile.

The book of Baruch is sometimes called 1 Baruch to distinguish it from the noncanonical apocalypses designated *2 (Syriac) Baruch* and *3 (Greek) Baruch*, as well as *4 Baruch* (the *Paraleipomena* ["Things Left Out"] *of Jeremiah*). According to the book of Jeremiah, Baruch the son of Neriah served as scribe and secretary to the prophet Jeremiah (see Jer. 36:27-32; see 45:1-5). It is unlikely that this Baruch was the author of the book. There is no evidence that Baruch was ever in Babylon; there are many historical inaccuracies in the narrative framework; and the three remaining parts depend on biblical texts that were not yet written in Baruch's own time. Therefore, like the other books ascribed to Baruch, this book should be understood as having been composed under Baruch's name (as pseudonymous). Since Jeremiah prophesied the destruction of Jerusalem and the exile, it was regarded as appropriate that his scribe Baruch should continue the process of theological reflection on the exile and the hope of return.

The Greek text of Baruch appears in the major manuscripts of the Septuagint and served as the basis for the versions in other ancient (Latin, Syriac, Ethiopic, etc.) and modern languages. There is now, however, general scholarly consensus that all the parts of the book were composed in Hebrew and translated into Greek. Although nothing of the Hebrew original was found among the Dead Sea Scrolls or in other discoveries of ancient texts, a good case for a Hebrew original can be made on the basis of the literary style and the reliance on parallelism, the clarity gained when the text is translated back into Hebrew, and the occasional instances where the Greek translator apparently misunderstood or mistranslated a Hebrew word or phrase.

Although the work is set in Babylon, the composition in Hebrew and the strong interest in the Jerusalem community in the first and fourth parts suggest that Palestine was the place of origin. It could have been written at any time from the early sixth century B.C.E. to the second century C.E. Most scholars place it in the period from 200 to 50 B.C.E. It may reflect the national revival under the Maccabees when the project of Antiochus IV Epiphanes and his Jewish collaborators was defeated. Part of that revival would have involved explaining how Judah had returned from exile and came back to national independence in the second century B.C.E. The extensive use of Daniel 9 in the exiles' prayer (1:15–3:8) would fit this setting well. But one must admit that there is no certainty on the date of Baruch's composition.

Content

A. The *Narrative Framework* (1:1-14) consists of a prescript (1:1-2), a "historical" scene (1:3-9), and an instruction (1:10-14). It is intended to provide a single setting for the three (quite different) sections that follow.

The prescript (1:1-2) identifies the (fictive) author and compositional setting. The author is Baruch, the secretary of Jeremiah; here he is given a more extensive genealogy than in Jeremiah 32:12. He is said to have written this book in Babylon, though according to Jeremiah 43:5-7 Baruch went into exile to Egypt with Jeremiah. The date formula "in the fifth year, on the seventh day of the month" is peculiar for its omission of the name of the month. But the time of the composition seems to be associated with the anniversary of the Babylonian capture and burning of Jerusalem either in 597 or 587 B.C.E.

The "historical" scene (1:3-9), which is probably not historical at all, portrays Baruch reading his book to the exiled king of Judah named Jeconiah (Jehoiachin) and to all the members of the exiled community in Babylon by the River Sud (otherwise unknown). Their response to his reading the book is appropriate to a communal commemoration of Jerusalem's capture and destruction: "they wept, and fasted, and prayed before the Lord" (1:5). The exiles resolve to take two practical actions. First, they take up a collection to support the priests and the people who remained in Jerusalem (1:6-7). And then Baruch is to return to Jerusalem the sub-

94

stitute set of temple vessels that King Zedekiah had made to replace the set carried off by the Babylonians (1:8-9). According to Ezra 1:7-11, the original temple vessels were returned to Jerusalem by the Persian king Cyrus in 538 B.C.E. These two actions suggest that services were still being held at the Jerusalem temple, and so perhaps we are to imagine a setting in 592 B.C.E. — before the complete destruction of the first temple.

These gifts are accompanied by an instruction from the Jewish exiles in Babylon to those Jews who remained in Jerusalem (1:10-14). First they are to use the money to buy supplies for use in the sacrifices offered at the temple (1:10). Then they are to pray for the Babylonian king Nebuchadnezzar and his "son" Belshazzar (who actually was the son of Nabonidus; see Daniel 5 for the possible source of this error). That prayers should be offered at the Jerusalem temple for foreign rulers was not unusual in Second Temple times (see Ezra 6:10). They should also pray for the exiles (1:13). Here the exile is interpreted as punishment for Israel's sins: "for we have sinned against the Lord our God, and to this day the anger of the Lord and his wrath have not turned away from us." Finally the Jerusalem community is told to read this scroll (that is, the book of Baruch) in "the house of the Lord" on certain days — most likely on the Day of Atonement and the anniversary of Jerusalem's capture.

B. The *Exiles' Prayer* (1:15–3:8) consists of a confession of sinfulness (1:15–2:10), a prayer for God's mercy (2:11-35), and a concluding summary (3:1-8). It uses words and phrases taken from various biblical books, especially from Daniel 9 and Jeremiah.

The confession first (in 1:15-18) contrasts the righteousness of God and the shame that has come upon all Israel, and attributes this shame to Israel's sin in not heeding the voice of the Lord and in not walking in God's Law (see Dan. 9:7-10). Then in 1:19–2:5 it traces Israel's disobedience throughout its history from the time of the exodus to the present (which is the early sixth century B.C.E. in the narrative setting). Israel's failure to heed God's voice has resulted in "the calamities and the curse." Nevertheless, Israel continued in its sinful ways and went so far as to serve other gods (see Dan. 9:12-13). The culmination of Israel's sinfulness took place in Jerusalem, according to 2:3, when parents engaged in cannibalism by eating the flesh of their own children. Therefore God used the surrounding nations as a means of punishing the people. Finally in 2:6-10 the confession returns to words and themes used in 1:15-18 to contrast God's righteousness and Israel's shame, and to explain this shame in light of failure to walk in God's Law (see Dan. 9:7, 12-14).

95

The prayer that begins in 2:11 addresses God directly (as in Dan. 9:15): "And now, O Lord God of Israel." First it acknowledges the power of God displayed in the exodus from Egypt (see Dan. 9:15-19) and Israel's sinfulness as the cause of its exile (2:11-13). The first reason why God should grant favor to Israel in the sight of its conquerors is "so that all the earth may know that you are the Lord our God" (2:15). What is at stake is the honor of God. The second reason is that Israel itself, in the midst of its suffering, will declare God's glory and righteousness (2:18).

The basis for this prayer can only be the mercy of God, not the righteous deeds of the exiles' ancestors or kings (2:19-26). Even though the people were warned by the prophet Jeremiah to surrender to the king of Babylon, they refused to do so and so have suffered the consequences prophesied by Jeremiah: the desecration of graves, exposure of bones to the elements, death by various causes, and the desolation of the Jerusalem temple.

Even the punishments visited upon Israel, according to 2:27-35, were illustrations of God's kindness and compassion. Indeed, as God was giving the Torah to Moses on Mount Sinai, he gave through Moses a preview of Israel's future experience of sin, exile, and return. (See Deuteronomy 30 and Jeremiah for many of the words and ideas, though what follows in 2:29-35 is not a verbatim quotation.) The "biblical quotation" attributes Israel's future experience of exile to its refusal to obey God (2:29-30a), foretells Israel's repentance and return to God in the land of its exile (2:30b-33), looks forward to its resettlement in the land promised to Abraham (2:34), and holds out God's promises of an everlasting covenant with Israel and its dwelling in the land forever (2:35). In the narrative setting of a book written and read in the exile community of Babylon (see 1:1-14), these promises were a sign of hope in the midst of suffering — a hope based upon the promises and the mercy of God.

The concluding summary (3:1-8) appeals to God to hear the exiles' prayer and to remember that God's power and name are at risk during Israel's continued humiliation. It begins by contrasting the sufferings of sinful Israel and the sovereignty and mercy of the God of Israel: "you are enthroned forever, and we are perishing forever" (3:3). It goes on to admit the sins of God's people in the past (3:4-5a) and to remind God that God's own honor is at stake and that without Israel there will be no one to praise God (3:5b-6). It concludes in 3:7-8 with the exiles affirming that they have put fear of God in their hearts and rejected the sins of their ancestors, and yet still find themselves suffering for the sins of their ancestors.

C. The *Poem About Wisdom* (3:9–4:4) consists of five stanzas. The first (3:9-14) and fifth (4:1-4) concern wisdom and the Law, while the second (3:15-23) and fourth (3:29-38) deal with the difficult search for wisdom, and the middle stanza (3:24-28) joins the two themes together in an indirect way. The development of the two main themes — the identification of wisdom and the Torah, and the elusive character of wisdom — parallels or is dependent on Sirach 24 and Job 28. The poem is loosely connected with the narrative setting of Israel in exile by comments in 3:10-11 and 4:2-3.

The first stanza (3:9-14) calls Israel to hear "the commandments of life" and to learn "wisdom," thus placing the Law and wisdom in synonymous parallelism right at the start (see Sir. 24:23). Then in 3:10-11 it asks why Israel is now in exile ("in the land of your enemies") and as good as dead ("that you are counted among those in Hades"). The answer is that Israel has "forsaken the fountain of wisdom," which is the Law and the "the way of God" (3:12-13). And so Israel is told to learn where wisdom is — and with it strength, discernment, length of days, and light for the eyes and peace (note the five "where" clauses in 3:14).

The second stanza (3:15-23) develops the theme of the search for wisdom and its elusive character (see Job 28). It begins with parallel rhetorical questions: "Who has found her place? And who has entered her storehouses?" (3:15) The answer is that no human being has done so. Neither powerful rulers nor those who have amassed silver and gold have done so (3:16-21). In fact, there has been a succession of generations that have tried to capture or buy wisdom, but without success. Nor is wisdom to be found, according to 3:22-23, in other countries and peoples (Canaan, Teman, etc.), or even among whose make a public profession of wisdom ("the story-tellers and the seekers for understanding").

The middle stanza (3:24-28) calls on Israel to recognize "how great is the house of God" — most likely a reference to the universe rather than to the Jerusalem temple. Among the largest creatures that the world has seen are the mysterious giants of Genesis 6:1-4 (a topic of great interest and speculation in some circles in Second Temple Judaism; see *1 Enoch*). It explains their demise as due to their lack of wisdom. The foolish perish.

The fourth stanza (3:29-37) takes up again the theme of the second stanza — the elusive character of wisdom. It first establishes in 3:29-31 that human beings have not obtained wisdom despite all their efforts. Then in 3:32-34 it acknowledges that only God ("the one who knows all things") knows wisdom, and has made all creatures in the universe and continues to direct them according to wisdom. Finally (3:35-37), this same God ("our God") has given to Israel the whole way to knowledge in the gift of the Torah. The statement that "she appeared on earth and lived with humankind" (3:37) refers to the idea of wisdom dwelling among human beings (see Prov. 8:22-31; Sir. 24:8-12; Wisdom of Solomon). It is important background for the early Christian identification of Jesus as the Wisdom of God in general and for the particular confession that "the Word became flesh and dwelt among us" (John 1:14).

The fifth and final stanza (4:1-4) takes up again the theme of the first stanza — wisdom and the Law: "She is the book of the command-ments of God, the law that endures forever" (see Sir. 24:23). Those who cling to wisdom/the Law will live, whereas those who do not do so will die (see Deut. 30:15-20). Then in 4:2 there is a call for Israel to take hold of wisdom/the Torah and walk toward her light. If Israel fails to do so, it will lose its glory and privileges as the people of God. A beatitude ("happy are we, O Israel") closes the poem. Israel's happiness or blessedness con-sists in its knowing what is pleasing to God — which is wisdom through the Torah.

D. The *Poem of Consolation* (4:5–5:9) consists of an introductory exhortation to the exiles (4:5-8), addresses by Jerusalem personified to the neighbors of Zion (4:9-16) and to the exiles (4:17-29), and an exhorta-tion by the narrator to Jerusalem to look forward to the exiles' return home (4:30–5:9). The poem freely gathers phrases, motifs, and ideas from that part of the book of Isaiah (chaps. 40–66) devoted to encourag-ing the exiles to return from Babylon to Jerusalem.

The introductory exhortation (4:5-8) calls the exiles those who "perpetuate Israel's name" and reminds them that, even though the exile was caused by Israel's sins (especially idolatry), its purpose was not the de-struction of God's people.

Personified, Jerusalem's first address (4:9-16) reminds "you neigh-bors of Zion" that she has endured great sorrow in being bereaved of her children because they turned aside from God's Law, that all this took place under the sovereignty of God "the Everlasting" (4:10, 14), and that God used the savagery of a distant and ruthless nation (the Babylonians) to lead away her beloved sons. Her second address (4:17-29) promises the exiles that God who has brought these calamities upon them will also bring about their deliverance and eventual homecoming (4:18; see also 4:29). She offers to pray on their behalf (4:20) and encourages them to trust in the mercy of God (4:22). She foresees that the nations that have captured Israel will see "your salvation by God" and will themselves be destroyed (4:24-25). What is needed now is Israel's repentance: "For just as you were disposed to go astray from God, return with tenfold zeal to seek him" (4:28).

The narrator's exhortation to Jerusalem (4:30–5:9) falls into three parts, each one signaled by a call to Jerusalem: "Take courage, O Jerusalem" (4:30); "Look toward the east, O Jerusalem" (4:36); "Arise, O Jerusalem" (5:5). The first part (4:30-35) describes the fall of "wretched" Babylon as part of Israel's consolation. The "Everlasting" will reverse Babylon's fortunes, and bring fire upon it so that it becomes an abode of demons. The second part (4:36–5:4) urges personified Jerusalem to look to the east and see her children returning from exile. In response she should take off her garments of sorrow and put on "the robe of righteousness that comes from God." From now on she will be called "Righteous Peace, Godly Glory." The third part (5:5-9) summons Jerusalem to look again for her returning children and to see God making smooth their way (see Isa. 40:9-11): "For God will lead Israel with joy, in the light of his glory, with the mercy and righteousness that come from him" (5:9).

Significance

What unifies the four parts of Baruch is the social suffering of Israel in exile and the attempt to explain this suffering against the horizon of Israel's past and future. The basic theological dynamic that runs through the book consists of four themes: sin, exile, repentance, and return.

The reason for the exile is Israel's sinfulness in not walking "in the statutes of the Lord that he set before us" (1:18). This failure to heed the voice of God led Israel into idolatry (see 1:22) and even into cannibalism (see 2:3).

No doubt is expressed about the sovereignty and justice of the God of Israel. Rather, it is assumed that God used the Babylonians as his instruments to punish Israel for its sinfulness. However, the attitude toward the Babylonians is complex. The exile community directs those still in Jerusalem to pray for King Nebuchadnezzar and his son (1:11). But Mother Zion/Jerusalem promises her children that "you will soon see their destruction and will tread upon their necks" (4:25). This complexity, of course, reflects what one also finds in the Hebrew Bible.

While admitting its sinfulness, Israel nevertheless prays that God will remember his own power and name (see 3:5). By hearing Israel's prayers for deliverance, God will put into effect the promises made to God's people and will vindicate his own honor in the sight of all the nations of the world. Israel for its part must repent of its sins and walk according to the Torah. Its repentance will issue in a return from exile to the temple city of Jerusalem.

The poem about wisdom in 3:9–4:4 approaches the topic of the exile from the perspective of how hard it is for human beings to grasp real (divine) wisdom and to understand the ways of God in allowing the exile to happen. In many respects the poem echoes the language and content of Job 28. At two points, however, the poem makes important theological contributions on its own — by identifying wisdom and the Torah (see 3:9; 4:1), and by portraying wisdom as a female figure who "appeared on earth and lived with humankind" (3:37). Thus Baruch deserves a place in the tradition history of wisdom as a personal figure that links the two Testaments.

Another important theological motif in Baruch is the personification of Jerusalem in the poem of consolation (4:5–5:9). Mother Zion addresses her children in highly emotional terms, but she is also addressed by the poet and is told to take courage and look for Israel's return from exile. Indeed, Mother Zion symbolizes the entire experience of exile and return. Just as Jerusalem suffered with those who were taken off to exile, so she is to rejoice as she sees her children returning from Babylon to Jerusalem.

Issues. The major problems raised by the book of Baruch are its unity, originality, and theological persuasiveness.

Despite their general thematic unity, the four main parts are quite different in form and mood. The introduction (1:1-14) provides a historical setting in a narrative format. The prayer (1:15–3:8) is a long and somewhat repetitive confession of guilt and a plea for deliverance. The poem about wisdom (3:9–4:4) is a carefully structured meditation on how difficult it is to understand God's ways. The poem of consolation (4:5–5:9) moves from the depths of sorrow to the heights of joy with its personification of Jerusalem as a mother. Were these four different parts composed by one person? Or were they separate pieces that have been joined by an editor (who perhaps supplied the narrative introduction)?

The question of originality is associated with the obvious use of biblical sources in each main part. The prayer echoes the language found in Daniel 9, while the poem about wisdom is based on Job 28, and the poem of consolation uses material from Isaiah 40–66. The language, images, and ideas are deeply rooted in the Hebrew Bible. What did the author(s) or editor(s) hope to achieve by reformulating these biblical models? Are we to dismiss the work as lacking originality? Or does the very combination of classic themes — sin, exile, repentance, and return — in several different genres and from several different perspectives itself constitute an original contribution?

The question of persuasiveness concerns the adequacy of the theological explanation for the exile that is offered in this and other Jewish writings from exilic and postexilic times. Does the complex of sin, exile, repentance, and return offer a really satisfying historical or theological interpretation of what happened to Israel? To what extent is blaming the exile on Israel's sinfulness a case of blaming the victim? Or is this explanation a case of theodicy or even cognitive dissonance, that is, a way of preserving faith in the sovereignty and justice of God in the face of what seemed to be the end of Israel's history? But if this explanation is judged to be inadequate, what interpretation would be more satisfying, and to whom?

Influence. The (hypothetical) Hebrew original of the book of Baruch is not included among the canonical writings of the Hebrew Bible. Whether its exclusion owes to historical accident or conscious decision is impossible to know. Since Protestants generally follow the Hebrew canon of the Old Testament, it is not regarded as canonical by them. The Greek version is part of the Septuagint (which served as the basis for the Latin Vulgate), and the work is regarded as canonical by the Roman Catholic as well as Greek and Russian Orthodox churches.

There is, however, little ancient evidence for the book of Baruch's influence among either Jews or Christians. Neither the figure of Baruch nor the book bearing his name is mentioned in the New Testament or in the Apostolic Fathers. Yet, the book does appear in Christian canon lists from the fourth century onward, and a few Church Fathers commented on it. Most Church Fathers, however, attributed quotations from Baruch to Jeremiah. In some regions, especially Latin-speaking ones, the book of Baruch evidently did not circulate independently of the book of Jeremiah. What was (and is) most attractive to Christians is its description of wisdom in personal terms: "Afterward she [wisdom] appeared on earth and lived with humankind" (3:37). This verse evokes the New Testament equation of Wisdom and Christ as well as the doctrine of the incarnation (see John 1:1-18; Col. 1:15-20; Heb. 1:1-4).

For both Jews and Christians today, the effort to explain theologically Israel's catastrophes of the early sixth century B.C.E. highlights the even more difficult task of explaining theologically the Holocaust or Shoah of the Jewish people in Europe in the mid-twentieth century C.E. However one judges the adequacy of Baruch's explanation (sin, exile, repentance, return), the Holocaust raises even more difficult and controversial questions about causes (the lack of correspondence between the people's "sin" and the punishment visited upon them) and results (the extent to which one may speak of national "repentance," and whether Zionism and the State of Israel should be given a religious significance).

For Further Study

Burke, David G. *The Poetry of Baruch: A Reconstruction and Analysis of the Original Hebrew text of Baruch 3:9-5:9*. Chico, Calif.: Scholars Press, 1982.

Moore, Carey A. *Daniel, Esther and Jeremiah: The Additions*. Anchor Bible 44. Garden City, N.Y.: Doubleday, 1977.

Tov, Emanuel. *The Book of Baruch, also Called I Baruch (Greek and Hebrew)*. Missoula, Mont.: Scholars Press, 1975.

CHAPTER 8

The Letter of Jeremiah:
The Folly of Idolatry

Basic Information

The Letter of Jeremiah purports to be a warning against the dangers of idolatry from the prophet Jeremiah to those who will soon be exiled to Babylon. It gives advice to Jews on how they should evaluate and respond to the idol worship to which they will be exposed in exile. The idea that the prophet wrote to Jewish exiles came from Jeremiah 29. Some of the content derives from Jeremiah 10, and there are echoes of other biblical polemics against idolatry (see Isa. 40:18-20; 41:6-7; 44:9-20; 46:1-7; Pss. 115:4-8; 135:15-18; Deut. 4:27-28). While appropriate to the early sixth century B.C.E., the work could fit almost any time during the Second Temple period or even into the rabbinic age.

When, where, and by whom the work was composed are not clear. The apparent reference to it in 2 Maccabees 2:1-3 and the dating of a Greek fragment from Qumran Cave 7 suggest an origin before 100 B.C.E. The problems provoked by Jewish exposure to idolatry would have been serious issues both in the land of Israel and in the Diaspora at almost any time from the exile onward. By adopting the persona of the prophet Jeremiah and by expanding and developing ideas found in Jeremiah 10, the author presents a long and detailed polemic against idolatry second only to that in Wisdom 13–15. The book is a guide to the folly of idol worship from a Jewish perspective

103

and a plea for Jews to remain faithful to the God of Israel and to the ways of righteousness.

Throughout the letter/sermon there are hints at a contrast between the powerful God of Israel (vv. 34-38, 53-55, 60-63, 66-67) and the powerless idols of the pagan peoples (which, of course, are not gods at all but only human fabrications). But what about the exile of the Jewish leaders? Does it not show the powerlessness of the God of Israel? The author anticipates this objection in his very first sentence: "Because of the sins that you have committed before God, you will be taken to Babylon as exiles" (v. 2). He attributes the exile to the sinfulness of Israel rather than to the powerlessness of the God of Israel. And he holds out the hope that in "seven generations" (v. 3) God will bring the exiles back to their homeland.

The Letter of Jeremiah is not an objective report written by a professor of comparative religion. Rather, it is partisan polemic against other peoples' religious beliefs and practices. It is written from the perspective of a Jew whose religion forbade physical representations of God (see Exod. 20:4-5; Deut. 5:8-9). Whether the author had direct experience of "idol worship" or derived his descriptions of idols and their temples from biblical texts and popular rumors, he shows no sympathy for religions that represented their gods with statues. For him, the God of Israel is the only true God, and what other people worship as gods are human creations. There is no indication from the author that the devotees of these idols may have regarded them simply as signs or representations of their deities.

The "letter" (which is really a sermon) consists of a brief introduction that sets the scene (vv. 1-7) and ten warnings or reflections on the folly of worshiping idols. Each unit ends with a refrain to the effect that, since the idols are not gods, there is no reason to worship ("fear") them.

The primary text is in Greek, though a Hebrew original is possible. In the Greek manuscript tradition it appears as a separate composition between Lamentations and Ezekiel, whereas in the Latin manuscript tradition it is attached to the book of Baruch as its sixth chapter.

The author's positive ideal is stated in verse 6: "It is you, O Lord, whom we must worship." Its implications for life are expressed in the final sentence: "Better, therefore, is someone upright who has no idols; such a person will be far above reproach" (73). The body of the letter/sermon charges that the idols are helpless, useless, lifeless, powerless, and senseless. Because they are human fabrications, they cannot do what the real God can do. In fact, they are less powerful and useful than human beings or parts of a house or the forces of nature. They are "like a scarecrow in a cucumber field" (v. 70).

Content

Setting (1-7). The opening section presents the work as a letter from Jeremiah to Jews about to go into exile in the early sixth century B.C.E. The prophet warns them against worshiping the idols that they will see in Babylon and reminds them that "it is you, O Lord, whom we must worship" (6).

Ten Warnings (8-73). The body of the letter is a series of ten warnings against idolatry. Each section explains why it is foolish to worship idols, and concludes that because the idols are not gods but only human creations there is no reason to worship them.

The *first warning* (8-16) stresses the helplessness of the idols. Although the idols have beautifully carved tongues overlaid with gold and silver, they cannot speak. Although the idols are dressed in beautiful garments, they cannot preserve themselves from rust and corrosion and from dust. Although the idols have symbols of power such as scepters and daggers, they cannot defend themselves. The charge is made that their priests take the gold and silver for their own use or even give it to prostitutes. From this, "Jeremiah" concludes, "it is evident that they are not gods; so do not fear them" (16; see also 23, 29, 65, 69).

The *second warning* (17-23) charges that idols are useless — as useless as a broken dish. Their eyes are full of dust, and their faces are blackened by smoke. Their temples need to be locked securely because they cannot defend themselves. The lamps burning in their temples do nothing to make them see. They suffer corruption from insects and degradation from birds and cats. They are not gods and so do not deserve "fear" (that is, the worship and respect due to the one true God).

The *third warning* (24-29) focuses on the lifelessness of the idols ("there is no breath in them"). They need someone to wipe off the tarnish from their metal. They had no feeling when they were being created. They cannot walk, and so they need to be carried around. Again the charge is made that only the priests and their families profit from the idols. They are touched by women in their ritual impurity (through menstruation or childbirth). Thus they are not gods and therefore do not deserve "fear."

The *fourth warning* (30-40a) emphasizes the powerlessness of the idols. Women serve them meals, and their priests act foolishly and steal their garments for use by their own children. The real problem is that the idols lack all power: "Whether one does evil to them or good, they will not be able to repay it" (34). They cannot do what the true God can do — set up and depose kings, give wealth, enforce the fulfillment of vows, and so forth. It is foolish to expect such powers from material objects manufactured by human hands, and even more foolish to imagine that they are gods.

The *fifth warning* (40b-44) stresses the foolishness and shamefulness involved in worshiping idols. On the one hand, worshipers of Bel (a name for the Babylonian god Marduk) pray that a mute person may speak to an idol who cannot speak. On the other hand, women eagerly prostitute themselves as if such shameful behavior made them superior to other women. How could anyone imagine that these idols are real gods?

The *sixth warning* (45-52) contends that, since the idols are the works of human hands, they cannot be regarded as divine. They have been made by the hands of craftsmen who are themselves mortal. In times of calamity or war, their priests have to hide the idols away, since they are incapable of defending or saving themselves. And so Jeremiah asks, "Who then can fail to know that they are not gods?"

The *seventh warning* (53-56) returns to the powerlessness of the idols. Because "they have no power," they cannot do what the true God does — set up kings, give rain, judge their own cause, and deliver one who is wronged. In the case of fire the idols are destroyed, and in the case of conquest they can offer no resistance. And so Jeremiah asks, "Why then must anyone admit or think that they are gods?"

The *eighth warning* (57-65) returns to the helplessness and uselessness of the idols, and deduces that they are not gods at all. Their helplessness is illustrated by their inability to protect themselves from robbers. Their uselessness is shown by a series of comparisons designed to prove the inferiority of the idols. Not only are they less useful than a courageous king. They are even less useful than a common utensil or a door or a pillar in a house. At the least the forces of nature — the sun, moon, stars, lightning, clouds, and fire — serve useful roles in carrying out the commands of God. The idols by contrast do no such thing. They are not gods at all.

The *ninth warning* (66-69) repeats the charge that idols cannot do what God does. It also compares the idols negatively to wild animals. At least the animals "can flee to shelter and help themselves."

The *tenth warning* (70-73) likens the idols to "a scarecrow in a cucumber field, which guards nothing." Despite their superficial splendor, the idols are at best like a thornbush on which birds perch and at worst like a corpse thrown out in the darkness. Jeremiah's conclusion describes the ideal for the Jew in exile: "Better, therefore, is someone upright who has no idols; such a person will be far above reproach" (73).

Significance

The sustained attack on other peoples' religious practices in the Letter of Jeremiah proceeds from the conviction that the God of Israel is the only true God. With this theological presupposition the writer explores the folly of idolatry from different directions and argues that the "gods" of other nations are powerless and useless. They cannot do what the God of the Bible does (see vv. 34-38). Therefore the author's advice to Jews (and to others) is expressed in his statement, "'It is you, O Lord, whom we must worship'" (v. 6).

The God of the Bible is powerful and just, whereas the idols are powerless and lack all justice (because they are nonexistent). The priests who promote their worship are immoral, showing no compunction about stealing and consorting with prostitutes. Idolatry breeds moral corruption. Israel's exile, however, is also a sign of God's power and justice, since the exile was just punishment for Israel's sins and in God's plan will last for only "seven generations" (vv. 2-3). God disciplines his people for a limited time, but those who worship idols wallow in folly and immorality forever.

Issues. How much did the writer know about the religions that he parodies? As a Diaspora Jew he must have had some exposure to them, and his graphic description of cultic prostitution with reference to the cult of Bel/Marduk (vv. 42-43) is confirmed by ancient nonbiblical sources. Much of his language, however, echoes biblical polemics against idolatry and sounds formulaic.

The formulaic character of the language should not obscure the enormity of the theological claim that the God of Israel is the only true God. Whereas the early parts of the Hebrew Bible give the impression that Yahweh is one god among many, there gradually developed among Jews in Second Temple times the boldness to say that the only true God is the God of Israel. The Letter of Jeremiah is important evidence for the development of early Jewish monotheism.

Influence. The attack against idolatry is a common feature in Second Temple Jewish writings. Among the Apocrypha, the best known and most sophisticated treatment appears in Wisdom 13–15. The story of Bel and the Dragon is a narrative exposé of deceitful pagan priests who use the cult of idols for their own gain. The later rabbinic tractates on "foreign worship" (*'Abodah Zarah)* continue the tradition of Jewish criticism of pagan religious practices.

Paul's reflection on idolatry as the origin of ignorance and sin in Romans 1:18-32 breathes the air of Hellenistic Judaism, as does the Letter of James ("You believe that God is one," James 2:19). The First Epistle of John ends with a call that summarizes the Letter of Jeremiah: "Little children, keep yourselves from idols" (1 John 5:21).

For Further Study

Moore, Carey A. *Daniel, Esther and Jeremiah: The Additions.* Anchor Bible 44. Garden City, N.Y.: Doubleday, 1977.

CHAPTER 9

The Additions to Daniel:
Who Is the Living God?

Basic Information

Within the Hebrew Bible, the book of Daniel presents some anomalies. Parts of it are in Hebrew (chaps. 1, 8–12), and parts of it are in Aramaic (chaps. 2–7). The stories and visions that it recounts are set in the sixth century B.C.E. at the courts of Babylonian and Persian kings. But these stories and visions in their present form clearly address the crisis of 167-165 B.C.E. when Antiochus IV Epiphanes and his Jewish collaborators threatened to destroy traditional Judaism and worship at the Jerusalem temple.

As it stands in the Hebrew Bible, the book of Daniel consists of six narratives (chaps. 1–6) about Daniel and three Jewish courtiers told in the third-person style, and three visions (chaps. 7, 8, 10–12) and a communal lament/confession (chap. 9) told in the first-person style. The narratives involve conflicts about food (chap. 1), worship (3), and prayer (6), as well as contests about interpreting the vision of the statue (2), a dream (4), and the handwriting on the wall (5). The visions concern "one like a son of man" (7), the ram and the he-goat (8), and Jewish history and the future (10–12). The book is the product of a nonrevolutionary Jewish religious group that looked to God alone for deliverance from the threat posed by Antiochus IV Epiphanes around 165 B.C.E.

The Greek versions of the book of Daniel include further material called the "Additions." Between 3:23 and 3:24 are the Prayer of Azariah and the Song of the Three Jews. The Story of Susanna appears at the beginning of some manuscripts and at the end (as chap. 13) of some others. And the Story of Bel and the Dragon also occurs at the end of the book (as chap. 14). These "additions" take different forms: a communal lament/confession (Prayer of Azariah), a benediction (the Song of the Three Jews), a detective story (Susanna), and parodies on idolatry (Bel and the Dragon). Each deals in its own way with the theological problems of suffering and theodicy. How they do so is discussed in each case under the heading "Significance." General observations about issues and influence are presented at the end of the chapter.

Addition 1: The Prayer of Azariah and the Song of the Three Jews (between 3:23 and 3:24 in the Greek Version)

A. The Prayer of Azariah (vv. 1-22)

This addition consists of a prose introduction (vv. 1-2) and a communal lament/confession along with a prayer for deliverance (vv. 3-22). Azariah functions as the spokesman for Israel and interprets the exile as God's just punishment for the people's sins. His prayer contains an address to God (vv. 3-4), a confession of sins (vv. 5-9), and a petition for deliverance (vv. 10-22).

The language of Azariah's prayer is thoroughly biblical, and it was probably composed in Hebrew and translated into Greek. Its present narrative setting in the Greek version of Daniel 3 is Babylon in the sixth century during the reign of Nebuchadnezzar. However, the references in verse 9 to "lawless and hateful rebels" and to "an unjust king, the most wicked in all the world" may reflect the coalition between "progressive" Jews and Antiochus IV Epiphanes that appears in 1 Maccabees 1. Thus the prayer may have addressed the crisis in Judea in 167-165 B.C.E. that is reflected in most of the book of Daniel. The historical setting envisioned in verses 15 and 17 fits equally well the sixth or the second century B.C.E. — which is the case in the rest of the book of Daniel.

Content

The prose *Introduction* (vv. 1-2) follows the report in Daniel 3:23 that Shadrach, Meshach, and Abednego were cast into the furnace of flaming

110

fire. Even though the surrounding narrative was in Aramaic, Abednego is given his Hebrew name Azariah ("the Lord is my help"). Moreover, there is some tension between the introduction ("singing hymns and blessing the Lord") and the confessional tone that predominates in Azariah's prayer for deliverance.

The *Address* (vv. 3-4) to God emphasizes the divine justice ("you are just . . . all your judgments are true") and so prepares for the *Confession* of sins (vv. 5-9). As a spokesman for Israel, Azariah attributes the "true judgments" executed upon Israel to the people's sins, especially Israel's breaking God's Law. The references to rebels and to the "unjust king" in verse 9 may link the composition to the crisis of 167-165 B.C.E.

The *Petition* (vv. 10-22) consists of two parts, each one introduced by "And now" (vv. 10 and 18). The first part (vv. 10-17) contrasts the shame that exiled Israel endures and the glorious "name" of God, the faithful and merciful one. It appeals to God's promise to Abraham (vv. 12-13) to make Israel a great nation through Isaac (see Gen. 22:17). Then it reflects in vv. 14-15 on the sad state to which Israel has been reduced: "no ruler, or prophet . . . no burnt offering . . . no place to make an offering." Since under present conditions no temple sacrifice is possible, Azariah prays that God will regard "a contrite heart and a humble spirit" as the equivalent of a sacrifice offered at the Jerusalem temple (vv. 16-17).

The second part (vv. 18-22) is a prayer for deliverance from the present situation. Along with an emphasis on God's "abundant mercy" and "marvelous works," there is a contrast between Israel's (and God's) shame if God does not intervene and the glory that will accrue to God's name if God does act. The thrust of Azariah's petition is summed up in the final sentence: "Let them know that you alone are the Lord God, glorious over the whole world" (v. 22).

Significance

As a communal lament/confession, the Prayer of Azariah concerns the sufferings and hopes of God's people. It affirms the power and justice of God, and appeals to God's fidelity and mercy as the only source of deliverance. It attributes the people's present sufferings in exile to its sins in breaking God's Law. It derives hope from the conviction that God's honor is at stake in the crisis.

The degradation of Israel in the exile (or under Antiochus IV Epiphanes) for its sins is admittedly a source of shame for the God who has entered into covenant relationship with Israel. And so Azariah asks God to intervene for "your name's sake" (v. 11). His hope is for a miraculous rescue: "Deliver us in accordance with your marvelous works" (v. 20). When the narrative resumes in Daniel 3:24, we are told how God brought about the miraculous rescue and punished the enemies of the Jewish courtiers.

B. The Song of the Three Jews (vv. 23-68)

This addition purports to describe the sentiments of Hananiah, Azariah, and Mishael in the furnace of flaming fire. After a prose introduction that explains how they remained unharmed by the fire (vv. 23-27), the three courtiers bless God directly (vv. 28-34) and call upon all creation to join in blessing the Lord (vv. 35-68). The two prayers are highly formulaic and invite public recitation or singing. Only the concluding tag in verses 66-68 relates all the benedictions to the situation of the three Jews in the furnace.

The language of the song is thoroughly biblical (see especially Psalm 148), and the text may have been composed in Hebrew. The narrative setting is the exile in Babylon under Nebuchadnezzar, though some expressions in verses 31-32 may assume that the Jerusalem temple still stands (in contrast to the situation described in vv. 15-17). In the narrative of the Greek version of Daniel 3, the three courtiers are not yet rescued from the fiery furnace. And so their prayer of blessing anticipates their deliverance and bears witness to their firm faith in God's power and mercy.

Content

The prose *Narrative* (vv. 23-27) describes the materials used to feed the fire ("naphtha, pitch, tow, and brushwood") and the height of the flames (14 cubits = 27 feet) pouring out of the furnace and burning the Chaldeans. It also identifies the mysterious fourth figure in the furnace as "the angel of the Lord" and explains how Azariah and his companions were protected from burns because the angel kept the inside of the furnace "as though a moist wind were whistling through it."

The *Blessing* (vv. 28-34) addresses God directly ("Blessed are you") and praises God six times as both "the God of our ancestors" and the one who presides over all creation "in the firmament of heaven." The references to the temple and the cherubim in verses 31-32 would appear to refer to the Jerusalem temple (see, however, vv. 15-17). But they may simply describe God's heavenly court with earthly temple images. The refrain accompanying each blessing varies slightly, but all of them reserve the highest praise for God ("to be praised and highly exalted forever"). The combination of a fixed formula and some slight variations serves to celebrate God as the truly blessed one.

The *Benediction* (vv. 35-68) calls all creation to bless God and follows an even more fixed pattern: "Bless the Lord" + the addressee + "sing praise to him and highly exalt him forever." After a general invitation to "all you works of the Lord" to bless the Lord (v. 35), the addressees fall into four major categories: what is in the heavens (vv. 36-41), what comes down from the heavens (vv. 42-51), what lives on the earth and in the seas (vv. 52-59), and various classes of human beings (vv. 60-65). By way of conclusion (vv. 66-68) the three courtiers call upon themselves to praise and thank God for their (anticipated) miraculous deliverance.

Significance

The Song of the Three Jews is presented as a prayer that is appropriate to those who hope for rescue from suffering and death. In the Greek book of Daniel it looks forward to a miraculous deliverance, which is then described as chapter 3 proceeds. It assumes the justice of God in saving the innocent courtiers and praises God as ruler over the heavens and the earth. The song is thus a witness to firm faith in God's sovereignty and justice in the midst of suffering. It suggests that the proper attitude in the midst of suffering is benediction ("blessed be the Lord . . . bless the Lord").

Addition 2: Susanna (Chapter 13 of the Greek Version)

The story of Susanna combines religion, sex, and death. The beautiful and God-fearing Susanna is accused by two "dirty old men" (who happen to be elders and judges in the Jewish community at Babylon) of committing adultery with a "young man." In fact, Susanna is totally innocent of the charge, and the accusation comes from the frustration of the two elders at having been refused sexual favors by Susanna. The innocent woman is saved from execution only when God stirs in Daniel a "holy spirit," and Daniel devises a way to prove the falsity of the accusation.

The story of Susanna reads like a detective story. It is set in Babylon and takes as its motto: "Wickedness came forth from Babylon" (see Jer. 29:20-23). But in this case the wickedness comes from the Jewish community. The narrative was probably composed in Hebrew or Aramaic in the land of Israel or in the Eastern Diaspora. It presupposes the strict legislation of the Torah regarding the penalties for adultery (see Lev. 20:10) and for false accusation (see Deut. 19:18-21).

Content

The *Accusation of Adultery* (vv. 1-27) is raised against Susanna, who is introduced in verses 1-4. Her righteous parents had trained her in the Law of Moses. She is beautiful and God-fearing. She married a wealthy man of good reputation named Joakim. The garden adjoining her husband's house had become a gathering place for Jews living in Babylon.

The accusation is raised by two elders who had become judges. Since they frequented Joakim's house, they saw Susanna often and "began to lust for her" (v. 8). On becoming aware of each other's lust for her, they plan to find her alone and to satisfy their desires for her. They hide in the garden. And when Susanna comes into the garden and sends her maids away, they confront her with a legal and moral dilemma. If she agrees to have sexual relations with them, she will commit the sin of adultery and run the risk of death by stoning as the punishment. If she refuses, the elders will claim that a young man was with her and she will face the same accusation and penalty. Susanna refuses their proposition and puts her life in God's hands.

When Susanna cries out for help (v. 24), the two elders cry out against her and open the garden doors to make it appear that the "young man" had fled. When people from the household come into the garden, the elders tell their version of the story and manage to convince the servants of Susanna's guilt.

The *Trial and Condemnation* (vv. 28-41) take place in the garden on the next day. The elders, frustrated in their lust for Susanna, now seek to have her put to death as an adulteress. They order that Susanna be brought forward for a public trial in the presence of her parents, husband, and children (v. 30). They even order that Susanna be "unveiled" so that she may be further shamed and so that they can "feast their eyes on her beauty" (v. 32).

As the elders begin their false accusation, Susanna looks heavenward "for her heart trusted in the Lord" (v. 35). The elders accuse her of having committed adultery with a "young man" who got away when they tried to capture him. As elders and judges, the two men naturally have great credibility. And on this matter the Torah is clear: "If a man commits adultery with the wife of his neighbor, both the adulterer and the adulteress shall be put to death" (Lev. 20:10; see John 7:53–8:11). And so on the (false) testimony of the elders, Susanna is condemned to death (v. 41).

The *Rescue of Susanna* (vv. 42-64) comes as an answer to her prayer in which she professes her innocence before God (vv. 42-43). As she is led off to execution, God inspires Daniel to shout: "I want no part in shedding this woman's blood!" (v. 46). Daniel demands that her case be reviewed, and his request is granted because he too is an "elder" (v. 50) despite his young age (see v. 45).

Then Daniel the detective goes into action. He separates the two elders, and asks each one to identify the tree under which he supposedly saw Susanna and the "young man" having sexual relations. One says that it is under a mastic tree (v. 54), and the other says that it was under an evergreen oak (v. 58). Their testimony does not agree, and so Daniel has caught them in a lie. And their punishments fit the tree: being "cut in two" *(schisei)* for the one who said it was a mastic tree *(schinon)*, and being "split in two" *(prisai)* for one who said it was an evergreen oak *(prinon).*

The whole assembly (vv. 60-62) confirms Daniel's finding and sentences the elders/judges to death according to the Torah for their false accusation (see Deut. 19:18-21). The assembly recognizes in Daniel's intervention the action of God to spare innocent blood. Finally Susanna is reunited with her parents and her husband, and acquitted of having done any "shameful deed" (vv. 63-64). The episode serves to launch the career of the young Daniel as a wise counselor for Jews and Gentiles alike. Thus in some Greek manuscripts the Susanna story precedes the rest of the book of Daniel.

Significance

Susanna is an innocent sufferer. She is a victim of two men's lust and of their false accusation. Her reputation is ruined, and she is led off to execution for adultery. She had done nothing wrong. Instead of acceding to the elders' lust, she steadfastly places her trust in God's justice "rather than sin in the sight of the Lord" (v. 23). When falsely accused by the elders at her trial, she looks toward heaven through her tears (v. 35). As she is led off to be executed, she reaffirms her innocence in a prayer to God (vv. 42-43).

The great turning point in the story comes with God's response to Susanna's protestation of innocence: "The Lord heard her cry" (v. 44). And Daniel emerges as the human instrument by which Susanna's innocence is proven and she is delivered from death and restored to her family. The message of the Susanna story is that God will vindicate the innocent sufferer. The episode illustrates the power of trust in God and of prayer in the midst of suffering, as well as God's use of the human wisdom displayed by Daniel.

Addition 3: Bel and the Dragon
(Chapter 14 of the Greek Version)

A. The Story of Bel (vv. 1-22)

This story is a parody on idolatry. The question is, Who is the living god? The Persian king Cyrus imagines that Bel (another name for the Babylonian god Marduk) is the living god because Bel apparently consumes the huge quantities of food and drink that Cyrus provides for him every day. But Daniel proves that the priests of Bel and their families were actually consuming the offerings, and so exposes Bel as a human creation and champions the God of Israel as the "living God."

The main characters are Daniel, Cyrus, and the priests of Bel. They come together in a neat plot in which Daniel once again shows the skills of a detective. In response to the test proposed by Cyrus, Daniel devises a way to catch the priests of Bel in the act of taking the food and drink offered to Bel. The story may have been composed in Hebrew or Aramaic, but the Greek version is now the primary text. The work's attitude toward idolatry fits well with those of the Wisdom of Solomon and Letter of Jeremiah.

Content

The *Setting* of the narrative (vv. 1-4a) is the court of the Persian king Cyrus, in which Daniel serves as a trusted counselor. Cyrus is portrayed as

116

a devout worshiper of the god Bel (Marduk), while Daniel continues to worship the God of Israel. Cyrus is so devoted to Bel that he provides a huge daily offering of flour, sheep, and wine. Since the sacrifices disappear every day, Cyrus assumes that Bel must have been consuming all the food and drink, and therefore is a living god.

The *Test* (vv. 4b-15) is occasioned by Cyrus's inquiry into why Daniel does not worship Bel. Daniel responds that he worships "the living God, who created heaven and earth and has dominion over all living creatures" (v. 5), not idols made by human hands. When the king protests that Bel is a living god, Daniel describes Bel as an idol that "never ate or drank anything" (vv. 6-7). So the king proposes an experiment or test to determine who is eating all the food. The penalty for failure in the test is to be death — either for the priests of Bel, or for Daniel (vv. 8-9).

The seventy priests of Bel, who along with their families had been eating the food, agree to the test (vv. 10-14a). They suggest that the king set out the food in the temple of Bel and seal the door shut with his own seal. They are confident, though, because they have devised a hidden entrance by which to get the food. Daniel, however, has ashes strewn inside the temple as a way of detecting the priests and their families as they took the food and drink offerings.

The *Result of the Test* (vv. 16-22) is shown on the next day. Daniel and Cyrus verify that the seal on the temple door remained unbroken. This moves Cyrus to proclaim, "You are great, O Bel, and in you there is no deceit at all" (v. 18). Daniel, however, points to the footprints in the ashes as proof that it was the priests, not Bel, who consumed the sacrifices (vv. 19-20). In a rage the king has the priests arrested and put to death after showing him their secret doors (vv. 21-22a). And Daniel is given the opportunity to destroy the idol and the temple (v. 22b). The test proves that the living God is the God whom Daniel worships, and that Bel and his priests are frauds.

Significance

Daniel believes so firmly that the idols are nothing and that the God of Israel is the only living God that he runs the risk of death by agreeing to the test. And the priests of Bel receive just punishment when their deception is exposed and they are arrested and killed. The test vindicates Daniel and the God whom he worships.

B. The Story of the Dragon (vv. 23-42)

This addition is a combination of three episodes: Daniel and the dragon (vv. 23-28), Daniel in the lions' den (vv. 29-32, 40-42), and Habakkuk's magical journey (vv. 33-39). The three episodes are loosely joined in a plot that vindicates Daniel and the God whom he worships, and are linked to the Story of Bel by verse 28 ("he has destroyed Bel, and killed the dragon").

The dragon episode is another parody on idolatry, while the lions' den episode is something like the conflict story in Daniel 6. The Habakkuk episode, with its fantastic voyage, interrupts the lions' den episode. All these episodes are evidence of the lively interest in the figure of Daniel.

Some scholars take "dragon" to mean "snake," and link the episode to Egypt and its religious practices (see Wisdom of Solomon). It is more likely, however, that these stories originated either in the land of Israel or in the Eastern Diaspora, and were originally composed in Hebrew or Aramaic.

Content

The *Episode of the Dragon* (vv. 23-28) concerns the question, Who is the living god? The dragon or snake eats, and so is clearly alive. Since the Babylonians are said to revere the dragon, they must consider it a living god worthy of worship. Daniel sets out to expose the falsity of this logic (vv. 23-26). He concocts cakes made of "pitch, fat, and hair" (v. 27), and so the dragon on eating them bursts open and dies. The dragon is not a living god. The Babylonians, however, protest that "the king has become a Jew," and that Daniel is destroying their gods and priests (v. 28).

The *Episode of Daniel in the Lions' Den* (vv. 29-32, 40-42) seems to be an alternative version of Daniel 6. When the Babylonians demand that Cyrus turn Daniel over to them (vv. 29-30), they throw Daniel into the lions' den. To make sure that lions will devour Daniel, the seven lions have been denied their daily ration of food consisting of two human bodies and two sheep. And yet Daniel remains unharmed for six days (vv. 31-32).

The *Habakkuk Episode* (vv. 33-39) interrupts the lions' den episode, and serves the purpose of getting food to Daniel during his ordeal. The prophet and his stew are miraculously transported to Babylon by the angel of the Lord. Daniel interprets this gift of food as a sign of God's care: "You have remembered me, O God, and have not forsaken those who love you" (v. 38).

The lions' den episode is resumed in verses 40-42 when Cyrus looks into the den and discovers Daniel alive and well after seven days. The king is so amazed and moved that he confesses: "You are great, O Lord, the God of Daniel, and there is no other besides you" (v. 41). When Daniel's accusers are thrown into the lions' den, they are devoured immediately.

Significance

In Bel and the Dragon, Daniel engages in more contests about who the living God is. By his deadly cakes he exposes the dragon/snake as no living god at all. By suffering imprisonment in the lions' den, he risks death and yet remains unharmed through divine protection. He takes the food brought by the prophet Habakkuk as a token of God's care for him. The two great theological assertions of this addition appear in verse 38 ("You have remembered me, O God, and have not forsaken those who love you"), and in verse 41 ("You are great, O Lord, the God of Daniel, and there is no other besides you!"). These statements affirm the sovereignty of God as well as God's care for those who love God in the midst of their sufferings.

Issues

The most difficult question raised by these additions is, How do they relate to the book of Daniel as it appears in the Hebrew Bible? It is not simply a matter of a few Greek compositions having been added when the translation from Hebrew/Aramaic to Greek was made.

There are two important Greek versions of the book of Daniel: the Septuagint and Theodotion. The latter version is closer to the Hebrew/Aramaic version. But was Theodotion a revision of the Septuagint, or an independent translation? Both Greek versions contain the additions, and it appears that the same translators were responsible for both the main text and the additions in both cases.

In almost every one of the additions, a good case can be made for assuming a Hebrew or Aramaic original, which in turn points to an origin

119

in the land of Israel or in the Eastern Diaspora. We know from the Dead Sea discoveries that the book of Daniel was very popular at Qumran and that there was a lively interest in the figure of Daniel as witnessed by several "pseudo-Danielic" compositions found there. The additions are further evidence for a "Daniel circle" that produced entertaining and edifying stories about Daniel and his companions.

What do the additions add? The prayers between 3:23 and 3:24 purport to represent the sentiments of Shadrach, Meshach, and Abednego in the furnace of flaming fire, but neither prayer need have been composed precisely for this context. The Susanna story is more about a false accusation against an innocent woman than about Daniel, who appears only near the end. It does show how the young Daniel gained a reputation for wisdom and holiness. The Bel and the Dragon episodes portray Daniel as a detective who exposes the folly of idolatry. Yet none of the additions fits neatly into the "conflicts and contests" pattern of Daniel 1–6. Rather, their inclusion is best explained in light of both a lively interest in Daniel and a desire to provide an expanded version of the book of Daniel at a time when a certain amount of fluidity characterized textual transmission.

Influence

The additions belong to the fuller edition of Daniel found in the Greek Bible and in those versions that are dependent on it. They are regarded as canonical in the Roman Catholic, Greek, and Russian Orthodox churches. The Theodotion version has been regarded as authoritative among Christians since the third century C.E.

The most familiar parts among the additions from use in Christian liturgical life are the Song of the Three Jews and the Susanna episode. The Susanna story has generated a rich artistic tradition. It has also become controversial in recent years among feminist interpreters who raise questions about the "male" perspective from which the story is told and about the possible voyeurism involved in it.

For Further Study

Collins, John J. *Daniel: A Commentary on the Book of Daniel.* Hermeneia. Minneapolis: Fortress, 1993.

Moore, Carey A. *Daniel, Esther and Jeremiah: The Additions.* Anchor Bible 44. Garden City, N.Y.: Doubleday, 1977.

Spolsky, Ellen, ed. *The Judgment of Susanna: Authority and Witness.* Atlanta: Scholars Press, 1996.

Steussy, Marti J. *Gardens in Babylon: Narrative and Faith in the Greek Legends of Daniel.* Atlanta: Scholars Press, 1993.

CHAPTER 10

1 Maccabees:
God's Dynasty

Basic Information

First Maccabees is aptly called a "dynastic history." It provides in narrative form the history of a second century B.C.E. Jewish dynasty through three generations. This family is called the Maccabees (after Judas's nickname "the hammer") or the Hasmoneans. The narrow focus on one family would allow the descendants of that family to ground their own claims to religious, military, and political authority in Israel.

The outline of the book reveals its purpose. After describing the crisis fomented by the Seleucid ruler Antiochus IV Epiphanes and the resistance begun by Mattathias (1:1–2:70), it recounts the exploits of Judas Maccabeus (3:1–9:22) and his brothers Jonathan (9:23–12:53) and Simon (13:1–16:24). The author wants to show how God used Judas and his brothers to remove the yoke of Seleucid oppression, and to explain how the Jewish high priesthood came to reside in this family. Judas and his brothers represent God's own dynasty. The book's perspective is illustrated in 1 Maccabees 5:61-62 when Joseph and Azariah try to gain military glory but suffer defeat because "they did not listen to Judas and his brothers. But they did not belong to the family of those men through whom deliverance was given to Israel."

The major characters in the book are the priest Mattathias, his five sons (John, Simon, Judas, Eleazar, and Jonathan), and Simon's son John

Hyrcanus. The book presents Judas, Jonathan, and Simon as bringing about Israel's "salvation," which is understood in a this-worldly historical sense of liberation from hostile political and military forces. The three brothers prove skillful in military, religious, and political matters. Judas is the great warrior. Jonathan is a shrewd politician. Simon consolidates and organizes the new Judean state.

In its narrative style the book imitates the biblical historical books of Samuel and Kings, thus suggesting a continuity between the heroes of Israel's past with the Maccabean dynasty. An important element in this program is the device of "biblical re-creations," that is, deliberate attempts at showing how the actions of the Maccabean dynasty stand in line with the words and deeds of the early heroes of the Bible. The underlying message is that the Maccabean dynasty carries on the great heritage of Israel's past.

The primary text of 1 Maccabees is the Greek version, which is part of the Septuagint. Most scholars assume that 1 Maccabees was composed in Hebrew and then translated into Greek, though it could conceivably have been composed in a Semitizing Greek. The present text is "biblical Greek," much like the Greek versions of the early historical books of the Greek Bible.

The book ends with a summary of the exploits of John Hyrcanus, who was the Jewish high priest from 134 to 104 B.C.E. The book was probably composed during his reign or shortly afterward in the early first century B.C.E. It incorporates several "official" documents (see 8:23-32; 10:18-20; 10:25-45; 11:30-37; 11:57-59; 12:5-23; 13:36-40). The authenticity of these documents is disputed, though current scholarship tends to support their basic authenticity. The poems, speeches, and prayers are best seen as the free compositions of the author (though based on biblical models). Some scholars argue that the authors used a common source in 1 Maccabees 1–7 and 2 Maccabees 3–15. However, given the complicated transmission of both books, it seems impossible to recover the text of this source now.

First Maccabees is the most important historical resource for studying the Maccabean movement from its inception around 165 B.C.E. to the reign of John Hyrcanus. Its style is generally straightforward and factual in comparison with the allusive book of Daniel and the dramatic 2 Maccabees. Where there are parallels between 1 and 2 Maccabees, there are some puzzling discrepancies, but 1 Maccabees at least gives the greater appearance of historical reliability.

123

A table of dates may help in following the narrative: *Hanukkah*

167: The temple cult is changed, and the persecutions begin. *Hanukkah*
164: The Jerusalem temple is recaptured, purified, and rededicated.
163: Antiochus V and Lysias mount a campaign against Judea.
161: Nicanor is defeated by Judas.
160: Judas is killed in battle, and Jonathan is acclaimed as his successor.
159: The high priest Alcimus dies, and the high priesthood is open until 152.
152: Alexander Balas replaces Demetrius I and appoints Jonathan as high priest.
142: Jonathan dies, and Simon replaces him.
134: Simon is killed, and John Hyrcanus succeeds him.

The appearance of objectivity in 1 Maccabees ought not to distract us from recognizing the rather narrow lens through which the author presents all events in relation to Mattathias, Judas, Jonathan, and Simon. He attributes the beginning of the resistance to Mattathias, and focuses on the military, religious, and political activities of his sons and grandson. He rejects the idea that others in Israel could succeed apart from the Maccabees (see 5:61-62), and comes close to equating the Maccabees with the "true Israel" and their Jewish opponents with "lawless men."

Part One: Crisis and Resistance (1:1–2:70)

A. The *Crisis* (1:1-64) occurs when the Syrian king Antiochus IV Epiphanes seeks to abolish the Jewish way of life built around Torah observance, temple worship, and circumcision. A sketch of Hellenistic history (1:1-10) from Alexander the Great (336-323 B.C.E.) to Antiochus IV (175-164 B.C.E.) highlights the themes of arrogance ("his heart was lifted up") and wickedness ("they caused many evils on the earth"). Although Antiochus is the primary villain, in 1:11-15 there are some indications of Jewish collaboration in his program: "Let us go and make a covenant with the Gentiles around us" (1:11). The program consists in observing a Gentile legal system (rather than the Torah), building a gymnasium, removing the marks of circumcision, and abandoning "the holy covenant" (traditional Jewish religion).

124

The crisis grows in 1:16-40 when in 169 B.C.E. on his return from Egypt Antiochus invades and plunders the Jerusalem temple, with the result that "all the house of Jacob was clothed with shame" (1:28). Then in 167 he sends a "chief collector of tribute" to plunder Jerusalem further and to set up a military garrison or citadel that will prove remarkably resistant to Jewish offensives over the twenty-five years of its existence: "the citadel became an ambush against the sanctuary" (1:36).

Having robbed the temple and established the citadel near the temple, Antiochus in 1:41-50 decrees the abolition of the temple service and its sacrifices, of observance of the Sabbath and the Jewish holy days, of circumcision of male children, and of the laws of ritual purity. The decree is accompanied, according to 1:51-61, by erecting "a desolating sacrilege on the altar of burnt offering" and other incense altars throughout Judah, destroying copies of the Torah, and putting to death women who had their sons circumcised. Although some acquiesced, "many in Israel stood firm" and willingly suffered death out of fidelity to their religious traditions (1:62-63). The crisis is summed up as follows: "Very great wrath came upon Israel" (1:64).

B. The *Resistance* (2:1-70) is led by the priest Mattathias and his five sons at Modein, a town about seventeen miles northwest of Jerusalem (2:1-14). When Mattathias sees the profanation of the Jerusalem temple and the program aimed at abolishing Judaism, he utters a lament ("Alas! Why was I born to see this, the ruin of my people, the ruin of the holy city?") and puts on the garments of a mourner.

The beginning of active resistance occurs in 2:15-28 when the king's officers come to Modein and try to force the people to offer sacrifice according to the "new order." When they try to enlist Mattathias as an example of Jewish cooperation, he refuses: "Far be it from us to desert the law and its ordinances" (2:20). When a Jew steps forward to offer sacrifice, Mattathias kills him and the king's officer. In the spirit of the zealous Phinehas (see Num. 25:6-15), he invites other Jews to join him in the revolt: "Let everyone who is zealous for the law and supports the covenant come out with me!"

The nature of the resistance is defined in part by the fate of a group of pious Jews who flee to the wilderness and refuse to defend themselves on the Sabbath (2:29-48). Their massacre leads the Maccabees to adopt a policy of self-defense: "Let us fight against anyone who come to attack us on the Sabbath day" (2:41). Joined by Hasideans ("mighty warriors of Israel"), they strike down sinners, tear down pagan altars, circumcise boys, and hunt down arrogant men, thus rescuing "the law out of the hands of Gentiles and kings" (2:48).

The first stage of the resistance reaches a climax with Mattathias's farewell to his sons and his death (2:49-70). He urges them to imitate great biblical figures who underwent testing and were rewarded by God for their fidelity, foretells the fall of Antiochus, appoints Simon as chief counselor and Judas as commander of the army, and tells them to "pay back the Gentiles in full, and obey the commands of the law" (2:68).

Part Two: The Exploits of Judas (3:1–9:22)

A. The *Early Victories of Judas* (3:1–4:61) make possible the recapture and rededication of the Jerusalem temple. After introducing Judas and quoting a poem celebrating his exploits (3:1-9), the author describes his surprising victories over Apollonius (the governor of Samaria) and over Seron at Beth-horon (3:10-26). Judas attributes his victories to the power of God: "It is not on the size of the army that victory in battle depends, but strength comes from Heaven" (3:19). When Antiochus IV goes off to Persia to raise money (3:27-31), he leaves Lysias in charge to mount a campaign against Jerusalem (3:32-37). But Judas defeats Lysias's generals Gorgias and Nicanor at Emmaus (3:38–4:25) and then Lysias himself at Beth-zur (4:26-35).

In these battles the rallying point for Judas's troops is the state of the Jerusalem temple: "The sanctuary was trampled down, and aliens held the citadel; it was a lodging place for the Gentiles" (3:45; see also 3:50b-53). Moreover, Judas conducts himself according to the Torah and evokes the example of biblical figures. In 3:56 he dismisses those exempted from battle by Deuteronomy 20:5-8, and in 4:9 he reminds his small group of men "how our ancestors were saved at the Red Sea, when Pharaoh with his forces pursued them." On their return from the victorious battle at Emmaus, they sing hymns and praises to God ("For he is good, for his mercy endures forever," 4:24). And before his battle with Lysias, Judas offers a benediction in which he reminds God that God gave David victory over Goliath and Jonathan over the Philistines (4:30; see 1 Samuel 14 and 17). Judas is very much a biblical warrior, one who depends on the power of the God of Israel for his victories.

The high-point of Judas's early career is the cleansing and dedication of the Jerusalem temple (4:36-61). As they approach Mount Zion,

Judas and his men find the temple in great disrepair (4:36-40). After sending a detail to hold off the hostile troops in the citadel, Judas restores the temple worship by choosing blameless priests, removing the stones of the altars that had been defiled and rebuilding the altars, and setting out new holy vessels (4:41-51). Then on the twenty-fifth of Chislev (December 14) of 164 B.C.E., on the anniversary of the temple's profanation, Judas and his brothers join the assembly in celebrating the new eight-day festival of Hanukkah (which means "Dedication"). The result was that "there was very great joy among the people, and the disgrace brought by the Gentiles was removed" (4:59). The first phase of Judas's leadership ends with him in control of the Jerusalem temple and environs, as well as the fortress of Beth-zur (about twenty miles south of Jerusalem).

B. The *Second Phase of Judas' sMilitary Leadership* (5:1–7:50) has Judas and his brothers waging battles against allies of the Seleucids and other enemies after the pattern of David (see 2 Samuel 8 and 10). They attack in all directions, including Idumea to the south (5:3-5, 65), Ammon and Gilead east of the Jordan River (5:6-13, 24-51), Galilee to the north (5:21-23), and the coastal plain (5:66-68). Their campaigns are presented as revenge for past harm done to Jews in those areas or attempts to prevent future harm to Jews. Whereas Judas and his brothers are greatly honored for their exploits not only among Jews but also among Gentiles, those who take military action apart from them — as Joseph and Azariah try to do in 5:55-62 — fail because "they did not belong to the family of those men through whom deliverance was given to Israel" (5:62).

The death of Antiochus IV (6:1-17) is traced to his shock at the military successes of Judas and the recognition that his death is a punishment for plundering the Jerusalem temple and killing the inhabitants of Judah. Whereas he appointed Philip as regent, Lysias made himself the guardian of the young King Antiochus V.

According to 6:18-31 Judas takes advantage of the confusion surrounding Antiochus IV's death to attack the citadel in Jerusalem. His boldness leads to complaints about him from those who escaped from the citadel, and in response the new king, under Lysias's guidance, mounts a full-scale campaign against the Maccabees. The account of the battle at Beth-zechariah (6:32-47) emphasizes the superior numbers of the Seleucid army and the courage of Eleazar, while glossing over the fact that Judas was defeated. Eleazar dies a hero's death when an elephant falls on him during his attempt to kill (one whom he perceived to be) the king. Then the Seleucid army takes Beth-zur and lays siege to the Jerusalem

127

temple (6:48-54). Just when the Seleucids are about to take the sanctuary, Lysias learns that his rival Philip has returned to Antioch. And so Lysias and King Antiochus V propose a peace treaty with Judas (6:55-63) in order to go back to Antioch and face Philip there. At the end of 162 B.C.E. the Maccabean revolt is in trouble. There have been military defeats. Eleazar is dead. The new king and his regent have weakened the Jewish defenses. And the peace is an uneasy one.

In 161 B.C.E. Demetrius I, the son of Seleucus IV, seizes the royal throne and has Antiochus V and Lysias killed (7:1-4). To stabilize the situation in Judea, he appoints Alcimus as high priest and sends Bacchides with a large army against Jerusalem (7:5-11). When the Hasideans throw their support to Alcimus, for no apparent reason he has sixty of them put to death (7:12-18). Faced with Judas's continuing guerrilla activity and unable to gain full control of Judah, Alcimus appeals to Demetrius for help (7:19-25).

Help comes in the person of Nicanor. However, Nicanor's plot to kill Judas fails, and he loses five hundred soldiers to Judas at Capharsalama (7:26-32). His threat to burn down the temple unless Judas is handed over (7:35) leads to another battle with Judas, in which Nicanor is the first to fall (7:43). In his prayer before the battle (7:41-42) Judas refers to the siege of Jerusalem under Sennacherib in 701 B.C.E. (see 2 Kings 19:35; Isa. 37:36), thus suggesting that he was greatly outnumbered. His prayer is answered, and so the thirtieth day of Adar becomes the annual celebration of victory over Nicanor (7:49).

C. The *Alliance with Rome* (8:1-32) gives the Maccabees a powerful ally against their hostile neighbors and gives the Romans another foothold in the Near East. After an idealized and somewhat inaccurate description of the Romans and their history (8:1-16), there is an account of how Judas sent emissaries to Rome to make a treaty (8:17-22). The (basically authentic) text of the treaty is given in 8:23-30. After an opening wish (8:23), there are parallel clauses stipulating that each side is to come to the aid of the other if war breaks out (8:24-26, 27-28), and a statement that alterations can be made only with the agreement of both parties (8:29-30). The postscript warning Demetrius (8:31-32) was probably not part of the original text.

D. The *Death of Judas* (9:1-22) comes in 160 B.C.E. when Demetrius orders Bacchides and Alcimus to make another attack on Jerusalem, this time with 20,000 foot soldiers and 2,000 cavalry against the 3,000 men in Judas's army (and only 800 after a massive desertion). Judas's strategy according to 9:8-10 is to seize the initiative and to surprise his numerically superior opponents. After a vivid description of the battle at Elasa, we are told that "the battle became desperate, and many on both sides were wounded and fell. Judas also fell, and the rest fled" (9:17-18). Judas's passing is recorded in the style of the biblical books of Kings, and the lament over him (9:21) is taken from 2 Samuel 1:19: "How is the mighty fallen, the savior of Israel." If the Maccabean movement is to continue, it will need a new leader and a new way of dealing with its enemies.

Part Three: The Exploits of Jonathan (9:23–12:53)

A. The *Accession of Jonathan* (9:23-73) brings a different style of leader to the movement. Whereas Judas was a brilliant and daring military leader, Jonathan was a skillful politician whose greatest successes came by playing off one claimant to the Seleucid throne against another, and thus gaining territory and security for his people. His political skill gave new life and direction to the Maccabean movement.

The situation after Judas's death (9:23-27) was grim. A great famine occurred. Many in Israel went over to the enemy. Bacchides put the "ungodly" in charge and persecuted the "friends" of Judas. There was "great distress in Israel." Against this background the friends of Judas choose Jonathan as their ruler and leader (9:28-31). While fleeing from Bacchides (9:32-34) Jonathan is betrayed by Nabateans who seize his brother John and put him to death. Jonathan and Simon get revenge by ambushing a Nabatean wedding party, and return to the marshes of the Jordan (9:35-42). Although Jonathan eludes his trap at the Jordan (9:43-49), Bacchides seems to have control over most of Judea and has taken as hostages at the citadel the sons of the leading men (9:50-53).

In 159 B.C.E. Alcimus orders the inner wall of the sanctuary to be torn down, thus giving access to pagans to areas reserved for Jews. But Alcimus suffers a stroke and dies a painful death (9:54-56). After two years of "rest," certain "lawless" ones try to convince Bacchides to destroy Jonathan and Simon. When he fails to do so, Bacchides comes to terms with the two surviving brothers (9:57-73). Thus Jonathan takes on a role reminiscent of the Judges of old: "Thus the sword ceased from Israel. Jonathan settled in Michmash and began to judge the people; and he destroyed the godless out of Israel" (9:73).

B. *Jonathan's Appointment as High Priest* (10:1-66) comes as the result of his political skill and good fortune. Events seem to have stood still between 157 and 152 B.C.E. What revived the Maccabean movement was the appearance of Alexander Balas (or Alexander Epiphanes), who claimed to be the son of Antiochus IV Epiphanes. Since both Demetrius and Alexander needed allies and since Jonathan seems to have been the only Jewish leader with whom they could bargain, Jonathan was free to play one off against the other.

The first offer (10:1-14) comes from Demetrius, who allows Jonathan to raise an army and commands that the Jewish hostages in the citadel be released. He also allows Jonathan to move back to Jerusalem and take control of territory previously held by Bacchides. Then in 10:15-21 Alexander Balas offers to appoint Jonathan the Jewish high priest and invites him to become one of the king's "friends" (special counselors). From the death of Alcimus in 159 to 152 B.C.E. there is no mention of a Jewish high priest in Jerusalem. But at the feast of Tabernacles in 152 B.C.E. Jonathan "put on the sacred vestments." The third offer (10:22-45) comes from Demetrius with promises so extravagant (exemption from taxes, handing over the citadel, release of Jewish captives, permission to celebrate holy days, and so on) that Jonathan and the people rightly discern that they were too good to be true, and they decide to side with Alexander (10:47). Their decision was wise, since Demetrius was killed in battle soon afterward (10:50). When Alexander arranges a marriage alliance with the Ptolemies, Jonathan is summoned to meet with the two kings, and he emerges wearing purple and bearing the titles of general and governor of the province (10:51-66).

C. *Jonathan's Further Political and Military Activities* (10:67–12:53) are intertwined with developments related to the Selecuid kings. In 147 B.C.E. Demetrius II, the son of Demetrius I, rises in opposition to Alexander, and so Jonathan is drawn into a new round of military and political involvement (10:67-89). When challenged by Apollonius, Jonathan and Simon take possession of Joppa, burn Azotus, and gain plunder from Ashkelon. The result is still greater honor for Jonathan ("a golden buckle, such as it is the custom to give to the King's Kinsmen") from Alexander Balas. But Alexander (11:1-19) is undone by his father-in-law Ptolmey VI, who in turn dies three days after Alexander's murder. And so Demetrius II becomes the Seleucid king in 145 B.C.E.

With political affairs so confused, Jonathan takes the opportunity to attack the citadel again (11:20). Then at a conference in Ptolemais (11:21-37), Jonathan wins Demetrius II over, has himself confirmed as

high priest and friend of the king, and even obtains some of the conces-
sions promised by Demetrius I. But when Demetrius II dismisses native
soldiers in favor of his own foreign troops (11:38-53), he sparks off a re-
bellion and has to appeal to Jonathan for help. In return for supplying
3,000 troops, Jonathan is promised that Seleucid troops will be with-
drawn from various strongholds, including the citadel. The Jewish troops
fight bravely and effectively, but Demetrius fails to keep his part of the
agreement. In 145 B.C.E. Antiochus VI Epiphanes with the backing of
Trypho gains control of Antioch and replaces Demetrius II. He confirms
Jonathan's privileges and makes Simon the governor of the coastal territory, thus also giving the two brothers opportunity for military activity at
Gaza, Kadesh in Galilee, and Hazor (11:54-74).

While Jonathan was willing to accept honors and privileges from
the various Seleucid rulers, he did not want to become totally dependent
on them. And so in 12:1-23 he sends a delegation to Rome to renew the
treaty made under Judas and also begins communication with the Spartans on the basis of an earlier contact between the Jewish high priest
Onias I (320-290 B.C.E.) and the Spartan king Arius (308-265 B.C.E.), as
well as an alleged relationship between the two peoples. Nevertheless,
Jonathan and Simon were drawn once more into the struggle for the
Seleucid throne, and so they undertook measures to strengthen their position, especially by trying to isolate the citadel from the rest of Jerusalem
(12:24-38). When Trypho attempted to become king in place of
Antiochus VI, he also sought to eliminate Jonathan (12:39). At Beth-
shan (12:40-45) Trypho backed away from battle with Jonathan, but at
Ptolemais he trapped Jonathan and took him captive (12:46-53). Thus
the public career of Jonathan came to an end. His brilliance as a politician
and strategist infused life into the Maccabean movement, and contributed greatly to making the people of Israel into an independent nation
once more.

Part Four: The Exploits of Simon (13:1–16:24)

A. The *Accession of Simon* (13:1-53) took place in 142 B.C.E. Although
Mattathias had appointed him as counselor, it was only after his four
brothers had passed from the scene that Simon got to head up the military and political operations of the Maccabean movement. In response
to Simon's offer to assume leadership (13:1-11), the people proclaim

him enthusiastically: "You are our leader in place of Judas and your brother Jonathan. Fight our battles, and all that you say to us we will do" (13:8-9).

In his invasion of Judea (13:12-30), Trypho decides to use Jonathan as a hostage. He claims to be holding Jonathan for nonpayment of taxes, and demands a hundred talents of silver and two of Jonathan's sons in exchange for Jonathan (13:15-16). If Simon refuses, it might seem that he wanted power for himself. But he knew that Trypho would not keep his word, and Trypho does not release Jonathan. Prevented by a heavy snowstorm from linking up with the troops in the citadel, Trypho goes off to Gilead and kills Jonathan on the way back to Antioch. When Simon recovers Jonathan's body, he buries him at Modein and erects a monument to the Maccabean family.

When Trypho kills Antiochus VI and becomes king in his place (13:31-42), Simon renews contact with Demetrius II, who confirms all his privileges and pardons all his offenses. In fact, Demetrius II had no real power, and his response was not very significant on the objective level. Nevertheless, for the author, Simon's accession in 142 B.C.E. was the beginning of a new era in Jewish history: "In the first year of Simon the great high priest and commander and leader of the Jews" (13:41). Thus Simon combines in his person the religious, military, and political leadership of the Jewish people.

After capturing Gazara/Gezer (13:43-48), Simon finally gains control over the citadel at Jerusalem (13:49-52), the last symbol of Seleucid power in Jerusalem. Chapter 13 ends by introducing John Hyrcanus, Simon's son, who will eventually succeed his father and carry on the Maccabean movement.

B. The *Reign of Simon* (14:1-49) is a great success. Despite the capture of his ally Demetrius II (14:1-3), Simon is acknowledged to be an effective leader by his own people and by others. A poem summarizes his exploits (14:4-7) and celebrates them in biblical language (14:8-15). After the alliances with the Romans and the Spartans are renewed, the people of Judea present a decree (14:25-45) expressing their appreciation for Simon's many benefactions to them. In it Simon is proclaimed as leader, high priest, and governor (14:41-42). The official character of this decree is indicated by its inscription on bronze tablets, its posting in the sanctuary, and the deposit of copies in the treasury (14:46-49). Under Simon, the Maccabean movement had gone further toward Jewish independence and nationhood than anyone could have imagined in 165 B.C.E.

C. The *End of Simon's Rule* (15:1–16:24) comes after further immersion in Seleucid dynastic intrigues. In 138 B.C.E. Simon receives a letter (15:1-9) from Antiochus VII Sidetes, the son of Demetrius I and brother of Demetrius II. He proposes to seize the Seleucid throne from Trypho, confirms Simon's privileges, and promises to bestow great honors on him and his people. But as the military action against Trypho proceeds (15:10-14, 25-36), Antiochus VII rejects Simon's help and demands that Simon return the cities and lands of Judea to him as the Seleucid ruler. Simon replies that these territories "had been unjustly taken by our enemies" and states that "we are firmly holding the inheritance of our ancestors" (15:33-34). In the meantime (15:15-24), the Romans wrote letters to Judea's neighbors warning them not to harm or make war against the Jews.

After Trypho's departure (15:37), the Seleucid general Cendebeus provokes and attacks the Jews but is defeated by Simon's son John Hyrcanus (15:37–16:10). The dynastic history that is 1 Maccabees comes to a somewhat inglorious end in 16:11-22, when in 134 B.C.E. Simon is killed while drunk at a banquet at the fortress of Dok near Jericho. His son-in-law Ptolemy, son of Abubus, tries to seize Simon's domain by killing him and his sons. But he fails to kill John Hyrcanus, who takes over from his father Simon. The book ends in 16:23-24 with a summary of John's achievements as the military, political, and religious leader of his people. It is written in the style of the summary reports about the kings of Israel and Judah contained in the canonical books of Kings.

Significance

The crisis faced in 1 Maccabees is the same as that faced in the book of Daniel and 2 Maccabees: the threat posed by Antiochus IV Epiphanes and his Jewish collaborators to the religious traditions and national identity of Israel. In Daniel there is an expectation that God will directly intervene against the enemies of God's people and bring about the kingdom of God. In 2 Maccabees God is the defender of the Jewish people and their temple, and will surely vindicate those Jews who remain faithful even to the point of martyrdom as the seven sons and their mother do (see chapter 7). The approach to the crisis of 167 to 164 B.C.E. in 1 Maccabees is more activist and materialist.

The God of 1 Maccabees is powerful and just, though perhaps

somewhat distant (God is generally referred to as "Heaven"). The Maccabees pray to God before their decisive actions and battles, and their (often surprising) victories are attributed to divine help. The crisis facing the Jewish people is the result of collaboration between the evil King Antiochus IV and the "lawless" within Israel. Throughout the careers of Judas, Jonathan, and Simon, the foreign rulers are treacherous and generally hostile to Israel. The Maccabees represent the "true Israel" within geographical Israel and indeed the world.

For the author of 1 Maccabees, the sufferings of Israel are obstacles to be removed largely by human activity, with the help of God. The author's models are Mattathias, Judas, Jonathan, and Simon — rebels against unjust and evil governments, men of action, guerrilla warriors, and practical leaders who know how to increase their power and influence. The result of their activism and militarism is political independence and the revival of national identity that had been submerged for over four hundred years through the Babylonian exile, the Persian period, and domination by the Ptolemies in Egypt and the Seleucids in Syria. The author's approach is not at all apocalyptic (waiting for God to act, as in Daniel), and he shows little sympathy for the pious Sabbath observers and the naive Hasideans who are killed off.

Issues. First Maccabees is our most important historical source for events in Jerusalem and Judea from ca. 167 to 130 B.C.E. — a very important period in the history of Israel. In his *Jewish Antiquities* (12.241–13.214) the Jewish historian Josephus gives a paraphrase of 1 Maccabees 1–13 in treating this period. The other sources — most obviously Daniel and 2 Maccabees, but also the Dead Sea Scrolls, Judith, the *Testament of Moses,* and perhaps other works — are far more allusive in their treatment of these events. And yet, despite its surface appearance of historical reliability, we must never lose sight of the fact that 1 Maccabees is a dynastic history, what some call "propaganda" for the Maccabean dynasty. And so the question is, How objective and reliable is 1 Maccabees as history?

Another issue is, How successful was the Maccabean revolt? One can point to the cleansing and rededication of the Jerusalem temple under Judas and to the capture of the citadel under Simon as the two great symbols of Maccabean success. And yet, especially under Jonathan and Simon, the Maccabean movement succeeded chiefly by entangling Jewish affairs with Seleucid dynastic struggles and by entering into treaties with Rome. And in military, economic, and even cultural matters, the Maccabees led the Jewish people further into the general milieu of Hellenism. While traditional Jewish religious observance was the rallying point for the Maccabees and their supporters, they gradually brought Jews into even closer contact with their neighbors. Their usurpation of the high priesthood from the Zadokite line was a bold and controversial move, one that horrified the traditionalists such as the group that eventually produced the Qumran Scrolls. Moreover, the treaties with Rome would bring about ever more direct interference by the Romans into Jewish affairs so that by 6 C.E. Judea became a Roman province overseen directly by a Roman prefect or governor (as Pontius Pilate was from 26 to 36 C.E.).

Influence. First Maccabees is part of the canon of Scripture in the Roman Catholic, Greek, and Russian Orthodox churches. It is not recognized as Scripture by Protestants and Jews. There has been, however, a puzzling ambivalence about 1 and 2 Maccabees in the Jewish tradition. Hanukkah, which celebrates the cleansing and rededication of the Jerusalem temple in 164 B.C.E. under Judas, is part of the traditional Jewish calendar of festivals. Although it is a minor holiday (except in countries where its proximity to Christmas has made it very significant), the "biblical basis" for it lies in books not regarded as canonical. Since it is likely that 1 Maccabees was composed in Hebrew, its absence from the canon of Hebrew Scriptures is somewhat puzzling.

These puzzlements have led some scholars to suspect that at some point in the first century there was a Jewish reaction against the Maccabees and what they stood for, and a deliberate attempt to push them out of the sacred tradition of Judaism. Perhaps "messianic" claims were being made about Judas Maccabeus or some other figure who traced his ancestry back to the Maccabean movement. Perhaps in light of failed uprising against the Romans by Jews claiming to follow the example of Judas and his brothers, the custodians of the Jewish tradition found the Maccabees too controversial and dangerous. The revival of interest in the Maccabees as men of action and noble warriors in the modern state of Israel suggests that these suspicions have some basis in fact.

The "messianic" dimension of the Maccabean movement may be reflected in the only New Testament passage that is explicitly tied to Hanukkah (John 10:22-39). The question about Jesus' identity as the Messiah, the charge that he makes himself equal to God, and the emphasis on the theme of eternal life suggest that the Hanukkah setting is part of John's effort in the "Book of Signs" (John 1–12) to show that in Jesus the Jewish festivals and institutions reach their fullness.

For Further Study

Bartlett, John R. *The First and Second Books of Maccabees.* Cambridge: Cambridge University Press, 1973.

————. *1 Maccabees.* Sheffield: Sheffield Academic Press, 1998.

Bickerman, Elias J. *The God of the Maccabees.* Leiden: Brill, 1979.

————. *The Jews in the Greek Age.* Cambridge, Mass.: Harvard University Press, 1988.

Dancy, John C. *A Commentary on I Maccabees.* Oxford: Blackwell, 1954.

Doran, Robert. "The First Book of Maccabees." In *The Interpreter's Bible,* vol. 4, 1-178. Nashville: Abingdon, 1996.

Goldstein, Jonathan A. *I Maccabees.* Anchor Bible 41. Garden City, N.Y.: Doubleday, 1976.

Harrington, Daniel J. *The Maccabean Revolt: Anatomy of a Biblical Revolution.* Wilmington, Del.: Glazier, 1988.

Sievers, Joseph. *The Hasmoneans and Their Supporters.* Atlanta: Scholars Press, 1990.

Tcherikover, Victor. *Hellenistic Civilization and the Jews.* Philadelphia: Jewish Publication Society, 1959.

CHAPTER 11

2 Maccabees:
God's Temple

Basic Information

The distinctive angle from which the author of 2 Maccabees views the events of the second century B.C.E. that he describes is the fate of the Jerusalem temple. The main part of the book (chapters 3–15) narrates three attacks on the temple and its successful defense by God and the people of Israel under the leadership of Judas Maccabeus. The first attack (3:1-40) takes place under Seleucus IV when Heliodorus tries to plunder the temple treasury. The second attack occurs under Antiochus IV Epiphanes (4:1–10:9) and results in the recapture of the temple and its rededication by Judas. The third attack happens under Antiochus V (10:10–15:36) and involves the defeat of his general Nicanor as he tries to capture and kill Judas. Two letters (1:1-9; 1:10–2:18) from Jews in Jerusalem encourage Jews in Egypt to celebrate Hanukkah, the festival of the rededication of the temple. These letters may have been attached to the copy of the work that was sent to Egypt in 124 B.C.E.

The best point of entry to 2 Maccabees is the author's own statements in 2:19-32 (the preface) and 15:37-39 (the conclusion). In the preface he describes the subject matter as the exploits of Judas and his companions against Antiochus IV and his son Antiochus V, and how with God's help these few men were able to recover the temple, free the city, and restore the laws. The author in fact is an epitomator or summarizer of a much larger (five-volume) work by Jason of Cyrene. In carrying out his digest, he views himself as both informing and entertaining, as he states both in the preface and the conclusion.

The main character is Judas Maccabeus — at least in the second and third defenses of the temple. Unlike 1 Maccabees, 2 Maccabees shows no interest in the Maccabean dynasty, never mentioning Judas's father, Mattathias, or his brothers, Jonathan and Simon. The work's real interest in Judas focuses solely on his function as the instrument of God in defending the temple. The author shows great interest in the righteous and noble high priest Onias III, and contrasts him with the scoundrels who succeeded him, Jason, Menelaus, and Alcimus. Moreover, he gives great attention to the heroic witnesses of the Jewish way of life — the martyrs Eleazar, the mother and her seven sons, and the Jerusalem elder Razis. He interprets their martyrdoms as atoning for the people's sins and so making it possible for Judas to reclaim the temple and restore it to its rightful place in Israel.

The narratives that constitute the main part of the book (chapters 3–15) have been described as "pathetic history" in the sense that the author plays upon the emotions *(pathē)* of the reader. The focus on God's temple as the center of Jewish life has also led the book to be labeled "temple propaganda." Within the larger narratives there are supernatural interventions or legends (see chapter 3), dialogues (see chapter 7), and dreams and prayers (see chapter 15).

This table of dates provides a framework for following the narrative:

175: Jason outbids Onias III for the high priesthood and imposes a program of forced Hellenization.
172: Menelaus outbids Jason for the high priesthood and robs the temple vessels. Antiochus IV also robs the temple.
167: The temple cult is changed, and the persecutions and martyrdoms ensue.
164: The Jerusalem temple is recaptured, purified, and rededicated.
163: Antiochus V and Lysias mount their campaign against Judea.
161: Judas defeats Nicanor.

The forthright and engaging way in which the author expresses himself in his preface can mask several critical problems in using 2 Maccabees as a historical source. The first problem concerns the relationship between the original five-volume work of Jason of Cyrene (now lost) and the one-volume work now known as 2 Maccabees. The original composition of both works seems to have been in Greek. But there is no way of knowing how closely the epitomator (as the author is often called) followed the style and vocabulary of Jason of Cyrene. Furthermore, there is no way of knowing what the epitomator left out or added into Jason's story in his efforts at being entertaining and telling the story from his own perspective. In particular, was Jason's work as focused on the defense of the Jerusalem temple as 2 Maccabees is?

The narrative ends in 161 B.C.E. with the defeat of Nicanor and before the death of Judas (in 160). The rather abrupt conclusion and the absence of any indication of Judas's death suggests that Jason could have written just about the time at which the story ends. But when did the epitomator do his work? Was it shortly after the original composition, or was it in the late second or even early first century B.C.E.?

Content

Part One: Two Letters and a Preface (1:1–2:32)

A. The *Letter to the Jews in Egypt* (1:1-9) is from Jews in Jerusalem and dated to 124 B.C.E. It encourages the former to celebrate the feast of the Dedication of the Jerusalem temple (Hanukkah). The letter may have been composed to accompany the copy of 2 Maccabees sent to the Jewish community in Egypt. It also subtly asserts the spiritual primacy of Jerusalem and its temple for Jews in the Diaspora. After the customary greetings (1:1), it presents a series of good wishes or prayers (1:2-6), recalls a previous communication (1:7-8), and requests that Hanukkah be observed in Egypt too (1:9).

B. The *Letter to Aristobulus* (1:10–2:18) is from the Jews in Jerusalem (including the senate and Judas) to a prominent Egyptian Jew named Aristobulus (the teacher of Ptolemy IV) and the other Jews in Egypt. If Judas is Judas Maccabeus and the letter is authentic, it must come from the period between late 164 (when the temple was rededicated) and 160 B.C.E. (when Judas was killed). It seeks to explain why Egyptian Jews should celebrate Hanukkah. After the customary greetings (1:10), the letter describes how the evil King Antiochus IV Epiphanes was driven out of Jerusalem by God, and how he died a disgraceful death while robbing another temple (1:11-17). Then in 1:18-36 it recounts as a precedent for

139

observing Hanukkah (which commemorates the "purification" of the temple) the miracle of the hidden fire that consumed Nehemiah's sacrifice, and presents Nehemiah's prayer that focuses on Israel as God's chosen people and the need for rescue from its enemies. Further biblical precedents for observing Hanukkah are put forward with reference to Jeremiah, Solomon, Moses, and Nehemiah (2:1-15). It is also said in 2:14 that Judas had collected books and established a temple library. The real reason why Jews in Egypt should observe the festival of Hanukkah is that in the events associated with the Maccabean revolt God "has saved all his people, and has returned the inheritance to all, and the kingship and the priesthood and the consecration, as he promised through the law" (2:17-18a).

C. The *Preface* (2:19-32) first summarizes the subject matter of the book: the exploits of Judas and his brothers against Antiochus IV and his son Antiochus V, and how with God's help these few men were able to recover the temple, free the city, and restore the laws (2:19-22). Then in 2:23 the writer describes his work as the digest of a longer work by Jason of Cyrene: "all this, which has been set forth by Jason of Cyrene in five volumes, we shall attempt to condense into a single book." In 2:24-32 he further describes his work as a condenser by comparing himself to a decorator at work in a house that has already been built. He hopes to entertain his readers ("to please those who wish to read," 2:25) and does not pretend to give an exhaustive treatment (2:31). With this preface the writer sets out his program of both entertaining and informing his readers.

Part Two: Heliodorus's Attack on the Temple (3:1-40)

Heliodorus's Attack on the Temple (3:1-40) is an overture or preview to the other two attacks described in the rest of the book. Heliodorus is sent by Seleucus IV (187-175 B.C.E.) to confiscate the wealth stored at the temple treasury. His mission is prompted by events within the Jewish community at Jerusalem (3:1-8). The author describes the Jewish high priest Onias III as an exemplary leader, so admired and successful that Seleucus IV had contributed to the upkeep of his temple and its services. But a certain Simon had a disagreement with Onias III about "the administration of the city market" (3:4). When Simon failed to get his own way, he went to the governor Apollonius with a report that the temple treasury in Jerusalem contained enormous amounts of wealth and that Seleucus could gain control over it. Apollonius told the king, who sent Heliodorus to check out the report.

The stage is set for the first attack on the temple (3:9-40). Even though the high priest Onias III tries to explain that there really is not much wealth in the temple treasury, he cannot dissuade Heliodorus from carrying out his mission (3:9-14a). The prospect of his profaning the temple sends the people of Jerusalem into panic (3:14b-21), and they beg God to intervene against Heliodorus. According to 3:22-28, just as Heliodorus and his companions arrive at the temple treasury, they are driven off by a frightening rider and two young men who defend the temple and beat Heliodorus to the point of death. Only through the mediation of Onias III (3:29-34) is Heliodorus rescued from death and restored to health. Heliodorus in turn acknowledges the power of the supreme God whose temple is in Jerusalem, and he shares with King Seleucus IV the lesson that he has learned from the incident: "If you have any enemy or plotter against your government, send him there, for you will get him back thoroughly flogged, if he survives at all; for there is certainly some power of God about the place" (3:38).

In several respects the Heliodorus episode is a preview of the two episodes that follow. There are tensions within the Jewish community at Jerusalem — in this case, between Onias III and Simon. When Simon appeals to the Seleucids, they involve themselves in Jewish affairs and threaten to profane the Jerusalem temple. The threat fails to materialize only because God intervenes to protect the temple and his people.

The chief difference between the Heliodorus episode and those that follow is that here the intervention seems to be miraculous or supernatural. The rider and the two young men appear out of nowhere, do their job, and disappear. They seem to be angelic rather than human. In the remaining two episodes, God works through the efforts of human beings — Judas Maccabeus and his companions.

Part Three: Antiochus IV's Attack on the Temple (4:1–10:9)

A. The *High Priesthood of Jason* (4:1-22) entails a shift to the "Greek way of life." Even after the Heliodorus incident, the intrigues surrounding the high priesthood in Jerusalem continued, when Simon accused Onias III of having incited Heliodorus to seize the temple treasury (4:1-6). At this point (4:7-8) the high priesthood passed from Onias III to his brother Jason because Jason promised Antiochus IV 360 talents of silver plus 80 talents more from another source. It was not unusual that the Seleucid king should have final approval over the Jewish high priesthood, or that the king needed money and so was willing to accommodate Jason, or that some Jews would have accepted Jason as high priest since he belonged to the legitimate high priestly family.

However, Jason's program for the high priesthood as described in 4:9-17 is very unusual. The author of 2 Maccabees presents it as a wholesale shift over to Hellenism. The shift includes the promotion of Greek institutions: the gymnasium (an institution for bodily exercise and for imparting Greek culture), the *ephēbete* (the youths enrolled in the gymnasium), and men of Jerusalem being enrolled as (honorary) citizens of Antioch. Moreover, the introduction of "new customs contrary to the law" suggests the abolition of the Torah as the official law in Israel. Both the placement of the gymnasium near the temple and the interest of the priests in the wrestling matches rather than in caring for the sanctuary and offering the sacrifices indicate disrespect for the Jerusalem temple. The author traces the evils about to befall Jerusalem to Jason's program of Hellenization.

When Jason sent envoys with 300 silver drachmas for a sacrifice to Hercules at the quadrennial games in Tyre, the envoys developed scruples and put the money toward the construction of ships (4:18-20). The incident shows that Jason's program did not meet with universal approval. According to 4:22, Antiochus IV was given a gracious welcome to Jerusalem by the high priest Jason and the people of Jerusalem in 172 B.C.E.

B. The *High Priesthood of Menelaus* (4:23–5:27) leads to even greater abuses. If the author was outraged by Jason, he was even more outraged by the accession to the high priesthood in 172 B.C.E. of Menelaus, the brother of Simon (4:23-29). Menelaus had no family qualifications for the office of Jewish high priest (he was from the tribe of Benjamin; see 3:4), and he obtained the office by outbidding Jason, just as Jason had succeeded Onias III.

The author describes Menelaus as "the chief plotter against his compatriots" (4:50), and in 4:30-50 he explains why that description is appropriate. When Menelaus was ordered by Antiochus IV to explain why he had failed to make his promised payments and while the king was distracted by revolts in Tarsus and Mallus (4:30), Menelaus confiscated the temple vessels to pay his debts and to raise money by selling them (4:32). When Onias III threatened to expose Menelaus's strategy, Menelaus plot-

ted with the Seleucid deputy Andronicus to have Onias killed. Even
Antiochus was outraged at this plot, and had Andronicus punished and
killed.

Menelaus's strategy of temple robbing also raised opposition in Jerusalem: "the populace gathered against Lysimachus, because many of the
gold vessels had already been stolen" (4:39). Lysimachus himself was
killed as "temple robber" in a popular uprising near the treasury. The Jewish opposition was allowed to plead its case against Menelaus before
Antiochus IV (see 4:44). Realizing that he was going to be convicted,
Menelaus bribed Ptolemy to win the king over to his side. The result was
that Menelaus was freed and his Jewish accusers were put to death (4:47).
The author notes that even the Tyrians recognized what a travesty of justice Menelaus had perpetrated (4:49).

During Antiochus's invasion of Egypt in 169 B.C.E., there was great
ferment in Jerusalem (5:1-10). When the false rumor arose that
Antiochus had died in Egypt, Jason tried to regain the high priesthood by
assaulting the city. But Menelaus was able to hold on to his power, and Jason had to flee. The author takes delight in describing the death of Jason:
"He who had cast out many to lie unburied had no one to mourn for
him; he had no funeral of any sort and no place in the tomb of his ancestors" (5:10).

Assuming that all Judea was in revolt (5:11-14) and smarting from
being forced out of Egypt by the Romans (see Dan. 11:30), Antiochus
put down the revolt with brutality, supposedly destroying 80,000 in three
days and selling as many into slavery. His arrival in Jerusalem and triumph there lead Menelaus to give him a tour of the temple and provide
the occasion to steal the temple vessels and votive offerings (5:15-16).
What outrages the author is that Menelaus served as Antiochus's guide.
This outrage in turn leads the author to reflect on God's purposes in allowing such a violation of the temple (5:17-20). It was a just punishment
for the "many sins" of the people of Jerusalem (5:18). Indeed, the author
discerns a close relation between the fate of the temple and the fate of the
people, and only when God becomes reconciled again to the people will
the temple be restored to its proper state.

After Antiochus's plundering of the Jerusalem temple with
Menelaus as his guide, there was even greater pressure on the Jews of Jerusalem and environs (5:21-26). Menelaus was still the high priest, barbarous governors were appointed at Jerusalem and Gerizim, and Apollonius
was sent to attack Jerusalem on the Sabbath. The first note of hope comes

with the introduction of Judas Maccabeus in 5:27: "But Judas Maccabeus, with about nine others, got away to the wilderness." Notice that, contrary to 1 Maccabees, there is no mention of Mattathias and the brothers of Judas. The author of 2 Maccabees, unlike the author of 1 Maccabees, has no interest in the Maccabean family or dynasty. His interest in Judas lies mainly in his exploits as God's instrument in defending and restoring the Jerusalem temple.

C. The *Stories About the Abomination of Desolation and the Martyrs* (6:1–7:42) are the most famous parts of 2 Maccabees. The material in 6:1-6 describes what the book of Daniel refers to as the "abomination of desolation." According to 6:2 this involved the transformation of the Jerusalem temple into a shrine to the Greek god Olympian Zeus and the Gerizim temple into a shrine to the Greek god "Friend-of-Strangers." The claim is made that cultic prostitution was involved (6:4), and this change in worship was part of a wider program to make Jews forsake the Torah and to prevent them from observing their religious festivals and even from confessing themselves to be Jews. Moreover, according to 6:7-9 they were forced to celebrate the king's birthday every month and to march in processions honoring Dionysus, the Greek god of wine and the grape harvest. The whole program is presented as an attempt to make the Jews "to change over to Greek customs." Two brief examples of the misery that came upon the Jewish people are presented in 6:10-11: Two women were tortured and killed for having their sons circumcised, and other Jews were burned while hiding in caves in order to observe the Sabbath.

The catalogue of horrors is interrupted by the author's reflection (6:12-17) on the purposes of God in allowing such events to happen to the Jewish people. His basic point is that these martyrdoms and other sufferings are a discipline applied by God in the short term. The other nations are given an opportunity to have their sins build up, so that their ultimate punishment will be worse than that of Israel. The author's faith in God's fidelity to Israel is complete: "Although he disciplines us with calamities, he does not forsake his own people" (6:16). His theology of the martyrdoms as divine discipline in the present allows him to preserve the identity of Israel as God's people while acknowledging the realities of suffering and death.

Eleazar the elderly scribe (6:18-31) refuses to eat pork (see Lev. 11:7-8). Indeed, he refuses even to pretend to eat pork, lest it be thought that he went over to "an alien religion" (6:24). In his speech (6:24-28) Eleazar holds out the prospect of judgment before God ("whether I live or die I shall not escape the hands of the Almighty") and proposes to "leave to the young a noble example of how to die a good death willingly and nobly for the revered and holy laws." The author comments that Eleazar left "an example of nobility and a memorial of courage" (6:31).

Chapter 7 tells the story of the martyrdoms of a mother and her seven sons. Each of the seven sons is brought forward before the king, is tortured, and explains why he is going through the suffering. At two points (7:20-23, 26-29) the mother intervenes. She dies last of all, after her sons (7:41). The mother and her sons are tortured and killed for the sake of the practices that made Jews distinctive in the Greco-Roman world: circumcision, Sabbath observance, and food laws. Among the motives that the martyrs bring forward for their fidelity in the midst of intense sufferings, the most prominent is belief in resurrection. The second son says that "the King of the universe will raise us up to an everlasting renewal of life, because we have died for his laws" (7:9). The third son offers his tongue and his hands, and says: "I got these from Heaven, and from him I hope to get them back again" (7:11). The fourth son says: "One cannot but choose to die at the hands of mortals and to cherish the hope that God gives of being raised again by him. But for you there will be no resurrection to life" (7:14). Finally, the mother counsels the seventh son: "Accept death, so that in God's mercy I may get you back again with your brothers" (7:29). In his own speech (7:30-38) the seventh son suggests that these sufferings are God's way of disciplining his people before being reconciled to them (7:33), and he expresses the hope that the sufferings endured by the martyrs may "bring to an end the wrath that has justly fallen on our whole nation" (7:38). This latter statement introduces the idea of vicarious or atoning sacrifice developed at length in 4 Maccabees. In the narrative structure of 2 Maccabees, the discipline learned through suffering and the atoning value of the martyrs' deaths made it possible for God to bring about the renewal of Israel and the purification of the Jerusalem temple under Judas Maccabeus.

D. The *Exploits of Judas Maccabeus* (8:1–10:9) issue in the purification of the temple in 164 B.C.E. As a champion for Israel, Judas along with his companions (8:1-7) first organizes a force of about 6,000 men and undertakes a series of guerrilla activities that are successful because "the wrath of the Lord had turned to mercy" (8:5). After Judas defeats Nicanor (8:8-29) as well as Timothy and Bacchides (8:30-33), Nicanor acknowledges the threat posed by Judas as God's instrument. He proclaims that "the Jews had a Defender [God], and that therefore the Jews were invulnerable, because they followed the laws ordained by him" (8:36). Throughout his battles, Judas behaves as the exemplary biblical warrior, faithful to the Torah and invoking biblical precedents by word and deed.

In 2 Maccabees (unlike 1 Maccabees) the death of Antiochus IV comes before the purification of the Jerusalem temple. After being repulsed in Persia and determined to attack Jerusalem, Antiochus is struck down by God with a foul disease (9:1-12). Recognizing that the disease is the "scourge of God" (9:11), Antiochus vows to free the city of Jerusalem and to become a Jew (9:13-18). Of course, this is all very doubtful and indeed impossible on the historical level. Having appointed his son Antiochus V as his successor, Antiochus IV dies (9:19-29).

The death of the persecutor sets the stage for the purification of the Jerusalem temple and the establishment of Hanukkah as a Jewish festival by Judas and his companions (10:1-9). After the remnants of foreign worship are taken away and Jewish worship is restored, there is a public prayer that such a catastrophe may never happen again. Hanukkah begins on the same day that the desecration of the temple began — on the twenty-fifth of Chislev (November-December). It is celebrated for eight days and is like the feast of Booths. The whole nation of Jews is to observe it annually. However, the use of "ivy-wreathed wands" (10:7) is curious, since they would be more appropriate to the cult of Dionysus (see 6:7) than to the "orthodox" Judaism that is supposedly being restored.

Part Four: Nicanor's Attack on the Temple (10:10–15:39)

A. The *Consolidation of Judas's Power* (10:10–12:45) is carried out by various military victories and diplomatic activities. Although the purification of the temple was an important symbolic event, it was necessary for Judas to try to increase his power and defeat his enemies. His success would eventually provoke the third major attack on the temple by the Syrian general Nicanor.

After noting the accession of Antiochus V Eupator (10:10-13), the author describes Judas's military victories over the Idumeans (10:14-23), Timothy (10:24-38), and Lysias at Beth-zur (11:1-15). Four pieces of correspondence illustrate Judas's political activity: Lysias to the Jewish people (11:16-21), Antiochus to Lysias (11:22-26), Antiochus to the senate of the Jews and the Jewish people (11:27-33), and two Roman envoys to the Jewish people (11:34-38). The thrust of this correspondence is that the Jewish people are to be left in peace and allowed to retain their ancestral customs.

With the advent of peace, the Jews sought to return to their farming, but some Seleucid governors "would not let them live quietly and in peace" (12:1-2). And so the shameful slaughter of two hundred Jews at Joppa arouses Judas to take revenge at Joppa and Jamnia (12:3-9). After defeating a force of Arabs (12:10-12), Judas attacks the fortified Gentile city of Caspin (12:13-16), captures Timothy and allows his release (12:17-25), marches against Carnaim and the temple of Atargatis (12:26), attacks Ephron and goes to Scythopolis (12:27-31a), and goes up to Jerusalem for the feast of Pentecost (12:31b).

After Pentecost, Judas defeats Gorgias (12:32-37). Having assembled his army and celebrated the Sabbath, Judas goes about the task of burying his fallen comrades (12:38-45). Judas discovers the reason why these Jewish soldiers fell in battle: They were wearing the sacred tokens of the idols of Jamnia under their tunics, "which the law forbids the Jews to wear" (12:40). The sin offering organized by Judas was most likely intended to avoid contaminating the living members of Judas's army (12:43). However, the author of 2 Maccabees takes it as proof of Judas's belief in the resurrection of the dead and the possibility of the living interceding on behalf of the dead. His reasoning is that if Judas "were not expecting that those who had fallen would rise again, it would have been superfluous and foolish to pray for the dead" (12:44). He goes on to describe Judas's sin offering as making "atonement for the dead, so that they might be delivered from their sin" (12:45).

B. The *Campaign of Antiochus V and Lysias* (13:1-26) is an all-out attack, with a very large force, against Judea (13:1-2). At first the high priest Menelaus supported the attack. But when God led Antiochus V and Lysias to recognize that Menelaus was responsible for all the trouble in Judea, they turned on him and had him executed (13:3-8). The author can hardly disguise his glee ("this was eminently just") at the fact that the lawbreaker Menelaus died in a pit of ashes without a burial.

The campaign of Antiochus V and Lysias was not successful. They were attacked first by Judas near Modein (13:9-17) and defeated again by him near Beth-zur (13:18-22). Their campaign was cut short by reports of a revolt back in Antioch. And so they decide to settle matters with the Jews by agreeing to observe all their rights (presumably allowing them to reestablish the Torah as the law of the land) and to honor the Jerusalem temple (13:18-26). So in 163 B.C.E. the Jews once more found themselves in a state of relative security.

C. *Nicanor's Attack* (14:1–15:39) takes place two years later (about 161 B.C.E.). Then there is a new Seleucid king, Demetrius I; a new Jewish high priest, Alcimus; and a new threat to the Jerusalem temple, the Syrian general Nicanor. Alcimus in 14:3-10 tries to convince Demetrius I to take action against Judas on the grounds that "as long as Judas lives, it is impossible for the government to find peace" (14:10). In response, Demetrius appoints Nicanor as governor of Judea and Alcimus the high priest (14:11-13), which gains support from the Gentiles throughout Judea (14:14).

When Nicanor arrives in Judea (14:15-36), he at first becomes a personal friend of Judas. But when Alcimus reports to Demetrius I that Nicanor was plotting with Judas, Nicanor is forced to carry out the king's orders and demands that Judas be handed over to him. The threat against Judas also becomes a threat against the temple when Nicanor warns: "If you do not hand Judas over to me as a prisoner, I will level this shrine of God to the ground and tear down the altar, and build here a splendid temple to Dionysus" (14:33).

The death of Razis (14:37-46), one of the elders of Jerusalem, is narrated as a kind of martyrdom (as in 6:18–7:42). He is said to have "most zealously risked body and life for Judaism" (14:38) and to have died with hope for resurrection (14:46).

Nicanor's plan to attack Judas and his men at Samaria on the Sabbath (15:1-5) does not succeed; indeed, it is presented as proof of Nicanor's arrogance in attempting to claim divine sovereignty for himself. In exhorting his men before the final battle (15:6-19) Judas recounts a dream in which he saw the good priest Onias III and the prophet Jeremiah praying for the Jews and the city of Jerusalem. Jeremiah gives Judas a golden sword by which he will strike down his enemies. In his prayer (15:22-24) Judas recalls the biblical precedent of Sennacherib's inability to conquer Jerusalem with a massive army in the eighth century B.C.E.

When the battle is joined (15:25-27), the Jews succeed in "laying low no less than thirty-five thousand men." Nicanor himself is slain. His corpse is recovered, and parts of it are exhibited as a reminder of his arrogance and of God's power to protect the Jerusalem temple: "Blessed is he who has kept his own place undefiled" (15:34). And there is a decree that Nicanor's Day — the thirteenth day of the twelfth month (Adar) — be observed as a festival.

The author brings his story to a close in 15:37-39 in the same engaging style that marks the preface in 2:19-32, reminding the reader that his purpose has been both to inform and to entertain.

Significance

In 2 Maccabees God is the defender of the Jerusalem temple and the protector of Israel. The three attacks on the temple are fended off both by supernatural means (3:1-40) and by Judas and his companions. Nevertheless, the events surrounding these attacks involve great suffering for God's people. Onias III is unjustly deprived of the high priesthood and replaced by a series of scoundrels. Many people are put to death for their fidelity to the Torah: two women who had their sons circumcised, the group that tried to observe the Sabbath while hidden in a cave, the elderly scribe Eleazar, the mother and her seven sons, and the elder Razis.

The author does not question the sovereignty or justice of God. He takes pleasure in the fact that some wicked persons — Heliodorus, Menelaus, Antiochus IV, and Nicanor — are justly punished in this life. But he also traces much of the people's suffering to their own sins. However, he regards their punishments in the present time as a sign of God's kindness inasmuch as God punishes Israel's sins quickly and does not let them reach "the full measure of their sins" (6:14). Thus, these sufferings are God's way of educating and disciplining Israel: "these punishments were designed not to destroy but to discipline our people" (6:12).

The dialogue between the wicked king and the mother and her seven sons in chapter 7 deals with suffering and theodicy from the perspectives of resurrection and judgment. The martyrs die in full confidence that they will be vindicated after death and live on with God. And they warn the wicked king that he will be punished after death. The justice of God is upheld, though its full manifestation is deferred to a personal afterlife. Furthermore, the martyrs' deaths seem to have an atoning or expiatory value. The seventh son says that their death will "bring to an end the wrath of the Almighty that has justly fallen on our whole nation" (7:38).

Issues. In the introduction above, we have already reflected on some of the problems involved in using the work as a historical source. Another factor in assessing 2 Maccabees as a historical source concerns the distinction between the events (and Jason's presentation of them) and the author's interpretation of them. That tension comes out in 2 Maccabees 12:38-45, where the author presents Judas's provision of a sin offering for the dead soldiers as proof of his belief in the resurrection of the dead and the efficacy of prayers for the dead.

An even more serious tension involves the basic interpretation of the threat posed by Antiochus IV Epiphanes. The author of 2 Maccabees portrays it as a systematic program of imposing the Greek way of life on Jews. Yet when he comes to describe what galvanized Jewish opposition to the program, he says that it was Menelaus's strategy of temple robbing (see 4:32, 39). What then was the real nature of the threat — a religious-cultural program imposed by Antiochus IV, or the perfidious behavior of an illegitimate high priest?

So in dealing with this source (and the other sources among the Apocrypha), we must be sensitive to the tensions between events and their interpretation, especially in writings from a culture in which events always received interpretations and there was little interest in objective reporting.

Influence. Second Maccabees is recognized as canonical by the Roman Catholic, Greek, and Russian Orthodox churches. Much of what was said about the influence of 1 Maccabees in Judaism and Christianity can be said about 2 Maccabees: it became a foundational document for the celebration of Hanukkah; Judas came to be identified as a military hero and became an inspiration to rebels in the name of God; and so forth.

The most distinctive and important contributions of 2 Maccabees to the Jewish and Christian traditions concern martyrdom and resurrection. The examples of the various martyrs, but especially that of the mother and her seven sons, have exercised enormous influence on Jews and Christians suffering for fidelity to their faith every age. The work known as 4 Maccabees (which is treated in this volume) greatly expands the tortures that the martyrs undergo and reflects at length on the role that belief in resurrection can play in the midst of suffering. The responses of the mother and her sons in 2 Maccabees 7 have shaped to a very large extent belief in the resurrection of the dead.

Two other areas in which 2 Maccabees has been particularly influential are the topics of *creatio ex nihilo* ("creation out of nothing") and prayers for the dead. The idea of creation out of nothing has often been read into the mother's comment in 7:28 ("God did not make them out of things that existed"), though it is doubtful that the author intended to attribute philosophical significance to her statement. The idea of prayers for the dead — a matter of controversy in early Judaism (see 2 Esdras/ 4 Ezra 7:104-5) — is based on the author's interpretation of Judas's organizing a sin offering on behalf of his fallen soldiers: "Therefore he made atonement for the dead, so that they might be delivered from their sin" (12:45). The passage (2 Macc. 12:38-45) was read at Catholic Masses for the Dead (Requiem Masses) for many centuries — one of the few Old Testament texts included in the pre–Vatican II lectionary.

For Further Study (see the books listed for 1 Maccabees)

Collins, John J. *Between Athens and Jerusalem: Jewish Identity in the Hellenistic Diaspora.* 2d ed. Grand Rapids: Eerdmans, 1999.

Doran, Robert. "The Second Book of Maccabees." In *The New Interpreter's Bible,* vol. 2, 179-299. Nashville: Abingdon, 1996.

—————. *Temple Propaganda: The Purpose and Character of 2 Maccabees.* Washington, D.C.: Catholic Biblical Association, 1981.

Goldstein, Jonathan. *II Maccabees.* Anchor Bible 41A. Garden City: Doubleday, 1983.

Henten, Jan W. van. *The Maccabean Martyrs as Saviours of the Jewish People: A Study of 2 and 4 Maccabees.* Leiden: Brill, 1997.

CHAPTER 12

1 Esdras:
Rebuilding the People of God

Basic Information

First Esdras tells the story of Israel's exile to Babylon and return in the sixth century B.C.E.. In the collection that we call the Old Testament Apocrypha, this book is important for its focus on the practical measures by which the people of God was rebuilt after its temple and capital city had been destroyed and its religious and political leaders were taken into captivity in Babylon. The rebuilding project was not confined to reconstructing the city walls and the temple. Indeed, even those measures were elements in the broader project of rebuilding the people of God.

The work known as 1 Esdras is part of the Greek Bible, where it is designated Esdras A to distinguish it from the books of Ezra (Esdras B 1–10) and Nehemiah (Esdras B 11–23; sometimes known as Esdras G, for *gamma*). In the Latin Bible tradition 1 Esdras is known as Esdras 3, whereas Ezra and Nehemiah are called Esdras 1 and 2. The Ezra apocalypse preserved in the Latin tradition is designated 2 Esdras or 4 Ezra.

The content of 1 Esdras closely parallels the content of 2 Chronicles 35–36, almost the entire book of Ezra, and some parts of Nehemiah (Neh. 7:6–8:12). It begins abruptly in the reign of King Josiah in the late seventh century B.C.E. and breaks off abruptly with the report of an assembly in 9:55. After telling the story of the exile and the first return (1:1–2:30), it describes the contest of the three bodyguards to determine "what one thing is the strongest?" (3:1–4:63) — a lively sapiential narrative not found in the Hebrew or Greek text of Ezra. Then rejoining the text of Ezra, it considers the rebuilding of the Jerusalem temple (5:1–7:15) and Ezra's mission to Jerusalem in the mid-fifth century (8:1–9:55).

The book is presented as a history. It is not easy to read, apart from the charming story in chapters 3–4. The other three main sections provide the stuff of history: descriptions of events, dates, lists of names, official documents, and so forth. The problems come mainly from the author's telescoped chronological framework, in which events that were spread out over several centuries are collapsed into what seems like a relatively short period. There are several different expeditions in which Jewish exiles return to their homeland, while there seems to remain in Babylon a large Jewish population and an apparently inexhaustible supply of "holy vessels" taken to Babylon under King Nebuchadnezzar and to be brought back to their rightful place in the Jerusalem temple. In fact, the impression of a gradual return to Jerusalem with several expeditions very likely corresponds to the historical reality of Israel's return from exile. But historical accuracy was not the author's main concern.

The main concern of 1 Esdras is the rebuilding of God's people through its religious and social institutions. In this rebuilding project, the priest Jeshua (known as Joshua elsewhere) and the governor Zerubbabel (the name means "seed of Babylon") as well as the priest-scribe Ezra play pivotal roles. (Nehemiah is all but absent, whether by design or accident is hard to say.) These great leaders stand in continuity with the pre-exilic King Josiah, whose reform based on the book of the Law found in the Jerusalem temple led to the ideal observance of Passover described in 1:1-22.

The means that the leaders used to rebuild God's people were the renewal of the system of sacrifices at the Jerusalem temple, the observance of the traditional festivals (Passover, Booths, etc.), the rebuilding the temple itself, the renewal of the priesthood, the clarification of who really belonged to what remained of the people of Israel (the tribes of Judah and Benjamin, as well as the priestly tribe of Levi), the prohibition of marriages with non-Jewish women, and the public reading of the Torah as the "law of the land." These were practical and effective means for rebuilding a people. They enabled the returnees to stand in continuity with pre-exilic Israel and gave an identity and a shape to the renewed people of God.

The history of the composition of 1 Esdras is complicated and uncertain. Most of the contest of the three bodyguards in chapters 3–4 probably existed separately in Aramaic (or Hebrew), which in turn may reflect an oral or written Persian original. Little or nothing in the account is distinctively Jewish until 4:41. The question ("What one thing is the strongest?") and the first three responses (wine, the king, and women) sound like pagan court wisdom. Even the addition about truth (4:33-41) to the third answer is not particularly Jewish or religious until the affirmation "Blessed be the God of truth" (4:40). The story only becomes Jewish with the obviously parenthetical identification of the third bodyguard as Zerubbabel (4:13) and most clearly by Zerubbabel's request in 4:42-63 that as his reward for winning the contest King Darius should remember his vow to rebuild the Jerusalem temple. These links to Zerubbabel and thus to Judaism may have been made before the story's incorporation into 1 Esdras, and thus inspired the author/editor to include it in his narrative. Or the author/editor may have made the link on his own.

The oldest extant text of 1 Esdras is the Greek version, which in all likelihood goes back to the second century B.C.E. The Greek version, however, seems to reflect a Semitic original, partly in Aramaic and partly in Hebrew (as in the canonical Esther and Daniel). The Semitic original was quite close to the Masoretic text of Ezra-Nehemiah. Although 1 Esdras contains some superior readings, there are many cases of textual corruption in names and numbers, as well as a certain freedom in translation style. Indeed, the much more literal translations of Ezra and Nehemiah now contained in the Greek Bible appear to have been made in the first or second century C.E. precisely to replace the free and textually corrupt 1 Esdras.

What then is 1 Esdras? Should we speak of an author or of an editor at all? The present form of 1 Esdras could simply be an excerpt from an early Greek translation of Chronicles and Ezra. This would explain the abrupt beginning and ending. Or 1 Esdras could be a composition based closely on biblical sources and intended to highlight Josiah, Jeshua and Zerubbabel, and Ezra as great leaders in the history of Israel. In either case, the major reason why 1 Esdras has survived and continues to be read is the inclusion of the story of the contest of the three bodyguards.

Content

Part One: Exile and Return (1:1–2:30)

A. *Josiah's Passover* (1:1-22; see 2 Chron. 35:1-19) introduces some of the book's major themes: the sanctuary at Jerusalem as the center of the people's religious life, the calendar of festivals providing the rhythm of life for the people, and the importance of a good leader. By his celebration of Passover at the Jerusalem temple in 622 B.C.E. (1:1-22), Josiah, the king of Judah from 640 to 609 B.C.E., sets the religious pattern and provides the continuity between the pre-exilic and the post-exilic people of God. The account presupposes the discovery of the book of the Law at the temple during repairs and the recognition that the people had not been obeying "the words of this book" (see 2 Kings 22 and 2 Chronicles 34). First Esdras begins abruptly (closely following 2 Chronicles 35) by describing how Josiah presided over the Passover rituals in the temple (rather than in private homes). He arranges the priests, Levites, temple singers, and gatekeepers in their proper hierarchical order. He gives gifts to the people as well as to the priests and Levites. The temple sacrifice inaugurates the seven-day festival of Passover and Unleavened Bread. The narrative emphasizes that "no Passover like it had been kept in Israel since the times of the prophet Samuel" (1:19). Thus Josiah's Passover reaches back to the period before the monarchy and serves as the model for future celebrations after the return from exile. Since Passover commemorated the pivotal event of ancient Israel's history — liberation from slavery in Egypt — its position in 1 Esdras points forward to the return from exile and the celebration of other festivals in the Jerusalem temple.

B. The *Death of Josiah* (1:23-33; see 2 Chron. 35:20-27) is interpreted as God's just punishment for Israel's sins — not so much for this king's sins (indeed, he was upright before God and his heart was full of godliness) but for the sins of "those who sinned and acted wickedly toward the Lord" (1:23-24). The occasion for Josiah's death was his attempt at fighting against the Egyptian Pharaoh Neco as the latter was attacking the Babylonians and Medes at Carchemish on the Euphrates in 609 B.C.E. (1:25-31). The author heightens the idea that Pharaoh Neco was an instrument of the God of Israel, and he portrays Josiah's wounding and death as the result of his failure to obey God's will made manifest through the prophet Jeremiah. The summary of Josiah's reign (1:32-33) notes that all the people of Israel lamented his passing, and that Josiah was outstanding for "his splendor and his understanding of the law of the Lord."

C. The *Last Kings of Judah* (1:34-58; see 2 Chron. 36:1-21) lead the people toward destruction and exile. This section covers events from 609 to 587 B.C.E. Since Josiah had provoked the Egyptians, the king of Egypt deposed Josiah's son Jeconiah and replaced him with the latter's brother Jehoiakim (1:34-38). The reigns of Jehoiakim (1:39-42), Jehoiachin

155

(1:43-46a), and Zedekiah (1:46b-58) follow a familiar pattern. Since each king did "what was evil in the sight of the Lord" (1:39, 44, 47), the God of Israel brings King Nebuchadnezzar of Babylon in each case to attack Jerusalem and take away some holy vessels from the temple of the Lord. In sinful deeds Zedekiah was joined by the leaders and the priests who committed sacrilege and polluted the temple. So persistent was Israel in refusing to heed the prophets sent by God that God finally "gave command to bring against them the kings of the Chaldeans" (1:52). Thus, blame for the destruction of Jerusalem and the desecration of its temple is placed upon the "ungodly acts" of its leaders and the people. At the same time, it is assumed that God not only allowed but even directed these events. And there is a time limit to Israel's exile — the "seventy years" prophesied by Jeremiah (see Jer. 25:11-12; 29:10). The justice and the mercy of God are at work.

D. The *First Return from Exile* (2:1-15; see 2 Chron. 36:22-23; Ezra 1:1-11) takes place in 539 B.C.E., in the first year of the Persian King Cyrus. The decree (1:1-7) of Cyrus is in keeping with his historical policy of allowing conquered and exiled peoples to return to their homes, but is cast very much in the language and theological perspective of Israel. According to the introduction (2:1-2), Cyrus acted to fulfill Jeremiah's prophecy about return from exile and under the inspiration of the Lord. The text of the decree (2:3-7) attributes to "the Lord of Israel, the Lord Most High" Cyrus's accession to kingship and his resolve to have the Jerusalem temple rebuilt. By way of response (2:8-15), the spirit of the Lord stirs up leaders of the two remaining tribes (Judah and Benjamin) as well as the priests and Levites to return home from exile, and even inspires their neighbors in Babylon to contribute supplies and other assistance toward their journey. Cyrus also directs that the holy vessels seized by the Babylonians from the Jerusalem temple be given to Sheshbazzar, who emerges as the leader of the returnees.

E. The *Local Opposition* (2:16-30; see Ezra 4:7-24) in the land of Israel communicates its fears to the Persian king. The author of 1 Esdras apparently thinks (wrongly) that Artaxerxes succeeded Cyrus, who died in 530 B.C.E. and preceded Darius, who became king in 522. In fact, Artaxerxes was king from 465 to 424 B.C.E. The opposition comes from the non-Jewish population, either indigenous peoples or more likely those peoples whom the Assyrians and Babylonians had settled in the land of Israel. In their letter to the king (2:17-25), the locals remind him that Jerusalem has been "a rebellious and wicked city" and warn him that if it is rebuilt it will refuse to pay taxes and may even rebel against the king. A special emphasis in the letter as it appears in 1 Esdras (as opposed to the text in Ezra 4) falls on the temple. The opponents accuse the Jews of laying the foundations for a temple and claim that the building of the temple is now going on (2:18, 20). The reply from the king (2:26-28) verifies that Jerusalem has been a rebellious city and orders that the rebuilding work there cease immediately. On receiving this response, the leaders of the local opposition take steps to stop the Jews from working on the temple. The work will be resumed only in the second year of Darius's reign (in 520 B.C.E.). Before that, there is an interlude featuring King Darius.

Part Two: The Contest of the Bodyguards (3:1–4:63)

A. The *Setting for the Contest* (3:1-17a) is the court of the Persian King Darius, who reigned from 522 to 486 B.C.E. The king holds a great banquet for the top officials of his empire (see Esther 1). Afterward he awakens from his sleep (see Esther 6:1; but why is this relevant?). Meanwhile, three young men (see Daniel 1) in the royal bodyguard propose a contest whose winner is to be decided by the king and his nobles. The contest is for the best answer to the question, "What one thing is the strongest?" The winner is to receive rewards that will make him rich and powerful. The boldness of the bodyguards in proposing this contest and its rewards goes unexplained.

The rules of the contest call on each of the three bodyguards to write out his statement and place it beneath the king's pillow (another bold step). Their three answers to what is the strongest are wine, the king, and women, respectively. But "above all truth is the victor" (3:12). One gets the impression that the section on truth has been tacked on to the section on women. When the king awakens, he summons his officials to judge the contest with him and calls in the three bodyguards to explain their answers.

B. The *Explanations* (3:17b–4:41) operate on the level of human experience and wisdom, not religion or theology. The strength of wine (3:17b-24) resides in its power to make people do things that otherwise they would not do. Wine has both positive effects (such as bringing joy and banishing sorrows) and negative effects (such as addling the mind and provoking fights).

157

The strength of the king (4:1-12) resides in his power to make his people and his armies obey his word. Even though the king is only one man, his word sends others off to war and makes them bring back the spoils of war to him.

The strength of women (4:13-32) resides in their indispensability to men from birth to death. Without women, men would not exist. Moreover, men give expensive gifts to women, leave their homes and native lands for them, expose themselves to all kinds of dangers on their behalf, and even become their slaves. This third answer is attributed in 4:13 to the Jew Zerubbabel, whose name means "seed of Babylon" and who links this episode to the main narrative of 1 Esdras. Zerubbabel goes on (boldly) to cite the example of Darius's own concubine Apame, who has shown her power over the king in various ways (4:28b-32).

The strength of truth (4:33-41) is greater than that of wine, the king, and women, according to Zerubbabel. His assertion is greeted with enthusiasm from the judges, who shout: "Great is truth, and strongest of all" (4:41). Thus Zerubbabel wins the contest.

C. *Zerubbabel's Request* (4:42-63) — another bold action — is that King Darius should keep his vow to rebuild Jerusalem and its temple (though there is no historical evidence for such a vow on Darius's part). The king gladly accepts Zerubbabel's request and orders Judah's neighbors to contribute to the reconstruction of Jerusalem and to the support of the temple personnel. He promises the Jewish exiles safe conduct on their journey to Jerusalem and hands over more sacred vessels. Thus Darius reinstates the policy of Cyrus and ends the ban on construction occasioned by the local opposition in Artaxerxes' time.

Zerubbabel attributes his victory in the contest to the power and wisdom of the God of Israel: "From you comes the victory; from you comes wisdom, and yours is the glory. I am your servant. Blessed are you, who have given me wisdom; I give you thanks, O Lord of our ancestors" (4:59-60). As the episode began with Darius's feast (3:1-3), it ends with a feast celebrated by the Jewish exiles for seven days (4:61-63).

Part Three: Rebuilding the Jerusalem Temple (5:1–7:15)

A. The *Return of the Exiles* (5:1-46; see Ezra 2 and Neh. 7:6-73a) is said to have taken place not in the reign of Cyrus (as in Ezra) but in March of 520 B.C.E., the second year of Darius's reign. According to 5:1-6 (material not found in the book of Ezra), Darius provided a large escort to lead the people of Judah on the long journey (six hundred miles) homeward. The festive character and the orderliness of the group make the journey into a religious procession. At the head of the people are the priest Jeshua and the leader Zerubbabel, who represent the tribes of Levi and Judah, respectively.

The names and numbers of the various groups listed in 5:7-46 generally parallel Ezra 2 and Nehemiah 7, though with many minor discrepancies. The list includes the Judean leaders (5:7-8), the various Judean families (5:9-23), the priests (5:24-25), the Levites (5:26), the temple singers (5:27), the gatekeepers (5:28), the temple servants (5:29-32), and the descendants of Solomon's servants (5:33-35). Also included are those who could not document their ancestry in Israel and whose cases were to be decided by some future high priest (5:36-40). The heads of the families pledge to rebuild the temple in Jerusalem and to contribute to its upkeep (5:44-45), and the various groups settle in Jerusalem and its environs (5:46).

B. The *Restoration of Temple Worship* (5:47-73; see Ezra 3:1–4:5) is the first task undertaken by the returnees. Under the leadership of Jeshua and Zerubbabel, they erect an altar and restore the order of sacrifices (5:47-53). The first great celebration takes place on the feast of Booths or Tabernacles — a fall harvest festival.

The next step is laying the foundations for the new temple (5:54-65). After procuring the necessary building supplies from the Sidonians and Tyrians, the people lay the foundations to the accompaniment of a joyful ceremony involving the priests and Levites. Their joy, however, is mixed with the weeping of some who had seen the first temple. Perhaps they wept because of the memories that the ceremony brought back. Or perhaps it was because the new temple seemed inferior to the old temple. At any rate, the dedication ceremony evolves into a noisy contest between the rejoicers and the mourners.

The noise at the temple site gets the attention of neighboring peoples (5:66-73). At first they offer to join in the construction work and in the temple worship. They claim to have been worshiping the God of Israel ever since they settled in the land of Israel some two hundred years before. But for Jeshua and Zerubbabel these peoples are foreigners and not real Jews. And so they refuse their offer: "You have nothing to do with us in building the house for the Lord our God" (5:70). This refusal in turn leads the neighbors to oppose the rebuilding project and to prevent its completion. Only those who can prove that they really belong to Israel (the reason for all the lists in the book) can join in worshiping the God of Israel at the Jerusalem temple.

C. The *Inquiry* (6:1-22; see Ezra 4:24b–5:17) comes from the governor of Syria and Palestine (the province called "Across the River" in the book of Ezra) and the local officials. The work on rebuilding the Jewish temple was proceeding under Jeshua and Zerubbabel, with the encouragement of the prophets Haggai and Zechariah (6:1-2). The officials want to know under whose authority the Jerusalem temple was being rebuilt. Their letter to King Darius (6:8-22) recounts the progress being made on the construction project, tells how they confronted the Jewish elders, and reports the response they got. The Jewish elders had explained that the first temple had been destroyed because "our ancestors sinned against the Lord of Israel" (6:15), and that King Cyrus had given permission for the temple to be rebuilt and had handed over the old temple vessels to Zerubbabel (not mentioned in Ezra) and Sheshbazzar. The officials suggest that a search be made in the Persian archives to determine whether the story told by the Jewish elders is correct, and that the king send word back to them whether the rebuilding should stop or go forward.

D. The *Permission to Continue* (6:23-34; see Ezra 6:1-12) is based on the discovery in the royal archives at Ecbatana of a scroll in which King Cyrus gave his official sanction for the Jerusalem temple to be rebuilt at his expense and for the old temple vessels to be returned (6:24-26). And so King Darius orders the local officials not only to allow the rebuilding to proceed but also to contribute to the support of the sacrificial system there. Again the key role of Zerubbabel is highlighted (6:27; not in Ezra). The king orders that sacrifices be offered on behalf of him and his children (6:31), and he calls upon the God of Israel to destroy every king and nation that interferes with the rebuilding of the temple (6:33).

E. The *Completion* (7:1-15; see Ezra 6:13-22) takes place with the active cooperation of the local officials (7:1-2; more so than in Ezra): "the holy house was finished by the twenty-third day of the month of Adar, in the sixth year of King Darius" (7:5), that is, in the early spring of 516 B.C.E. The dedication ceremony takes place in accord with "what was written in the book of Moses" (7:6). The first great festival celebrated at the newly completed temple is Passover. Thus the starting point of the book — the account of Josiah's Passover — comes into focus as a way of stressing the continuity between the old and the new temples. The identity of Israel as God's chosen people is highlighted by the ritual purification of the Levites (not in Ezra) and by Israel separating itself from "the abominations of the peoples of the land" (7:13). This Passover is an occasion for special joy because God had changed the will of the "king of the Assyrians" and allowed the Judeans once again to dedicate themselves to "the service of the Lord God of Israel" (7:14).

Part Four: Ezra's Mission (8:1–9:55)

A. The *Commission of Ezra* (8:1-27; see Ezra 7:1-28) comes from King Artaxerxes. Ezra is identified as both a priest ("son of Aaron the high priest") and "a scribe skilled in the law of Moses." He receives permission to lead a band of returnees in the "seventh year" of Artaxerxes' reign — 458 B.C.E., though one gets the impression of only a short interval between the expeditions of Zerubbabel and Ezra. In describing Ezra, the author places emphasis on his great knowledge of the Torah. The book will end with Ezra's public reading of the Torah in Jerusalem (see 9:37-55).

The written commission from Artaxerxes (8:9-24) highlights further the importance of the Torah in the renewed community. Ezra and his companions are sent forth to look into matters in Judea and Jerusalem "in accordance with what is in the law of the Lord" (8:12). At the Jerusalem temple they are to "let all things prescribed in the law of God be scrupulously fulfilled" (8:21). And Ezra is to appoint judges who know "the law of your God" (8:23) and to teach those judges who do not know it.

B. The account of *Ezra's Journey* (8:28-67; see Ezra 8:1-36) begins with a list of the leaders of the various clans and the numbers of those in their group (8:28-40). On inspecting the assembly at the River Theras (Ahava in Ezra), Ezra discovers that there are no priests or Levites, and he puts out a call for those remaining in exile to join the returnees (8:41-49). After fasting and prayer they all set out — without a military escort, since they told the king that their God would protect them (8:50-53). Particular attention is to be given by the priests and Levites to the silver and gold as well as the holy vessels that are being brought back to the temple in Jerusalem (8:54-60).

The journey is successful, and Ezra and his companions arrive safely in Jerusalem "by the mighty hand of our Lord" (8:61). On their arrival they transfer the silver and gold as well as the holy vessels to the priests and Levites in Jerusalem, offer sacrifices to the Lord, and deliver the king's

161

orders to the local officials who as a result "honored the people and the temple of the Lord" (8:67).

C. The *Report About Intermarriage* (8:68-96; see Ezra 9:1–10:5) comes from the leaders. They inform Ezra that all the people — including priests and Levites as well as leaders and nobles — have married non-Jewish women, thus mixing "the holy race" with the alien peoples of the land (8:68-70). In response to their report, Ezra adopts the posture of the mourner and the penitent interceding with God on behalf of the people (8:71-73).

Ezra's prayer (8:74-90) is both a confession of national guilt and a recognition that there must be a change. Ezra acknowledges that Israel's sins in the past caused the exile, and he proclaims that "we are in great sin to this day" (8:76). That Israel found favor with the Persian king and that many Jews had been allowed to return from exile were due to God's mercy. The land, however, was still polluted through intermarriage and the idolatry associated with it. The returnees are a "root" out of which a purified and renewed people can arise. Moved by Ezra's prayer, the leaders publicly confess the sin of intermarriage and determine to take strong measures to end this abuse (8:91-96).

D. The *Dissolution of Mixed Marriages* (9:1-36; see Ezra 10:6-44) takes place after Ezra's lament and the proclamation that all the returnees should assemble in Jerusalem (9:1-4). At the assembly Ezra demands that those in mixed marriages should confess their sin, give glory to the God of Israel, and separate themselves from the non-Jews in the land and from their foreign wives.

A procedure for investigating the individual cases of mixed marriage is set up. Judges are appointed, and the cases are heard over a period of two and a half months. The results of the investigation are summarized in a list of those in mixed marriages: priests (9:18-22), Levites (9:23), temple singers (9:24), gatekeepers (9:25), and Israel at large (9:26-35). The outcome is expressed as follows: "All these had married foreign women, and they put them away together with their children" (9:36). This measure was taken so that only the "holy race" represented by the "root" of returnees might constitute the renewed people of God.

E. The *Reading of the Torah* (9:37-55; see Neh. 7:73b–8:13) at the east gate of the temple (the Water Gate in Neh. 8:3) is the climax of 1 Esdras. At the new moon of the seventh month, Ezra assembles all the people and reads the Torah to them. Accompanied by other dignitaries, Ezra stands on a wooden platform. On opening the Torah he offers a benediction and the people answer with "Amen," lift up their hands, fall to the ground, and worship God. The Levites serve as interpreters by explaining to the people what is being read. (This practice is often cited as the origin of the Targums — the Aramaic translations/paraphrases of the Hebrew Scriptures.)

The governor (or someone named Atthartes; Nehemiah in Neh. 8:9) declares that this day of reading the Torah is a holy day, a day of special rejoicing and feasting. The text of 1 Esdras breaks off abruptly with the words: "And they came together." In Nehemiah 8:13-18 the people come to Ezra for further study of the Torah and learn how to observe the feast of Tabernacles by making booths and living in them.

Significance

By recounting the rebuilding of God's people, 1 Esdras deals with Israel's efforts at recovering from the traumatic sufferings of the exile. The power and justice of God are never questioned. Rather, the people's sufferings are traced to their own sinfulness. The last kings before the exile did "what was evil in the sight of the Lord," and the people refused to listen to the prophets (especially Jeremiah). And so the destruction of Jerusalem and the exile were just punishments from God's hand.

And yet the sufferings of God's people in exile are not permanent. Instead, the Lord stirs up the Persian King Cyrus to allow the exiles to return to Judah and Jerusalem, and to rebuild the temple. The various returns from exile are presented as providential opportunities to contribute to a new beginning in the history of Israel. This new beginning involves restoring old institutions: sacrifices, festivals, the temple, the priesthood, marriage within the people, and the Torah as the "law of the land." These are the principal means by which the returnees may put an end to their sufferings and once more function as God's people. Each leader pushes the people to a more perfect observance. Ezra focuses on the sensitive issue of marriage with non-Jews, proclaiming that because of this abuse "we are in great sin to this day" (8:76). The ideal Israel will follow the Torah as the law of the land.

Issues. What is 1 Esdras? The question concerning the work's nature and composition has already been addressed in the introduction. But it remains a source of many problems.

Is the religious vision of 1 Esdras (and Ezra and Nehemiah) the begin-

163

ning of Judaism? The return (or returns) from exile marked an important point in Israel's history as God's people. Earlier scholars often referred (generally in a negative way) to Ezra's reform as the beginning of "Judaism," which they sharply distinguished from the religion of Israel before the exile. The thrust of 1 Esdras, of course, is to assert a continuity between pre-exilic Judaism (represented by Josiah) and post-exilic Judaism. It offers an idealized picture in which the Jerusalem community systematically adopts religious institutions from temple to Torah that will insure its holiness and right relationship to God. Outside of the land of Israel there were other ways of being Jewish, and even within the land there was some opposition to the Second Temple as the replacement for Solomon's temple or as functioning the way God's temple should. Thus, to call 1 Esdras (and Ezra and Nehemiah) the beginning of Judaism is to overemphasize both the discontinuity and the normativeness of Ezra's reform.

Does 1 Esdras (and Ezra and Nehemiah) promote a kind of racism? There is opposition to the returnees from some of the local population, and they succeed at times in stopping the construction work. But when other peoples want to join in the work and worship at the temple, they are told by Jeshua and Zerubbabel that "you have nothing to do with us in building the house for the Lord our God" (5:70). Moreover, when Ezra points out the evils of marriage with non-Jews, the solution is that the men should put away their foreign wives together with their children. What happened to these people? In its defense, one can say that 1 Esdras never promotes violence against the enemies of Israel, nor does it ever assert the inferiority of non-Jews. Indeed, it paints a positive and respectful picture of the Persian kings. Nevertheless, its ideal is a purified "root" or "holy seed" from which a renewed people can grow and flourish. It is not interested in an all-inclusive people of God.

Influence. In the Greek and Russian churches 1 Esdras is regarded as canonical, whereas in the Roman Catholic Church it is not part of the canon and is relegated to an appendix in the Vulgate. Protestants and Jews do not accept it in their canons. The first-century Jewish historian Flavius Josephus used 1 Esdras as a source in books 10 and 11 of his *Jewish Antiquities,* probably because the more literal Greek translation of Ezra was not yet made or at least was not yet available to him. Early Christian writers cited 1 Esdras frequently and showed special interest in the contest of the three bodyguards. There are no references to 1 Esdras in Rabbinic literature. Its praise of truth ("Great is truth, and strongest of all," 4:41) has become something of a popular slogan.

For Further Study

Coggins, R. J., with Michael Knibb. *The First and Second Books of Esdras.* Cambridge: Cambridge University Press, 1979.

Myers, Jacob M. *I and II Esdras.* Anchor Bible 42. Garden City, N.Y.: Doubleday, 1974.

CHAPTER 13

The Prayer of Manasseh:
The Prayer of the Repentant Sinner

Basic Information

The Prayer of Manasseh consists of an invocation of God (vv. 1-7), a confession of sin (vv. 8-10), and a plea for forgiveness (vv. 11-15). It uses many biblical phrases and is written in accord with the conventions of Second Temple Jewish prayer. It addresses the "God of the righteous" (v. 8) and "the God of those who repent" (v. 13).

Manasseh was the king of Judah from 698 to 642 B.C.E. In 2 Kings 21:1-18 he is judged to have been the most wicked of all Judean kings; in 21:10-15 the fall of Jerusalem and Judah is blamed on his apostasy. He is said to have introduced foreign cults into Judah, erecting altars for worship of Baal and setting up the carved image of Asherah in the temple. According to 2 Kings 21:6, he "made his son pass through the fire; he practiced soothsaying and augury, and dealt with mediums and wizards." He is also said to have "shed much innocent blood" (21:16). There is no mention of his repentance in 2 Kings. In 2 Chronicles 33:1-20, however, after Manasseh is accused of the same evil deeds, he is said to have been captured by the Assyrians and led off to Babylon. While in captivity Manasseh "entreated the favor of the Lord his God" (33:12) and was restored to his throne in Jerusalem, where he engaged in a program of restoring the proper worship of the God of Israel.

What were the words of Manasseh's prayer? Inquiring minds wanted to know. According to 2 Chronicles 33:18-19 the words were preserved in "the Annals of the Kings of Israel" and in "the records of the seers." But neither of these books has been preserved. The Prayer of Manasseh represents what an anonymous author imagined that Manasseh should have said or would have said in his prayer. It was most likely composed in Greek and reflects the language and style of the Septuagint. It is included in some Septuagint manuscripts in a special section called "Odes." The most important versions are in Latin and Syriac, and it is included in church manuals from the third and fourth centuries C.E. *(Apostolic Constitutions* and *Didaskalia)*. The earliest evidence for the work's existence comes from the third century C.E., and so it could have originated at any time between the composition of 2 Chronicles and then. It was probably written by a Greek-speaking Jew outside the land of Israel, though Christian authorship is not impossible.

The purpose of the prayer is twofold: to supply the missing words of Manasseh's prayer mentioned in 2 Chronicles 33:12-13, 18-19; and to present a model prayer of repentance. If God can accept the confession and prayer of repentance from so great a sinner as Manasseh, repentance and forgiveness of sins are possible for anyone.

Content

A. Manasseh's *Invocation of God* (vv. 1-7) first calls upon the Lord Almighty, who is the God of Abraham, Isaac, and Jacob (v. 1). The mention of "their righteous offspring" suggests a division within Israel between those who are righteous and those who are not (see v. 8). Then in verses 2-3 he calls upon God as the creator. Using language from Genesis 1:1–2:4a and Job 38, he gives particular attention to the order that God imposed on creation, to the power of God's word in creation ("by your word of command"), and to God's sovereignty over creation ("sealed it with your terrible and glorious name"). The God whom Manasseh approaches in prayer is both the God of Israel and the all powerful creator and lord.

The appropriate response to this God is fear and trembling on the part of all creation (vv. 4-5). God's glory is so splendid that creatures cannot bear it, and for sinners the threat of God's anger cannot be endured. Nevertheless, what makes it possible for a sinner like Manasseh to approach God in prayer is God's "immeasurable and unsearchable" mercy (v. 6). The theme of God's mercy is developed at length in the final verse of the invocation (v. 7). The first part of verse 7 appeals to God's compas-

167

sion, patience, and mercy. The second part is absent from the two principal Greek manuscripts but present in other early versions; it was very likely part of the original text and omitted by accident in the transmission of the Greek text. It reflects Manasseh's position as a sinner who promises repentance and seeks forgiveness and salvation. The basis for his prayer is the mercy of God, not his merits or even his initiative in repenting.

B. Manasseh's *Confession of Sins* (vv. 8-10) is addressed to the "God of the righteous." Manasseh admits that righteous persons such as Abraham, Isaac, and Jacob did not sin against God and so had no need to repent. But as an egregious sinner, Manasseh did need to repent, and it was for sinners like him that God established repentance (v. 8; see Mark 2:17). In verse 9 Manasseh expresses his hesitation to approach God at all. On the one hand, his sins are "more in number than the sand of the sea." On the other hand, he is so burdened down by his sins that he regards himself as unworthy to look up to God in prayer. The themes of Manasseh's unworthiness and his sinfulness are developed in verse 10. He feels weighed down by his sins as "with many an iron fetter," and freely admits that he has done evil in God's sight and provoked God's anger by promoting idolatry.

C. Manasseh's *Plea for Forgiveness* (vv. 11-15) proceeds from a penitent heart ("now I bend the knee of the heart"). Twice he acknowledges that he is a sinner ("I have sinned"), and twice he seeks forgiveness from God ("forgive me"). Manasseh asks that God not destroy him with his sins, or be angry with him forever, or condemn him to eternal separation from God in "the depths of the earth" (Sheol). Rather, he implores "the God of those who repent" to save him "according to your great mercy" (vv. 13-14). In the narrative framework suggested by 2 Chronicles 33:12-33, salvation for Manasseh would be release from prison and restoration to his throne in Jerusalem. God's willingness to forgive Manasseh will be a manifestation of God's own goodness, and Manasseh in turn promises to praise God continually in concert with the entire heavenly host.

Significance

In some parts of the Hebrew Bible, there is a direct connection between suffering and sin. In the Deuteronomic History (from Deuteronomy to 2 Kings) the primary reason for the fall of the kingdoms of Samaria and Judah are the sins of the kings and of the people as a whole. The worst sin is idolatry. Indeed, the major criterion by which the kings are judged is their fidelity to the proper worship of God and to the Torah. Their sins bring suffering and death on the people of God.

In this theological framework King Manasseh of Judah must rank among the worst of sinners and as the cause of his own sufferings and those of his people. And so his prayer for forgiveness is a good example for all repentant sinners who have caused others to suffer. He acknowledges the sovereignty of God over creation and over Israel's history. His appeal is to the mercy of God, for he recognizes that he has sinned. He confesses his sins and is ashamed at their enormity. Indeed, he states in a straightforward way: "I have sinned, O Lord, I have sinned, and I acknowledge my transgressions" (v. 12). He seeks forgiveness because he views God as "the God of those who repent" (v. 13), and promises to amend his life and devote himself to the praise of God.

The Prayer of Manasseh presents in outline form the process of the forgiveness of sins in the Jewish and Christian traditions. The process involves the recognition and admission of one's sins, asking forgiveness from God on the basis of God's mercy rather than of one's own merits or even God's justice, and a firm resolve to serve God faithfully and to avoid sinning again.

There are cases, of course, where sin is the cause of suffering, where the sinful behavior of an individual, a group, or a whole people can visit suffering on others or on themselves. The Prayer of Manasseh provides an idealized example of the cycle of sin and suffering being broken by repentance and by seeking forgiveness from God.

Issues. The origin of the Prayer of Manasseh remains mysterious. It is clearly a development of what was perceived as an omission in 2 Chronicles 33. But its language is so general that it could fit many circumstances. Indeed, this is the genius of the prayer and the secret to its success. As is the case with many biblical psalms, its open and metaphorical language makes it possible for people from many very different times and places to use it as a spiritual resource in facing some of the most difficult experiences of human life.

Influence. The Prayer of Manasseh is not regarded as canonical by Jews, Protestants, or Roman Catholics. Since the Council of Trent, the Latin translation of it has been placed in an appendix to the Latin Bible. It is considered authoritative, however, by Eastern Orthodox churches. Regardless of its canonical status, readers throughout the centuries have found in this prayer an important resource for facing the reality of sin and the suffering that sin can cause.

CHAPTER 14

Psalm 151:
God's Care for David

Basic Information

In the Greek version of the book of Psalms, it is customary to include what is designated as Psalm 151. This is in fact a poetic summary of material in 1 Samuel 16 and 17, narrated by David in the first person. It recounts how God chose David to be king of Israel (vv. 1-5) and how David killed the Philistine Goliath in battle (vv. 6-7).

The discovery of a fuller and more coherent version of Psalm 151 in column 28 of the *Psalms Scroll* found in Qumran Cave 11 (11Q5 or 11QPs[a]) shows that the Greek Psalm 151 is a summary of two longer and distinct Hebrew compositions. The work is a rewriting of, or midrash on, 1 Samuel 16–17. Since the script of the Qumran manuscript can be dated to the first half of the first century c.e., the Hebrew original of Psalm 151 must have been composed before then. There is no indication of Essene sectarian concerns in it. Its inclusion in the Qumran psalms collection neither confirms nor denies that it was regarded as scriptural by the Qumran community. That decision depends on how one assesses the nature of the *Psalms Scroll* itself: Was it an early version of what came to be the traditional psalter of the Hebrew canon, an alternative psalter accorded scriptural status by the Qumran community, or just a hymnbook?

Content

A. The story of *God's Choice of David* (vv. 1-5) is a somewhat clumsy retelling of 1 Samuel 16. David is the speaker. In verse 1 he identifies himself as the youngest among his brothers and as a shepherd (see 1 Sam. 16:10-11). Next in verses 2-3 he speaks about musical work with the harp and lyre in soothing King Saul (see 1 Sam. 16:14-23), only to raise a question about the need for singing since the Lord is the source and goal of his music. Then in verses 4-5 he returns to the story of how Samuel picked him and anointed him, and how God chose him instead of his more handsome and taller brothers (see 1 Sam. 16:4-13). The Hebrew version found among the Dead Sea Scrolls (11Q5 col. 28) provides a fuller and more coherent text.

B. The story of *David's Victory Over Goliath* (vv. 6-7) is a brief account or epitome of 1 Samuel 17. Again David is the speaker. He claims that when he went out to meet Goliath for battle, his opponent "cursed me by his idols" (v. 6; see 1 Sam. 17:43). Then David notes that he beheaded Goliath with his own sword (see 1 Sam 17:51) and thus restored the honor of Israel. Again what is preserved of the Hebrew version (in 11Q5 col. 28) suggests that here too it had a fuller and more coherent text, and was originally separate from the first part.

Significance

Psalm 151 reflects the main themes of 1 Samuel 16–17: God chose David to be the king of Israel despite his being a young shepherd, and used David and his slingshot to defeat the powerful Philistine warrior Goliath. The theological lesson is that the God of Israel can and does rescue his people from their sufferings in surprising ways. In danger of being conquered by the Philistines, Israel was delivered by a young shepherd with a laughably weak weapon. The mighty and faithful God can and does use such weak means as a way of showing that God (and not the armies of Israel) was responsible for the people's deliverance. This theological theme runs through both Testaments from start to finish.

Issues. The discovery of Psalm 151 among the Dead Sea Scrolls has both illuminated the Greek version and made study of the text even more complicated. From the Hebrew version in the Qumran *Psalms Scroll,* we know that Psalm 151 was composed in Hebrew and that the Greek version is a shorter version (the summary of a summary?). The complicating factor is whether we can restore the "original" text by comparing the extant Hebrew, Greek, and other ancient versions. Or do we have to reckon with a certain textual fluidity in the transmission of Psalm 151, as is the case with so many other Jewish texts from the Second Temple period, that renders such efforts guesswork at best?

Influence. As the Greek superscription states, Psalm 151 is "ascribed to David as his own composition" but is "outside the number" of 150 canonical Psalms. It is not regarded as canonical by Jews, Protestants, or Catholics, but is customarily printed in Greek Bibles.

For Further Study

Flint, Peter W. *The Dead Sea Psalms Scrolls and the Book of Psalms.* Leiden: Brill, 1997.

Sanders, James A. *The Dead Sea Psalms Scroll.* Ithaca, N.Y.: Cornell University Press, 1967.

———. *The Psalms Scroll of Qumran Cave 11.* Oxford: Clarendon, 1965.

CHAPTER 15

3 Maccabees: Israel in Crisis and the Divine Deliverer

Basic Information

Despite its traditional title, 3 Maccabees narrates events that purport to have taken place in the late third century B.C.E. — some fifty years before the Maccabean revolt. It tells of two crises that Jews faced during the reign of the Egyptian king Ptolemy IV Philopator (221-204 B.C.E.) — the first at the Jerusalem temple (1:1–2:24), and the second at Alexandria in Egypt (2:25–7:23). The book shows how "the supreme God perfectly performed great deeds for their deliverance" (7:22b).

The main character is Ptolemy IV Philopator. In the first crisis his arrogant insistence on entering the Holy of Holies in the Jerusalem temple is stopped only by a stroke or seizure visited upon him by divine intervention. In the second crisis his plan to destroy the Jewish population of Egypt is foiled by "two glorious angels," and he then becomes the champion of the very Jews he planned to kill. The sudden shifts in his attitude and behavior are hard to explain except on the basis of the workings of divine providence.

In both crises the Jews appear as a collective entity, with prayers offered on their behalf in Jerusalem by Simon the high priest (2:1-20) and in Egypt by Eleazar, a priest who lived there (6:1-15). The people are fearful and devote themselves to prayer when faced with the desecration of their temple and with the loss of their property and destruction in Egypt.

Their prayers are heard by God, the "Deliverer of Israel," who rescues them miraculously.

The work is commonly described as a historical romance. Its starting point is the victory of Ptolemy IV Philopator at the battle of Raphia in 217 B.C.E. It features marvelous and even miraculous events that save the Jewish community at critical moments. It uses official-sounding letters (3:12-29; 7:1-9) from Philopator to summarize the narrative, as well as prayers by individual priests (2:1-20; 6:1-15) to express the hopes and fears of the Jewish people. The sufferings of the people (1:16-26; 4:2-9) are recounted in a highly emotional way designed to move the reader to pity and compassion.

The purpose of the book is to foster trust in God as the Deliverer of Israel. The miraculous resolution of both crises indicates that God can rescue Israel from any calamity visited upon it, provided the people remain faithful to prayer and the Torah. The large space given to the victory celebrations in 6:30–7:23 suggests a connection with an annual seven-day Jewish festival observed in Egypt. It is possible that 3 Maccabees provided the story, or foundational myth, for an otherwise unknown festival, much as the book of Esther did for Purim.

The events described in the book are set in the late third century B.C.E. Its descriptions of Philopator's victory at the battle of Raphia in 217 B.C.E. and of his erratic and dissolute behavior echo what is said by Polybius in his *Histories* (see 5.34 and 5.79-86). It is possible that Philopator visited the Jerusalem temple and wanted to enter the Holy of Holies (as others did), though there is no other evidence of it. The census and registration of Jews in Egypt may well reflect some historical event. But the author has transformed whatever it was into a full-scale (and otherwise unknown) persecution of Jews in Egypt. While the work has a historical framework, the author was more interested in showing his literary skills and promoting his theological message than in writing history.

The book could have been composed at any time between 217 B.C.E. (the battle of Raphia) and 70 C.E. (since in 1:1–2:24 the Jerusalem temple still stands). Most scholars place its composition during the Roman period, in the first century B.C.E. at Alexandria. The second and longest crisis takes place at Alexandria, and the book seems to have functioned as the foundational myth for a Jewish festival celebrated in Egypt. The book portrays the Jews of Egypt as loyal and cooperative citizens. Their arrest and condemnation are due to the madness of an arrogant king, the anti-Judaism of native Egyptians, and the malicious envy of the king's "Friends." There is no trace, however, of the philosophical interests displayed in the book of Wisdom and Philo's writings, and this difference suggests a diversity within Alexandrian Judaism.

Third Maccabees is found in some important manuscripts of the Greek Bible (Alexandrinus and Venetus) but not in others (Vaticanus and Sinaiticus). It was certainly composed in Greek, as its large vocabulary and elegant style show. The prayers of the priests Simon and Eleazar are cast in "biblical Greek," but there is no reason to assume the translation of a Hebrew original.

The author may have used Polybius's *Histories* (or something like it) as a source for the historical framework. He was apparently familiar with the conventions of Hellenistic official letters and of Greek romances. The account of the resolution of the crisis at the Jerusalem temple is reminiscent of the Heliodorus episode in 2 Maccabees 3. The parallels in function and content suggest knowledge of the book of Esther; indeed, the general situation in the story about persecution in Alexandria strongly resembles the scenario in Esther.

Content

Part One: The Crisis in Jerusalem (1:1–2:24)

A. The *Occasion* (1:1-7) for the first crisis is supplied by Philopator's victory at the battle of Raphia in 217 B.C.E. over Antiochus III (1:1). To thwart a plot to kill Philopator by the renegade Theodotus, an apostate Jew named Dositheus the son of Drimylus has "a certain insignificant man" take Philopator's place in the royal tent and be killed in the king's place (1:2-3). Then when Arsinoë — the king's sister and later his wife — rallies the Ptolemaic armies by promising them large sums of money, the tide of battle turns and Philopator comes away both alive and victorious (1:4-5). Elated by his victory, Philopator visits the neighboring cities and gives support to local shrines (1:6-7). Philopator's life being saved through the clever plan of Dositheus leads to the former's "beneficence" toward the local people and their gods — which leads ironically to a great crisis for the people of Jerusalem and the temple of the God of Israel.

B. The *Crisis* (1:8-29) begins with the friendly reception of Philopator by the Jewish leaders (1:8). When Philopator visits the Jerusalem temple (1:9-15), he offers sacrifices and thank offerings as befitted his recent victory and escape from death. The crisis comes when Philopator, so impressed by the beauty of the Jerusalem temple, wants to enter the Holy of Holies — a privilege granted only to the Jewish high priest on the Day of Atonement (see Exod. 30:10; Lev. 16:29-34). Even when the Law is read to Philopator, he insists that he should count as an exception. Since he had been granted access to every other temple in the area, he could see no reason, notwithstanding the Torah, why he should not go anywhere he pleased in the Jerusalem temple.

According to 1:16-26 Philopator's insistence throws the whole population of Jerusalem into a panic. The priests (1:16) go to the temple to pray, while the rest of the people — including young women (1:18), recently married women (1:19), and mothers and nurses (1:20) — take to the streets. The outrage of "the bolder of the citizens" is barely restrained by the elders (1:22-23). But nothing — not even the advice of his own counselors — seems able to dissuade the arrogant king from carrying out his desire to enter the Holy of Holies (1:24-27). So serious is the crisis that not only the people but even "the walls and the whole earth" enter into prayer and grief (1:28-29).

C. The *Prayer of Simon* (2:1-20) expresses the hopes of the people of Jerusalem. In his address (2:2a) the high priest affirms the sovereignty of God ("Lord, Lord, king of the heavens . . . the only ruler, almighty") and asks God to attend to the people's sufferings at the hand of the arrogant king (2:2b). Then Simon invokes three biblical precedents (2:3-8) in which God "the just Ruler" punished insolent and arrogant conduct: the giants before the flood (Genesis 6), the people of Sodom (Genesis 19), and the Pharaoh of Egypt (Exodus 5–15). In each case the arrogant evildoers were punished, and God's sovereignty and justice were vindicated.

In the second part of the prayer (2:9-20) Simon focuses on God's choice of Jerusalem as the place for the temple and on God's promise to listen to the people's prayers there in times of trouble (2:9-10). Simon affirms the justice of God ("you are faithful and true") and ascribes the people's present sufferings to "our many and great sins" (2:11-13). However, in the present crisis (2:14-18) what is at stake is the glory of God and the danger of God's temple being profaned by an arrogant king. Therefore in 2:19-20 Simon asks God for forgiveness of the people's sins and for divine mercy so that the present crisis might be averted: "Give us peace."

D. The *Rescue* (2:21-24) takes the form of a stroke visited upon Philopator ("paralyzed in his limbs . . . unable even to speak"). The author interprets the stroke as a "righteous judgment" and a "punishment" for the king's arrogance in daring to profane God's temple in Jerusalem. But Philopator recovers and learns nothing from his experience ("he by no means repented"). His recovery and return to arrogance set the stage for the second crisis facing Israel — this time in Egypt.

Part Two: The Crisis in Egypt (2:25–7:23)

A. The *Occasion* (2:25-33) for the crisis in Egypt is Philopator's decree, which the author explains as intended "to inflict public disgrace on the Jewish community." He ascribes the decree to Philopator's arrogance and dissolute behavior and notes that he was encouraged by his "Friends" (a technical term for the king's inner circle). The decree is posted publicly ("in stone on a tower in the courtyard"). The first part of the text (2:28-29) forbids those who refuse to sacrifice to the pagan gods from entering their own sanctuaries (thus preventing uncooperative Jews from going to their own synagogues), and subjects Jews to register for the poll tax. Those who refuse are to be put to death, while those who agree (reluctantly?) are to be branded with the ivy-leaf symbol of the god Dionysus (to whom Philopator was devoted) and to lose the political privileges granted to Jews in Egypt. After the author's parenthetical comment questioning Philopator's sincerity (2:30a), the second part of the decree (2:30b) promises full Alexandrian citizenship to Jews willing to be initiated into the mystery cult of Dionysus.

The response of the Alexandrian Jewish community (2:31-33) is mixed. Some accept Philopator's offer in the hope of advancing themselves socially and politically, while the majority rejects it in the hope of saving themselves by means of bribery. The latter regard the former as "enemies of the Jewish nation" and refuse to have anything to do with them.

B. In the *Growing Crisis* (3:1-10), the king's anger (and his decree) extends beyond Alexandria to Jews in the Egyptian countryside, and he appeals to the anti-Judaism of the local populace. The Jews, according to the author, were different — in their exclusive worship of the God of Israel, in their observance of the Torah, and in their food laws. But, in the author's opinion, the separateness of the Jews in no way detracted from their "goodwill and unswerving loyalty toward the dynasty" (3:3). Nevertheless, others viewed Jewish distinctiveness as hostility and disloyalty, and so the decree of Philopator found support among the local inhabitants of Egypt. But according to 3:8-10, the "Greeks in the city" — as opposed to the native Egyptians in the countryside — recognized the injustice of the decree and tried to help Jews on the grounds that "such a great community ought not to be left to its fate when it had committed no offense" (3:9).

C. The *Letter of Philopator* (3:11-30) recounts the story of the crisis from the king's perspective. After the customary salutation (3:12-13), Philopator explains in 3:14-19 how he went up to honor the Jerusalem temple but was prevented from entering it because of the Jews' "traditional arrogance." He ascribes the resolution of the Jerusalem crisis not to a stroke or to God's miraculous intervention but to his own benevolence, and blames the Jews for their "manifest ill-will toward us." Then in 3:20-21 he interprets the decree that occasioned the second crisis as an example of his willingness to accommodate himself to the Jews by giving them the opportunity to obtain Alexandrian citizenship and to participate in the cult of Dionysus.

In 3:22-24 Philopator blames the Jews for taking his generous offer "in a contrary spirit" and criticizes them for their hostility toward others and disloyalty toward him. He defends his policy on the grounds that he cannot allow "traitors and barbarous enemies" within his kingdom.

Finally in 3:25-29 Philopator directs those who receive his letters ("his generals and soldiers in Egypt and all its districts," 3:12) to send the Jews in their districts to him immediately "to suffer the sure and shameful death that befits enemies." He warns that those persons who shelter Jews will be tortured to death, those who turn them in will be rewarded (with Jewish property, cash, and freedom), and those places that protect Jews will be thoroughly destroyed. The crisis now involves all of the Jews of Egypt and threatens the complete destruction of the Jewish community there.

D. The *Arrest and Registration* (4:1-21) of the Egyptian Jews is accompanied by a public celebration at which the anti-Judaism of the local population is manifest (4:1). For the Jews, their arrest is an occasion for great lamentation since it appears to mean their "unexpected destruction." Their situation is so pitiful that it even moves some of their enemies to tears (4:2-5). Scenes of old men, brides, and young husbands being led off to the boats (4:6-8) add to the pathos. Being treated "like wild animals," they begin their river journey to Alexandria (4:9-10).

When the boats arrive at Schedia, three miles from Alexandria, the Jews are brought to a large race-course outside the city (4:11). From what follows, one gets the impression that the original purpose of the "arrest" was to bring Jews from the countryside to register them for a census (see Luke 2:1-5). However, the author presents the event as a plot to annihilate the Egyptian Jewish community (4:14). The Alexandrian Jews become involved when they try to help the other Jews (4:12-13). Despite the efforts of the king's officials, they fail to complete the census after forty days (4:15) and eventually run out of paper and pens (4:20). Because there were so many Jews in Egypt, the census was an impossible undertaking. The king meanwhile spends his time in "organizing feasts in honor of his idols" and "uttering inappropriate words against the supreme God" (4:16). The failure of the census is given a theological interpretation: "this was an act of the invincible providence of him who was aiding the Jews from heaven" (4:21).

E. The *Heat of the Crisis* (5:1-51) comes to a head when the king orders Hermon, the keeper of the elephants, to feed five hundred elephants (a fantastic number) with frankincense and strong wine — perhaps intended as a drug to drive them crazy, or perhaps associated with the cult of Dionysus. The plan is to set loose the crazed elephants to trample the Jews in the hippodrome. While to Gentile observers it appeared that "the Jews were left without any aid" (5:6), the Jews turned to God and prayed that the plot be averted and they be rescued: "So their entreaty ascended fervently to heaven" (5:9).

On the first day (5:10-22) Hermon goes to the palace to receive the king's command to set loose the elephants. But "by the action of the Lord" the king is so overcome by sleep that he does not awaken until late afternoon ("nearly the tenth hour," 5:14). At the banquet that same evening, however, the king vows that "tomorrow . . . the destruction of the lawless Jews" will take place (5:20). The king's savagery is said to be even worse than that of Phalaris, the sixth-century B.C.E. tyrant of Agrigentium who was famous for cruelty in roasting people alive inside a bronze bull and enjoying their screams (see also 5:42).

On the second day (5:23-44) a crowd gathers to observe the massacre and the Jews again turn to prayer. When Hermon comes to the palace, he finds that the king has no comprehension of the plan to annihilate the Jews and instead praises them for their great loyalty (5:31). The king's forgetfulness is described as "an act of God" (5:28) and "by the providence of God" (5:30). At the banquet that same evening, however, the king renews his plan to destroy the Jews and is again compared to Phalaris (5:42; see 5:20). And now he extends his plan to include marching against Judea and burning down the Jerusalem temple (5:43).

On the third day (5:45-51) Hermon has the elephants ready and there are massive crowds of spectators gathered at the hippodrome (5:45-47). The Jews on their part (5:48-51) prepare to die but implore "the Ruler over every power to manifest himself."

F. The *Prayer of Eleazar* (6:1-15), an elderly priest from the Egyptian countryside, expresses the people's hopes and fears. In his address (6:2) Eleazar first appeals to God's sovereignty ("Almighty God Most High") and mercy. In 6:2-8 he asks that God look upon Abraham's children "perishing as foreigners in a foreign land" and recalls the miraculous rescues of Israel in the days of Pharaoh (Exodus 5–15) and Sennacherib (2 Kings 18–19), of the three Jewish courtiers (Daniel 3), of Daniel (Daniel 6), and of Jonah. Then he appeals to God as "all merciful and protector of all" to save Israel from "abominable and lawless Gentiles" (6:9).

In his petition (6:10-15) Eleazar admits that his people have become "entangled in impieties in our exile" but appeals to the more important matter of God's honor. Eleazar calls upon God as the "Eternal One, who [has] all might and all power" (6:12). If Israel is destroyed, then its enemies will say: "Not even their god has rescued them" (6:11). But if Israel is rescued, the enemies will have to acknowledge that "you are with us, O Lord" (6:15). Whatever the sins of Israel may have been, what is really at stake in this crisis, according to Eleazar, are the power and justice of the God of Israel.

G. The *Resolution of the Crisis* (6:16-29) comes about through divine intervention by means of "two glorious angels." Just as Eleazar completes his prayer, the king arrives for the spectacle and the Jews turn to God in prayer (6:16-17). The angels, who are "visible to all but the Jews" (6:18), throw the soldiers into confusion, frighten the king so much that he forgets his "sullen insolence," and turn the elephants back to trample the king's army (6:19-21).

So complete is the king's forgetfulness that he blames his Friends for persecuting the Jews (6:22-29). He accuses them of harming his kingdom by mistreating the Jews, whom he now claims "faithfully kept our country's fortresses" and distinguished themselves "in their goodwill toward us." He orders his officials to release the Jews and to allow them to return home. The Jews in turn praise "their holy God and Savior," thus attributing their escape from sure death to the One to whom they prayed constantly during their ordeal.

H. The *Celebration* (6:30–7:23) begins in Alexandria, where the

king, once the enemy of the Jews, provides the funds for them to celebrate a festival for seven days (6:30-41). Those who had expected to be
put to death now celebrate "a banquet of deliverance" in praise of God
"their Savior and worker of wonders," whereas those who plotted their
death and registered them fear for their own lives. Even the king enters
into the celebration "for the unexpected rescue that he had experienced (!)" (6:33).

The celebration is described at such length that one gets the impression that the story served as the basis for a seven-day festival celebrated by
Egyptian Jews annually in summer. The festival is said to commemorate
the day "on which the Lord of all most gloriously revealed his mercy and
rescued them all together and unharmed" (6:39). Then the people ask the
king's permission to return to their homes.

The king's letter to his officials (7:1-9) repeats his charge that "certain of our friends" were responsible for arresting the Jews (7:3-5). But
now the king has come to see that "the God of heaven surely defends the
Jews" and that in fact the Jews have shown "friendly and firm goodwill"
toward him and his predecessors (7:6-7). Finally in 7:8-9 he gives his permission for the Jews to return home, warns that no harm should come to
them, and acknowledges the sovereignty of "the Ruler over every power,
the Most High God."

Before returning home, however, the Jews also receive permission
from the king in 7:10-16 to exact revenge not on their pagan persecutors
but rather on those Jews who apostatized during the crisis to save and "advance" themselves. They convince the king that those Jews who were not
faithful to the Torah will not be loyal to the king (7:11). The result is that
more than three hundred apostates are put to death (7:15), while those
who remained faithful to the Torah continue to celebrate "the one God of
their ancestors, the eternal Savior of Israel" (7:16).

The celebration then shifts to Ptolemais (7:17-21), where a seven-
day festival takes place, accompanied by the erection of a memorial pillar
and "a place of prayer" (a synagogue). When they return home, the Jews
find themselves treated with greater respect (since they now have the
king's public support) and recover their property (since it had been recorded in the registration).

The book ends in 7:22-23 first with a one-sentence summary ("So
the supreme God perfectly performed great deeds for their deliverance")
and then with a benediction ("Blessed be the Deliverer of Israel through
all times! Amen"). In two great crises facing Jews in Jerusalem and in

Egypt, their prayers were answered. The "Deliverer of Israel" intervened and rescued the faithful people of God.

Significance

The suffering of the Jewish people is the main topic of 3 Maccabees. In the crisis at Jerusalem, they face the desecration of their temple by Philopator. In the crisis in Egypt, they are arrested and brought to Alexandria to be killed. In both crises what is at stake is the honor of the God of Israel.

The prayers offered by the priests Simon and Eleazar (2:1-20; 6:1-15) emphasize God's power and justice: "Lord, king of the heavens, and sovereign of all creation . . . just Ruler . . . the Almighty. . . ." They appeal to God's past mighty acts in punishing evildoers and in rescuing the righteous. Simon attributes the threat against the Jerusalem temple to "our many and great sins" (2:13), and Eleazar alludes to the people having "become entangled in impieties in our exile" (6:10). Nevertheless, both prayers appeal to God's power and justice to overlook Israel's sins and to rescue Israel from its present distress. If God fails to act, then Israel's enemies will have the opportunity to defile God's temple and to boast that Israel's God is powerless.

The means by which God acts in each crisis is miraculous. Though Philopator suffers in Jerusalem what sounds like a stroke or seizure, the author attributes it directly to God ("God . . . scourged him who had exalted himself in insolence and audacity," 2:21). At Alexandria the king's command to destroy the Jews is prevented on three successive days by divine action: by the king's oversleeping ("the Lord sent upon the king a portion of sleep," 5:11), by his forgetfulness ("this was the act of God," 5:28), and by two glorious angels ("God revealed his holy face and opened the heavenly gates," 6:18). At each point the "Deliverer of Israel" intervenes.

In an indirect way 3 Maccabees illumines Jewish life in the Diaspora. The author portrays the Jews of Egypt as good citizens and as willing to cooperate with the king and his officials, provided their religious "separateness" is respected. Their sufferings are due to the king's arrogance and the prejudices of the native peoples. When the king comes to his senses, he publicly recognizes the Jews' services in maintaining fortresses for the Egyptians (as at Elephantine) and in showing loyalty to the rulers of Egypt. The native peoples resent the Jews because they insist on worshiping the God of Israel only, living according to the Torah, and avoiding certain foods (see 3:4).

The author shows a special dislike for apostate Jews. The cleverness of the apostate Dositheus in saving Philopator (1:3) provides the occasion for the two crises. Some Jews in Alexandria accept Philopator's offer of initiation into the mysteries of Dionysus and full Alexandrian citizenship (2:30-31). And the only vengeance that the Egyptian Jews seek is from apostate Jews, whom they contend are bad citizens also (7:10-16).

Issues. How much history is there in this historical romance? Most interpreters answer, Not much. At least, there is general agreement that 3 Maccabees cannot be used as a reliable historical source for Jewish history in the late third century. What it says about the battle of Raphia and about Philopator's character and lifestyle seem accurate enough and agree with Polybius. And Philopator could have visited Jerusalem and did order censuses to be taken. But these facts are simply elements of the historical setting in which the two crises are narrated.

More important and controversial is the question whether 3 Maccabees can be used as a serious historical source for later Jewish history. Josephus assigns the episode of the Jews and the elephants to the reign of Ptolemy VIII Physcon (144-117 B.C.E.) in *Against Apion* 2.53-55. Moses Hadas links the census of the Egyptian Jews to the poll tax instituted by the Roman emperor Augustus in 24/23 B.C.E. And other scholars have proposed a connection with the emperor Caligula's campaign (in 37-41 C.E.) to have himself worshiped as a god — an event that caused great consternation among the Jews of Alexandria, as Philo's *Embassy to Gaius* shows.

Influence. Third Maccabees appears in the Greek and Slavonic Christian Bibles. But it is not part of the Latin Vulgate or of the Catholic canon of Holy Scripture. There is little evidence for its influence in Rabbinic Judaism or in early Christianity. It is easy to dismiss 3 Maccabees as a historical romance or even as a "tear jerker." However, its analysis of the roots of Egyptian anti-Judaism as rooted in resentment against Jewish "separateness" is an early and important witness in the history of anti-Semitism. And its highly emotional portrayals of Jews being dragged from their homes and brought to a central camp for destruction (see 4:1-21) find chilling parallels in the "final solution" of the Nazis.

For Further Study

Collins, John J. *Between Athens and Jerusalem: Jewish Identity in the Hellenistic Diaspora.* 2d ed. Grand Rapids: Eerdmans, 1999.

Hadas, Moses. *The Third and Fourth Books of Maccabees.* New York: Harper, 1953.

Kasher, Aryeh. *The Jews in Hellenistic and Roman Egypt.* Tübingen: Mohr Siebeck, 1985.

Schäfer, Peter. *Judeophobia: Attitudes toward the Jews in the Ancient World.* Cambridge, Mass.: Harvard University Press, 1997.

CHAPTER 16

2 Esdras: Prophecies and Visions of Ezra

Basic Information

The work known as 2 Esdras is in fact three separate compositions. In them Ezra functions not as the architect of Israel's return from exile but rather as a prophet and a visionary. In 2 Esdras 1–2 (also known as 5 Ezra) Ezra prophesies about God's rejection of Israel as God's people and its replacement by the Church. This is a Christian work composed in Greek in the mid-second century C.E. In 2 Esdras 3–14 (also known as 4 Ezra) Ezra engages in dialogue about the meaning of Israel's sufferings and is granted visions that reveal what God is going to do in the near future on Israel's behalf. This is a Jewish work written in Hebrew around 100 C.E. The material contained in 2 Esdras 15–16 (also known as 6 Ezra) consists of oracles of doom against the enemies of God's people (the Church) and advice on how those enduring persecution should behave. This is a Christian work composed in Greek in the third century C.E.

Thus 5 Ezra, 4 Ezra, and 6 Ezra (for the identity of 1, 2, and 3 Ezra, see the introduction to 1 Esdras) are loosely related through the figure of Ezra cast as a prophet and visionary. The original language versions (Greek and Hebrew) of the three works have been lost. The primary text now is the Latin version. The composite text is included in the Slavonic Bible as 3 Esdras and in the appendix to the Latin Bible as 4 Esdras.

While 2 Esdras has little claim to canonical authority, it remains very important for the glimpses into early Christian history that 5 and 6 Ezra provide, and especially for the treatments of the mystery of suffering and theodicy in 4 Ezra. Each of the three compositions will be treated separately.

2 Esdras 1–2 (5 Ezra):
A Christian Prophecy and Apocalypse

The part of 2 Esdras known as 5 Ezra (chapters 1 and 2) consists of Ezra's prophecy about Israel's rejection as God's people (1:1–2:9) and its replacement by the Church (2:10-48). It makes abundant use of the language and conventions of biblical prophecy ("Thus says the Lord Almighty") and ends with a vision of the victorious martyrs and the Son of God. Ezra serves as the vehicle for God's prophecies, and gets help from the angelic interpreter in understanding his vision.

In the narrative setting, Ezra serves as the prophet and spokesman for the Jews in exile under the Persian empire in the fifth century B.C.E. In the historical setting of the work's composition, Ezra expresses the views of Christians in the second century. The author was familiar with the biblical historical narratives as well as with prophecy and apocalypticism. The many phrases and motifs also found in the New Testament (the Gospels of Matthew and Luke, and especially Revelation) suggest that those books or the traditions behind them were major sources also. The author wrote his work most likely in Greek during the second century C.E. The primary version is the Latin text included in the Vulgate.

Content

A. *Ezra's Prophecy of Israel's Rejection as God's People* (1:1–2:9) takes place during Persian rule (1:1-3). The Lord first summons Ezra in 1:4-11 to "declare to my people their evil deeds" and to tell them that the evils that have befallen them are due to their failure to obey God's law. In a series of prophetic oracles introduced by the formula "Thus says the Lord (Almighty)" (see 1:12, 15, 28, 33; 2:1), God complains to Ezra that despite God's many acts of mercy toward Israel from the exodus through the arrival in the land, Israel has repeatedly refused to obey God's law. Therefore God has determined to abandon Israel as his people: "Because you have forsaken me, I also will forsake you" (1:25). In the final oracle (2:1-9) God enlists Mother Zion ("I am a widow and forsaken") and Ezra the prophet as witnesses against Israel. God decrees that the names of those in Israel should "be blotted out from the earth, because they have despised my covenant" (2:7).

B. *God's Election of the Church as God's People* (2:10-48) is expressed first in an oracle from God (2:10-32) and then in Ezra's speech to the nations (2:33-41) and in his vision (2:42-48). Ezra is told to announce to "my people" (to be identified as the Church, even though this term is never used) that God will give them "the kingdom of Jerusalem" (the heritage of God's people), and the "Mother" (again, the Church) is told to embrace her children. Particular attention is given to the theme of resurrection ("I will raise the dead from their places," 2:16) and to the paradise that awaits the new people of God. In the meantime, Mother Church is to nourish her children so that they "may not see hell" (2:29).

In 2:33-41 Ezra tells the nations to wait for their Shepherd (who is Christ, although this term is not explicit): "he will give you everlasting rest, because he who will come at the end of the age is close at hand" (2:34). His coming is near, because the full number of those clothed in white (the martyrs) is now complete. In Ezra's vision on Mount Zion (2:42-48), he sees a multitude praising God with songs and "a young man of great stature" in their midst. An angel implies that the multitude of those being crowned and receiving palms are the martyrs, and identifies the young man as the Son of God.

Significance

The work called 5 Ezra is a Christian composition presented in a Jewish narrative setting. It follows the biblical tradition emphasizing Israel's failure to observe God's law as the reason for its sufferings. It also stresses God's patience and mercy toward Israel as God's people. However, it goes beyond the biblical tradition in affirming that Israel's infidelity is so complete that God gives up on Israel and transfers its identity as God's people to the church. In forsaking God, Israel has forsaken itself, and gets the punishment that it deserves. From the author's Christian perspective, this transfer is warranted by the justice of God.

Issues. The replacement of Israel as God's people by the Church raises a very important theological question. How can the biblical pledges of God's eternal covenant with Israel be fulfilled? The Christian answer (and 5 Ezra is a very early witness of it) is that since Israel had failed as God's people, it was only just that the Church led by Jesus the Son of God should replace Israel as God's people and succeed Israel as the heir to God's promises to Israel. This approach (called *supersessionism*) has been traditional in Christian theology for many centuries. But it has had disastrous results in the history of Christian-Jewish relations. Modern theologians are concerned to replace this supersessionist approach with one that is more faithful both to Hebrew Scripture and to the approach taken by Paul in Romans 9–11 (see especially 11:25-26), and that is more conducive to a positive relationship between Christians and Jews today.

Influence. The presence of 5 Ezra in the Latin Vulgate, even if only as an appendix, has influenced (for good or for ill) how the Church has regarded itself as replacing Israel and thus has shaped Christian-Jewish relations for many centuries.

2 Esdras 3–14 (4 Ezra): A Jewish Apocalypse

The part of 2 Esdras (chapters 3–14) known as 4 Ezra is a masterful Jewish apocalypse written around 100 C.E. It is one of the longest and most theologically significant books included among the Old Testament Apocrypha.

A large part of 4 Ezra is devoted to three dialogues (3:1–5:20; 5:21–6:34; 6:35–9:25) in which Ezra the scribe raises theological questions about the exile and the angel Uriel responds mainly with predictions about the future and the "signs" that will accompany the end of "this age" and the beginning of the "age to come." The dialogues are followed by three dream visions and their interpretations: the mourning woman (9:26–10:59), the eagle and the lion (11:1–12:51), and the man from the sea (13:1-58). The final part (14:1-48) contains God's instructions to Ezra and a description of Ezra's work as a scribe. Within the dialogues and dream visions there are many smaller literary forms: addresses, questions and answers, lists, prayers, small apocalypses, narratives, and so forth.

There is a longstanding debate about the literary unity of 4 Ezra. At first glance it can look like seven small units brought together into an artificial unity. Moreover, scholars in the past have detected several sources within the seven units. At present, however, the general tendency is to view 4 Ezra as the work of a single author who may have used some preexisting material.

The major characters are Ezra and Uriel. Ezra the scribe functions as the representative of Israel in exile and asks the hard theological questions that life in exile has raised. It is possible to detect in the portrayal of Ezra a kind of personal development (as in Job) in which he passes from constant and fruitless questioning of God's purposes to an acceptance of God's will in the present and a hope for a better life in the age to come. Uriel fills the role of the angelic interpreter, a common feature in Jewish apocalypses. He answers Ezra's questions and explains the meaning of various features in the dream visions. At several points it appears that God rather than Uriel has become the speaker, or it is hard to discern who is speaking. This shift between the Lord and the angel of the Lord is common in the Hebrew Bible. Whether Ezra or Uriel was intended to express the author's own viewpoints is also hard to know. It is probably better to regard both characters as expressing the tensions and struggles within the author's mind.

The various literary forms and characters in 4 Ezra are vehicles for exploring the serious theological issues raised by Israel's experiences in seeing Jerusalem and its temple in ruins and in living under foreign domination. This book raises very difficult questions: Why have these terrible things happened to God's chosen people? Why have Adam's sin and the "evil heart" exercised so much influence? Why are there so many wicked people? In light of these facts, how can anyone regard God as just? Why do Israel's enemies seem to have the upper hand? When will this age end? How will we know when the end is near? What will life be like after death and in the age to come? Is God faithful to the promises made to Israel as God's people?

The narrative setting of 4 Ezra is the Babylonian exile in 557 B.C.E. Despite the fact that the historical Ezra led a group of returnees to Jerusalem some 100 or 150 years later, here he serves as the spokesman for the Jewish exiles in the sixth century B.C.E. However, the historical setting of 4 Ezra's composition seems to be the late first century C.E. This becomes most obvious in the vision of the eagle and the lion (11:1–12:51) where the eagle is clearly Rome and there are abundant references to the Roman emperors of the first century C.E. And so the Babylonian exile of the sixth century B.C.E. becomes the literary occasion for exploring the theological issues raised by the recent destruction of Jerusalem and its temple in 70 C.E. under the Romans. The eagle vision reaches its climax with reference to the three "heads" — the late first-century C.E. Roman emperors

189

Vespasian, Titus, and Domitian — who were responsible for the destruction of Jerusalem and for the harassment of Jews afterward. Thus it appears that 4 Ezra was composed around 100 C.E. in the expectation of the imminent end of "this age" (and the Roman empire) and the beginning of "the age to come" (and the vindication of the righteous within Israel).

There is general agreement among scholars that 4 Ezra was composed in Hebrew and translated into Greek. Since both of these texts have been lost, the primary version is the Latin text supplemented by the versions in other languages (Syriac, Ethiopic, Arabic, Armenian, etc.). The original composition in Hebrew and the focus on Jerusalem indicate the land of Israel as the place in which the work was written.

The chief biblical source and model is the book of Daniel, a Jewish apocalypse composed in the second century B.C.E. in the land of Israel. There are also many affinities in language and content with *2 Baruch,* a Jewish apocalypse from roughly the same time and place as 4 Ezra. Whether one work was the source of the other, or both depended on a common source or reflect a common milieu, is a matter of debate among scholars. There are also affinities with Pseudo-Philo's *Biblical Antiquities,* an imaginative history of Israel composed in Hebrew in the first century C.E.

Content

Part One: The First Dialogue (3:1–5:20)

A. Before *Ezra's Address* (3:4-36) the introduction in 3:1-3 provides basic information about the time (the thirtieth year after Jerusalem's destruction = 557 B.C.E. in the narrative setting but perhaps 100 C.E. in the historical setting), the place (Babylon in the narrative setting; perhaps Rome or more likely the land of Israel), the visionary ("I, Salathiel, who am also called Ezra" = Ezra the scribe in the narrative setting), and the purpose (his need to understand the disparity between the desolation of Jerusalem/Zion and the prosperity of Babylon).

In the first part of his address (3:4-27) to "the Most High" (the most prominent title for God in the book), Ezra gives a review of history from Adam to the exile of 587 B.C.E. in which he highlights the presence of an "evil heart" that led to the transgression of God's commands and punishments for sin. Ezra objects that God has not taken away "their evil heart" and so has frustrated the purpose of the Torah. Adam serves as both the

190

cause and the model of human sinfulness: "For the first Adam, burdened with an evil heart transgressed and was overcome, as were all who were descended from him" (3:21).

In the second part (3:28-36) Ezra questions the justice of God with regard to Babylon's (and Rome's) dominion over Zion: "Are the deeds of Babylon better than those of Zion?" (3:31). As an expatriate in Babylon for thirty years, Ezra witnessed the sinfulness of the Babylonians, and so he challenges God to "weigh in a balance our iniquities and those of the inhabitants of the world" (3:34). By allowing the evil inclination to continue to exist in humans and by punishing Israel rather than Babylon (whose sins are greater), the Most High seems to be unfair.

B. The *Dialogue Between Uriel and Ezra* (4:1-25) begins in 4:1-4 with Uriel criticizing Ezra's arrogance in trying to understand "the way of the Most High." Uriel offers to explain "why the heart is evil" if Ezra can solve three problems.

The three problems (4:5-12) concern weighing fire, measuring wind, and calling back the past day. When Ezra objects that these problems are impossible for him to solve, Uriel reminds him that fire, wind, and the day are part of his everyday experience. If Ezra cannot understand these matters, how can he expect to comprehend the way of the Most High? But Ezra is not satisfied and contends that it would be better not to have been born than "to suffer and not understand why" (4:12).

The parable (4:13-21) concerns a forest of trees that plans to make war against the sea, and the waves of the sea that plan to make war against the forest. But the forest is prevented by fire, and the sea by the sand. The lesson is that each has been assigned its own place, and it was foolish for the forest or the sea to try to impinge on each other's territory. The application to Ezra's situation is that humans "can understand only what is on earth" (4:21).

In response (4:22-25) Ezra again expresses his dissatisfaction. What he wants to know does pertain to life on earth. He wants to know why Israel has been given over to the Gentiles, why the Torah and the covenants are no more, why Israel has not obtained mercy from God, and what God is going to do about the disgrace that has attached to God's name.

C. *Ezra's Questions About the Future* (4:26-52) take as their starting point the prediction that this age or world is "hurrying swiftly to its end" (4:26). The end will come, however, only when the grain of evil seed sown in Adam's heart reaches its harvest or full measure. The idea is that the quota of evil must be filled before the end can come (4:26-32).

Ezra's first question (4:33-37) is, "How long? When will these things be?" Uriel's answer is that Ezra should not be in a greater hurry than the Most High is. Moreover, there seems to be a second quota or measure, that of the souls of the righteous. The end will not come until that quota too is met.

Ezra's second question (4:38-43) concerns whether the sins of human beings are delaying the end. The answer is that the end will come in God's good time. It can be delayed or hurried no more than a pregnant woman can be.

Ezra's third question (4:44-50) is "whether more time is to come than has passed, or whether for us the greater part has gone by" (4:45). The answer takes the form of a parable about a flaming furnace and a trail of smoke, and about a cloud full of rain and a few remaining drops. And so the quantity of time that has passed is far greater, but "drops and smoke remained." In other words, most of the allotted time has passed, and the end will come soon.

Ezra's fourth question (4:51-52) is, How soon? Will the end come in his lifetime? Uriel claims not to know about Ezra's case but offers to tell him about the signs that will accompany the end of this age or world.

D. The *Signs* (5:1-20) by which Ezra (and anyone else) can know that the end is coming are provided by Uriel. The first signs (5:1-4a) are the triumph of unrighteousness over truth and the destruction of "the land that you now see ruling" (Babylon in the narrative setting, but Rome in the historical setting). Then there will be cosmic portents (with the sun, the moon, etc.), the rule of the "antichrist," the outbreak of chaos, and the disappearance of wisdom and righteousness (5:4b-12). And Uriel promises to tell Ezra "yet greater things than these" (5:13).

As Ezra emerges from his dream (5:14-15), he is very disturbed and needs reassurance from Uriel. When Phaltiel comes to him as a representative of the exiled community, he begs Ezra not to abandon the people "like a shepherd who leaves the flock in the power of savage wolves" (5:18). However, Ezra asks to be left alone for seven days during which he fasts and laments the state of his people.

In the first dialogue Ezra has asked some difficult questions about the state of God's people in exile. He has raised theological concerns about the justice of God, human sinfulness and human/divine responsibility, Babylon's (Rome's) prosperity and Israel's suffering, and his inability to understand the present suffering. Uriel, however, has not given Ezra any direct answers. Rather, he has appealed to the inability of humans to comprehend the ways of the Most High and to what God will do in the near future to vindicate his justice.

Part Two: The Second Dialogue (5:21–6:34)

A. Before *Ezra's Address* (5:23-30) the introduction in 5:21-22 describes how after seven days he recovered his "spirit of understanding" and began to address God once more. The first part of his address (5:23-27) uses various images to remind God that God chose Israel as his people. Several of these images — the vine, the dove, and the sheep — have traditional associations with Israel. The three most obvious and important reminders concern Jerusalem ("you have consecrated Zion for yourself"), Israel as God's people ("you have gotten for yourself one people"), and the Torah ("you have given the law that is approved by all"). Then in the second part (5:28-30) Ezra wants to know why God has handed Israel over to other nations for punishment. He says boldly: "If you really hate your people, they should be punished at your own hands" (5:30).

B. The *Dialogue Between Uriel and Ezra* (5:31-40) begins with a round of comments (5:31-35) in which Ezra again voices his desire to "understand the way of the Most High." When Uriel assures him that he cannot, Ezra wonders why he has been born at all. Again Uriel answers Ezra (5:36-40) with a list of things that he cannot do: He cannot count up those who have not yet come, gather up scattered raindrops, make withered flowers bloom again, and so forth. When Ezra admits that he does not know how to do these things, he is told: "so you cannot discover my judgment, or the goal of the love that I have promised to my people" (5:40).

C. *Ezra's Questions About the Future* (5:41–6:10) begin with his query (5:41-42) about those who have already died or are still yet to be born. What will their fate be at the end? The answer is that God's judgment is like a circle (rather than a straight line) and so Ezra's linear conception of time does not apply.

Ezra's second question (5:43-44) concerns whether God could have created everyone all at once, and so have hastened the judgment. He is told that God has his own schedule ("the creation cannot move faster than the Creator"), and moreover the earth could not hold all those people at once.

Ezra's third question (5:45-49) makes the objection that if all creatures existed at one time, then creation could sustain them all. He is told that just as a woman can bear ten children one after another but cannot

193

do so all at once, so the earth can bear only so many people at once. Again the idea is that God has his own schedule.

Ezra's fourth question (5:50-55) concerns the imminence of the end: "Is our mother (the earth) . . . still young? Or is she approaching old age?" The answer he receives is curious. The assumption is that young women bear large children and old women bear small children. Now in comparison with earlier times — perhaps a reference to Genesis 6:4 and the myth of the "giants" is presumed — the children of Ezra's day are supposed to be smaller. Those who will follow Ezra "will be smaller than you, as born of a creation that already is aging and passing the strength of youth" (5:55).

In his fifth question (5:56–6:6) Ezra wants to know "through whom you will visit your creation?" The answer is that just as all things have been made by God alone, so the end will come through God alone and not through another.

Ezra's sixth question (6:7-10) returns to the timing of the end. With reference to the births of Esau and Jacob (see Gen. 25:24-26), Ezra is told that Esau (a traditional Jewish cipher for Rome) is the end of this age, and Jacob (also known as Israel) is the beginning of the age that follows. In other words, the new age will be ushered in when Rome's domination ends and it will belong to Israel as God's people.

D. The *Signs* (6:11-34) are presented in response to Ezra's request (6:11-12) and delivered by a voice that makes the earth shake (6:13-17). In fact, the speaker is God, who describes what will happen as he visits the earth "when the humiliation of Zion is complete" (6:19). The visitation will mark the end of the old age (with God's judgment upon it) and the beginning of the new age. The list of signs (6:20-28) includes unnatural happenings and terrifying events. Those who remain will "see my salvation and the end of my world." What will remain is a new earth without evil and governed by faithfulness and truth — the exact opposite of conditions in the present age.

At the close of this second dialogue (6:29-34) Uriel assures Ezra that "the Mighty One has seen your uprightness" and that after seven more days he will declare to him "greater things than these."

Part Three: The Third Dialogue (6:35–9:25)

A. *Ezra's Address* (6:35-59) takes place after seven days of fasting, and is delivered "in distress" (6:35-37). In the first part (6:38-54) Ezra speaks directly to God ("O Lord, you spoke . . .") and presents a rewriting of the six days of creation in Genesis 1. He gives special prominence to God's word or command: "For your word went forth, and at once the work was done" (6:43). The version of the fifth day (see Gen. 1:21) is notable for its treatment of Behemoth and Leviathan as the great land and sea monsters who are to be eaten when and by whom God wishes (at the end of this age).

In the second part (6:55-59) Ezra complains that if God created the world for Israel, and if the other nations are nothing ("like spittle . . . a drop from the bucket"), why do these nations have power over God's chosen people? And why does Israel not possess the world as its inheritance? And how long will this be the case?

B. The *Dialogue Between Uriel and Ezra* (7:1-25) takes as its starting point two parables: a huge sea whose entrance is set in a narrow place (7:3-5), and a great city with a narrow entrance (7:6-9). One can gain access to them only by "passing through the appointed danger."

Then God in 7:10-16 draws out the implications of these parables for Ezra's questions from his address. Even though God created the world for Israel, the entrances have been made narrow because of Adam's sin. Therefore human beings must pass through "difficult and futile experiences" and especially through death before they can enjoy "what is to come."

When Ezra invokes the law of retribution in 7:17-18 (see Deut. 8:1), God responds in 7:19-25 that the Torah provides the criteria for rewards and punishments, and that Israel's sufferings are due to its disobedience with regard to the Torah. Those who are empty of piety will be empty of rewards, whereas those who are full of piety will be full of rewards.

C. *God's Prediction* (7:26-44) features an eschatological scenario in which "my son the Messiah" plays a major role. With the appearance of the New Jerusalem and the Holy Land, there will be also a revelation of the Messiah and his four-hundred-year reign — after which the Messiah will die (7:26-29). Then, after the world returns to silence for seven days (7:30), the last judgment will take place (7:31-43). When the dead come before the throne of the Most High for judgment, they can expect only the truth, not mercy or patience. The wicked are destined for "the pit of torment" and the righteous for "the place of rest." The Most High will then explain to the Gentiles that they have denied God and not served God, and despised the divine commandments. The day of judgment will

195

last for seven years ("for a week of years") and will be illumined only by "the splendor of the glory of the Most High." The prediction ends in 7:44 by noting that this scenario has been revealed only to Ezra.

D. The *Dialogue Between God and Ezra* (7:45-74) concerns Ezra's fear that very few persons will enjoy the delights of the world to come. The reason for his fear is that almost all are sinners because "an evil heart has grown up in us" (7:48). God answers that he is concerned mainly with those precious few (like gold) who prove righteous. God rejoices over "the few who shall be saved" (7:60) and does not grieve over "the great number of those who perish" (7:61).

Dissatisfied with God's response, Ezra in 7:62-69 laments about the human condition, over the fact that "all who have been born are entangled in iniquities, and are full of sins and burdened with transgressions" (7:68). He even envies the animals because they do not have to face the divine judgment. The angel responds in 7:70-74 that those who are consigned to punishment from God get what they deserve. Even though they were given understanding, the commandments, and the Torah, they have failed to obey God's directives. Indeed, the existence of so many wicked persons is proof of God's patient observance of his own timetable.

E. The *Prediction* (7:75-115) concerns life after death and before the final judgment. Immediately after death a person's spirit returns to God and "adores the glory of the Most High" (7:78). The wicked suffer in seven ways (7:79-87), with their worst torment being fear "at seeing the glory of the Most High" before whom they have sinned. The righteous "have rest in seven orders" (7:88-99), the greatest of these being their desire to see God's face and receive their rewards.

When informed that there is a seven-day interval between death and final assignment (7:100-101), Ezra asks in 7:102-103 whether the righteous can intercede with God for the ungodly on the day of judgment. He is told in 7:104-105 that "the day of judgment is decisive" and that no one can pray for another on that day. When Ezra in 7:106-111 objects that there is a long tradition of intercessory prayers throughout Israel's history, he is told in 7:112-115 that those prayers belonged to the present world, whereas "the day of judgment will be the end of this age and the beginning of the immortal age to come" (7:113).

F. The *Dialogue Between Ezra and Uriel* (7:116–8:3) begins with Ezra's lament (7:116-126) about the human condition, especially as this has been shaped by Adam's sin: "the fall was not yours alone, but ours also who are your descendants." He goes on to complain that the fact that

God has created wonderful things for humankind — immortality, everlasting hope, safe and healthful habitations, glory, paradise, and eternal splendor — does no good, since on account of their wicked lives most humans will fail to attain these gifts and merit only sufferings after death. Uriel responds in 7:127-131 that human existence is a contest and a struggle, and how it ends depends on the basic choice one has made: "Choose life for yourself, so that you may live" (Deut. 30:19). And he repeats the idea that in God's perspective joy over those who are saved is more important than grief over those who fail to choose life.

Ezra's second contribution to this dialogue (7:132-140) is a meditation on the attributes of God based loosely on the list in Exodus 34:6-7: The Most High is merciful, gracious, patient, bountiful, abundant in compassion, beneficent, and the judge. He suggests that without these attributes there would be even fewer humans ("not one ten-thousandth of humankind") who might have life. Uriel responds in 8:1-3 that "the Most High made this world for the sake of many, but the world to come for the sake of only a few." Just as there is much clay and only a little gold dust in the earth, so "many have been created, but only a few shall be saved."

G. *Ezra's Prayers* (8:4-36) mark a development in his relationship with God. In his first prayer (8:4-19) Ezra calls upon his own soul to drink its fill of understanding and calls upon God "that we may pray before you" (8:4-5). He celebrates God's care in creating, bringing to birth, nurturing, and guiding every human being through divine righteousness, the Law, and wisdom. He acknowledges that God has dominion over human life and death, but wonders why God so quickly destroys what is the product of so much labor (8:6-14). Then in 8:15-19 he breaks off talking about humankind in general and returns to the present sorry state of Israel as the people of God. He asks permission to pray upon Israel's behalf.

Ezra's second prayer (8:20-36) begins with praise of God as sovereign over creation (8:20-23), calls upon God to hear his petition (8:24-25), asks God to look not "on the sins of your people but on those who serve you in truth" (8:26-30), confesses the people's sins but appeals to God's mercy (8:31-35), and closes with a promise that God's righteousness and goodness will be declared "when you are merciful to those who have no store of good works" (8:36).

H. *Ezra's Questions About the Future* (8:37-62a) are answered by God, who reiterates his intention of focusing on the righteous and their fate (8:37-41). He uses the analogy of a farmer who sows many seedlings and recognizes that not all will take root. And so "those who have been sown in the world will not all be saved" (8:41). Ezra, however, rejects this analogy on the grounds that God has shaped Israel and created all things for Israel, and concludes that therefore God should "have mercy on your inheritance" (8:42-45).

God's scenario for the future (8:46-62a) begins by distinguishing the present and the future (8:46), rebuking Ezra for suggesting that he loves creation more than God does (8:47a), and praising Ezra for his humility and promising him future glory (8:47b-49). Next, after referring to the many miseries that will afflict the proud (8:50), God paints a picture of the age to come in which the righteous will share in God's glory and there will be no more evil, illness, or death (8:52-54). Then in 8:55-60 he advises Ezra to stop obsessing about the fate of the wicked, precisely because they had an opportunity to choose life but instead "despised the Most High, and were contemptuous of his law, and abandoned his ways" (8:56). Finally God proclaims that "my judgment is now drawing near" and observes that he has revealed his plans "only to you and a few like you" (8:61-62a).

I. The *Signs* (8:62b–9:25) are given by God in response to Ezra's request (8:62b-63) that he be shown when God will act in the last times. In response (9:1-6) God gives a list of signs ("earthquakes, tumult of peoples, intrigues of nations, wavering of leaders, confusion of princes") that will precede God's visitation of the world. Then God distinguishes between the fate of those who will be saved "on account of their works or on account of their faith" and the fate of those who refused to acknowledge God in their lifetimes (9:7-13).

Ezra again brings up the fact that "there are more who perish than those who will be saved" — just as a wave is greater than a drop of water (9:14-16). In response God explains that since this world is already lost through sin, he has decided to save one grape from the cluster and one plant from the great forest (9:17-22). Finally God instructs Ezra to eat only the flowers of the field and to pray continually for seven days, and promises that there will be another revelation.

Part Four: The Vision of the Mourning Woman (9:26–10:59)

A. *Ezra's Address* (9:26-37) takes place in the field called Ardat (otherwise unknown) after seven days of eating flowers (9:26-28). His address begins with a reflection on God's gift of the Torah after the exodus from Egypt and on God's plan for the Torah in Israel: "For I sow my law in you, and it shall bring forth fruit in you, and you shall be glorified through it for-ever" (9:31). The problem was that the people who received the Torah did not observe it. Nevertheless, the Torah did not perish; it is eternal. The Torah "does not perish but survives in its glory" (9:37).

B. *Ezra's Vision of the Mourning Woman* (9:38–10:28) concerns a woman who had been barren for thirty years before God heard her prayers and gave her a son. The son grew up to be his parents' pride and joy, but on his wedding night he died suddenly. Despite her neighbors' ef-forts at consoling her, the woman came to the field in order to mourn and fast until her death.

In 10:5-17 Ezra grows impatient with the woman's apparent self-centeredness, and tells her to compare her loss of her one son with all the children lost by Mother Zion and by the earth itself. And he consoles her by saying that "you will receive your son back in due time" — in life after death (10:16). When the woman rejects Ezra's efforts at consoling her (10:18), he goes into great detail about "the sorrow of Jerusalem" — about what happened to the temple and to the people of the city (10:19-24). Then the woman's face begins to shine, and suddenly she disappears, only to be replaced by a city with huge foundations (10:25-28).

C. The *Interpretation* (10:29-59) of this "bewildering vision" is given by the angel in keeping with the apocalyptic convention of the an-gelic interpreter (10:29-37). The angel identifies the mourning woman as Zion, her thirty years of barrenness as the three thousand years before the Jerusalem temple was built, her raising her son as the period of Jewish res-idence in Jerusalem, and her son's death and her mourning for him as the destruction that befell Jerusalem. The angel also tells Ezra that as a reward for his efforts at consoling the woman (Zion) he was granted a vision of "the brilliance of her glory" (10:50) and a preview of the New Jerusalem. By way of conclusion (10:55-59), the angel invites Ezra to inspect the new city, and to await another vision about what "the Most High will do to those who inhabit the earth in the last days" (10:59).

Part Five: The Vision of the Eagle and the Lion (11:1–12:51)

A. *Ezra's Dream* (11:1–12:3a) begins with the vision of an eagle rising from the sea — an eagle with "twelve feathered wings and three heads" (11:1). As the following interpretation will make clear, the eagle is a (tra-ditional) symbol for Rome, and its wings and heads refer to the Roman emperors of the first century B.C.E. and C.E. The eagle's power is signified

by its spreading its wings over the whole earth (11:2-6). The eagle instructs the wings to take their proper turns as emperors but assigns the
reign of the three heads to the end (11:8-9). The sequence of wings (emperors from Julius Caesar onward) moves forward until it reaches the
time (70 to 96 C.E.) of the three heads: the emperors Vespasian, Titus,
and Domitian (11:29-35).

The second part of Ezra's dream vision (11:36–12:3a) features a lion
(who is the Messiah). The lion identifies the eagle as the fourth and final
kingdom (Babylonians, Persians, Greeks, and Romans), and indicts the
eagle for its oppression, injustice, and arrogance: "Your insolence has
come up before the Most High, and your pride to the Mighty One"
(11:43). The lion proclaims that the eagle's times have ended and that it
and its wings (the emperors) will disappear "so that the whole earth, freed
from your violence, may be refreshed and relieved, and may hope for the
judgment and mercy of him who made it" (11:46). The next thing that
Ezra sees is the disappearance of the third head (Domitian) and of the last
two wings (his short-lived successors as emperor), and the whole body of
the eagle is burned. Thus the dream vision purports to describe the last
days of the Roman empire in the late first or early second century C.E.

B. The *Interpretation* (12:3b-51) is introduced by Ezra's request to
be shown the meaning of this dream vision (12:3b-9). The angelic interpreter identifies the eagle as the fourth kingdom (Rome), the twelve
wings as the Roman emperors, the three heads as the three mighty and
oppressive emperors (Vespasian, Titus, and Domitian), the two little
wings as their successors, and the eagle as the Messiah who will bring the
eagle to judgment and destroy it. The result of the Messiah's intervention
is that "in mercy he will set free the remnant of my people" (12:34). By
way of conclusion (12:36-39), Ezra is told to write down his visions in a
book and put it in a hidden place, to teach the wise, and prepare for another dream vision. When the people complain that Ezra is neglecting his
tasks as their leader (12:40-45a), he replies (12:45b-49) that he came to
this place "to pray on account of the desolation of Zion, and to seek
mercy on account of the humiliation of our sanctuary" (12:48).

Part Six: The Vision of the Man from the Sea (13:1-58)

A. *Ezra's Dream* (13:1-13a) concerns a man who comes up from the heart
of the sea and overwhelms even the forces of nature. As an "innumerable
multitude" prepares to make war against him, he carves out a great moun-

tain from which he wages war and defeats the enemy not with military weapons but rather with what comes forth from his mouth alone. Then he calls to himself and receives "another multitude that was peaceable."

B. The *Interpretation* (13:13b-58) comes in response to Ezra's request for enlightenment (13:13b-20). The angelic interpreter identifies the Man from the Sea as God's Son (the Messiah), whom God will use as an instrument to defeat the enemies of God's people; the mountain as Mount Zion; and the peaceable multitude as the nine tribes that were taken from the northern kingdom of Israel under Assyrians in the eighth century B.C.E. These people had gone off to a far country called "Arzareth" (otherwise unknown), and at the Messiah's appearance they will be gathered in once more to the people of God at Mount Zion. Once more (13:53b-58) Ezra is told that he has been and will continue to be the recipient of special revelations.

Part Seven: Ezra the Scribe (14:1-48)

A. *God's Final Instruction to Ezra* (14:1-18) first relates him to the figure of Moses, to whom God revealed many things, especially insofar as God instructed Moses to publish some of them openly and to keep others a secret (14:3-6). Then in 14:7-12 God promises that Ezra will be taken up to heaven (like Enoch and Elijah) and "live with my Son and with those who are like you, until the times are ended." Finally, in 14:13-18 God instructs Ezra to set his house in order, since the power of evil is increasing and the eagle (Rome) "is already hurrying to come."

B. *Ezra's Work as a Scribe* (14:19-48) must be completed before he joins God's Son and the others. Since "your law has been burned" in the destruction of Jerusalem, Ezra volunteers to rewrite everything (14:19-22). God accepts Ezra's offer, and assigns him and his five assistants forty days in which to do their work. God promises to inspire Ezra and tells him to make some things public and to deliver other things in secret to the wise (14:23-26). Before beginning the work, Ezra addresses the people (14:27-36). He explains that their present state of exile is due to Israel's failure to keep the Torah, and holds out the possibility that if they now keep the Torah, they will live in the present and live again after death when the judgment comes. To help in carrying out the scribal work (14:37-48), God gives Ezra a potion that inspires him to dictate to the five assistants. After forty days they produce ninety-four books — twenty-four of which are to be made public (the books of the Hebrew Bible), and seventy of which are given to the wise (the Apocrypha). These latter books are said to be "the spring of understanding, the fountain of wisdom, and the river of knowledge" (14:47).

Significance

Among the Old Testament Apocrypha, 4 Ezra is the fullest and most profound exploration of suffering and theodicy. Its focus is the communal suffering of Israel deprived of its temple and its Mother Zion (Jerusalem). If Israel is God's chosen people and if the world has been created for God's people, how can such terrible things be happening to Israel in the narrative setting (557 B.C.E.) and in the historical setting (100 C.E.)?

According to 4 Ezra, the reason for Israel's present suffering is its sin — the standard biblical and early Jewish explanation of the exile. In general, Ezra accepts this explanation. But he also raises questions about the origin of sin and its domination of most human beings. The sin of Adam is both the prototype and the cause of subsequent sin. As a result, the "evil heart" or "evil inclination" is so powerful that humans can hardly escape from sinning. This leads Ezra to question the justice of God. Especially galling is the fact that other nations (such as Babylon and Rome) far more wicked than Israel now exercise dominion over the chosen people of God.

The book offers a sustained exploration of the justice of God. Uriel (and God) does not directly answer Ezra's hardest questions in much depth but proposes as a solution to Israel's present plight the new age that God is about to usher in. The present age is so dominated by sin that there is no hope for it. But when God brings in the new age, then God's justice will be fully manifest and fully operative. The book insists many times that only a few righteous persons like Ezra will fully enjoy life in the age to come. Therefore it is imperative to choose life now.

The beginning of the new age will be marked by cosmic signs and by the appearance of "my son the Messiah" (who will eventually die). The sovereignty and justice of God will be fully vindicated in the great judgment at which the wicked will be punished and the righteous will be rewarded. For 4 Ezra, as for other apocalypses, the justice of God is at work in the present but will be fully visible to all creation only at the end of the present age.

Issues. The major questions debated among scholars have been

202

raised in the introduction and the exposition. Does 4 Ezra constitute a literary unity? Is there development in the character of Ezra? Where is the author's own point of view to be found (in Ezra's questions, Uriel's and God's responses, in both)? What about the theological questions raised by Ezra but left unanswered? Is the apocalyptic solution to the mystery of suffering convincing? Does deferring the judgment of God to the end-time solve the problem of theodicy? These are perennial issues of interpretation that admit of no easy answer, and part of the appeal of studying 4 Ezra is the challenge of trying to answer them anew on each rereading.

Influence. The work known as 4 Ezra has exercised little direct influence on the Jewish tradition. Its inclusion in the appendix to the Latin Vulgate, however, has made it very influential among Christians. We get the notion of "apocryphal" or hidden books in addition to the canonical Scriptures from Ezra 14. And the part of chapter 7 (vv. 36-105) that is missing from most Latin manuscripts but was surely part of the original composition is best understood as having been suppressed because of its rejection of prayers for the dead (an idea that was offensive to many Christians). Moreover, it is said that Christopher Columbus pointed to the multitude from the nine tribes driven into exile by the Assyrians (see 13:39-50) as a theological warrant for his expeditions to the New World.

For Christians, 4 Ezra is especially important for its many parallels to the New Testament. Within the general apocalyptic framework, the most striking parallel comes in the references to "my son the Messiah," though this Messiah dies and disappears from the scene, and his death has no redemptive significance. The focus on Adam's sin and its consequences for all humans illumines what Paul says about original sin in Romans 5–6. And the use of apocalyptic language and conventions contributes greatly to our understanding of New Testament apocalypticism. This is especially the case with regard to the book of Revelation — a work composed at roughly the same time as 4 Ezra and one especially concerned with the evils visited upon God's people in the last days of this age and with the hopes of their vindication in the full manifestation of God's reign in the age to come. All in all, then, 4 Ezra is important in its own right and in the light that it sheds on the apocalyptic worldview of the New Testament.

2 Esdras 15–16 (6 Ezra): A Christian Prophecy

The part of 2 Esdras known as 6 Ezra (chapters 15 and 16) consists of oracles of doom uttered against the nations (15:1–16:34) and advice to the people of God, who are suffering persecution (16:35-78). Although Ezra is not mentioned by name, the proximity of 6 Ezra to 4 Ezra 14 suggests that Ezra delivers the oracles and the advice as God's prophet.

Much of the language, imagery, and thought is familiar from the prophetic books of the Bible as well as from Jewish and Christian apocalypses. Thus it is difficult to be certain about the work's historical setting. But some material in the oracles against the nations (see 15:28-34) suggests a setting in the eastern Roman empire in the third century c.e. It appears to be a Christian work, though there is not nearly as much explicitly Christian material as there is in 5 Ezra (2 Esdras 1–2). The original language was likely to have been Greek, though the Latin version is now the primary text. The book sought to encourage Christians in the Roman empire to remain faithful during the persecutions that they faced, in the conviction that God was about to intervene definitively against their persecutors.

Content

A. The *Oracles of Doom Against the Nations* (15:1–16:34) are based largely on biblical phrases and images. Again Ezra is enlisted as the prophet of God (15:1-4), and he proclaims that God will soon bring evils upon the nations of the world because of the "ungodly acts that they impiously commit" (15:8). These nations will be punished especially for their persecutions of "my elect" (15:21), which in this context refers most likely to Christians. Those nations that will experience the wrath of God include Babylon, Asia, Egypt, and Syria (16:1). In this context Babylon is again a code name for Rome. The enemies of Rome, especially the Persians, will serve as God's instrument in bringing chaos and destruction to the persecutors of God's people. God's judgment on their adversaries is irreversible: "The sword has been sent upon you, and who is there to turn it back?" (16:3). The punishments include "famine and plague, tribulation and anguish . . . sent as scourges for the correction of humankind" (16:19).

B. The *Advice to the Persecuted* (16:35-78) tells the "servants of the

Lord" that the calamities are drawing near, and so they should prepare themselves to be "like strangers on the earth" (6:40-50). They are warned in 16:51-67 to cease from all sins, and especially not to try to hide their sins from God, "who certainly knows everything that people do" (16:54). They are encouraged to remain steadfast in the midst of the persecutions that will surely come their way. In particular, they are to resist eating food sacrificed to idols (16:68). Indeed, the persecutions will be an opportunity for "the tested quality of my elect" to be made "manifest, like gold that is tested by fire" (16:73). The advice concludes in 16:74-78 with an assurance that the calamities are imminent and a promise from God to the elect who remain faithful: "the days of tribulation are at hand, but I will deliver you from them" (16:74).

Significance

This work addresses people undergoing persecution. It encourages them to put their trust in the sovereignty and justice of God. While the persecutors may seem to have the upper hand, God will soon visit upon them terrible calamities and so destroy the persecutors. Those who suffer in the present are urged to avoid sin and to resist their persecutors by remaining faithful to God. Their deliverance is imminent. The persecution will test them and show what they are made of (gold).

The addressees are most likely Christians in the Roman empire during the third century C.E. If that is so, it is striking how completely a Christian writer has assimilated the Jewish apocalyptic solution to the mystery of suffering and the question of theodicy, and how little attention is given to the distinctive features of Christian faith vis-à-vis Judaism in this situation.

Issues. The major issue is the tension between the generic biblical-apocalyptic language of 6 Ezra and the precise historical setting that generated it. Much suggests a persecution of Christians in the eastern Roman empire during the third century C.E. But there are few concrete details that make this certain and much very traditional and general language in the book.

Influence. In providing a glimpse into early Christian life under the Roman empire, 6 Ezra is a valuable source. It also is important evidence for the influence of the book of Revelation or the traditions in it. As in Revelation, Rome is given the code name Babylon and is threatened with

205

punishments from God for having subjected God's people to eating food sacrificed to idols and other persecutions. As in Revelation, there is an expectation that God will soon intervene decisively on the side of God's people. Thus 6 Ezra is a link in the tradition of Christian apocalypticism adapting the conventions and concepts of Jewish apocalypticism.

For Further Study

Bergren, Theodore. *Fifth Ezra: The Text, Origin, and Early History.* Atlanta: Scholars Press, 1990.

———. *Sixth Ezra: The Text and Origin.* New York and Oxford: Oxford University Press, 1998.

Knibb, Michael A., with R. J. Coggins. *The First and Second Books of Esdras.* Cambridge: Cambridge University Press, 1979.

Longenecker, Bruce. *2 Esdras.* Sheffield: Sheffield Academic Press, 1995.

Myers, Jacob M. *I and II Esdras.* Anchor Bible 42. Garden City, N.Y.: Doubleday, 1974.

Stone, Michael E. *Features of the Eschatology of IV Ezra.* Atlanta: Scholars Press, 1989.

———. *Fourth Ezra.* Hermeneia. Minneapolis: Fortress, 1990.

Thompson, A. L. *Responsibility for Evil in the Theodicy of 4 Ezra.* Missoula, Mont.: Scholars Press, 1977.

CHAPTER 17

4 Maccabees:
The Sovereignty of Devout Reason

Basic Information

For over two thousand years Jewish and Christian thinkers have been trying to integrate theology and philosophy. One of the earliest and most successful attempts is 4 Maccabees. The author has a clear and simple thesis: devout reason is sovereign over the emotions. The adjective "devout" specifies that reason is guided by the Torah, and the word "emotions" refers to what are sometimes also called the "passions" — the feelings that might lead one to hasty and inappropriate actions.

A short preface (1:1-12) delineates the topic and explains how the thesis will be developed. The first part (1:13–3:8), which deals with "the main principle," provides definitions (1:13-30a) and illustrates the thesis with various examples from the Torah (1:30b–2:23) and the life of David (2:24–3:18). The second part (3:19–18:24) is a greatly expanded version of the martyrdom episodes in 2 Maccabees 6–7 ("their story"). After background information (3:19–4:26), it takes up in turn the martyrdoms of Eleazar (5:1–7:23), the seven brothers (8:1–14:10), and their mother (14:11–17:6), and concludes with a final encomium (17:7–18:24).

After using first-person language ("I") in the preface, the author adopts first the persona of the philosophy professor with his thesis and definitions, and then the persona of the preacher with biblical incidents to illustrate his thesis. In his accounts of the Maccabean martyrs, he

207

writes as a narrator who sketches each confrontation between the wicked King Antiochus and the martyrs with help of emotional dialogues, gruesome tortures, and defiant speeches. The details of the tortures are intended to evoke sympathy from the reader and serve to highlight the principle that devout reason is sovereign over the emotions.

Among the martyrs there is a progression with regard to the reader's expectations. It may be surprising that an elderly sage like Eleazar could withstand terrible tortures by his fidelity to the Torah and the power of reason. And it is even more surprising that the seven youngsters could do so. And most surprising of all is that their mother could do so. If such persons could control their emotions under such extreme circumstances by exercising "devout reason," how much more should adult males be able to do so.

The narrative setting is the persecution of Jews under Antiochus IV Epiphanes around 167-164 B.C.E. The major source for the bulk of the book is 2 Maccabees 6–7. Though there was surely religious persecution in Judea at this time, the specific incidents narrated in 2 Maccabees 6–7 are literary-theological creations to a large extent. The revised and greatly expanded versions in 4 Maccabees are even further removed from historical fact.

Besides 2 Maccabees 6–7, the author makes use of many biblical incidents as examples, showing a particular fondness for the stories about Abraham and Isaac in Genesis 22 and about Daniel and his companions. The use of 2 Maccabees and Daniel points to a date of composition in the first century C.E. The original language was certainly Greek. Most scholars prefer to place the book's origin in Antioch of Syria rather than Alexandria.

Various expressions scattered throughout the book suggest that it may have been composed for a particular occasion: the commemoration of the Maccabean martyrs in Antioch. Whether we are to imagine the martyrdoms taking place in Jerusalem or Antioch, it does seem that a cult of the Maccabean martyrs developed in Antioch. The work gives the impression of having been written for oral presentation. And its concluding encomium (17:7–18:24) includes some conventions associated with a memorial service: the epitaph (17:9-10), the athletic metaphor (17:11-16), and the benefits derived from the hero's life and death (17:17–18:5).

The discourse is philosophical both in style (thesis and proofs) and content (the traditional cardinal virtues, the passions or emotions, immortality, etc.). For the author, the faithful Jew is the true philosopher.

There is no conflict for him between Judaism and philosophy. Indeed, the Torah provides the content that guides reason in controlling the emotions. Since the divinely revealed Torah commands abstention from pork and meat sacrificed to idols, it is rational to obey its commands.

The author gives a distinctive interpretation to the martyrs' deaths. They not only present a good example of reason, self-control, and courage, but also exercise a beneficial effect on behalf of the Jewish people. Their deaths bring about "the downfall of tyranny" over Israel (1:11) since by their sufferings they atone for the sins that brought about the crisis in the first place.

Content

Preface (1:1-12)

The subject of the book is "whether devout reason is sovereign over the emotions" (1:1a) — an issue of importance for all who seek knowledge and virtue (1:1b-2). Devout reason — reason informed by the Torah — is the key to practicing the other cardinal virtues of self-control, justice, and courage, and to controlling whatever may hinder their practice. Rational judgment, while not destroying the passions, can control them (1:3-6).

In 1:7-12 the author proposes to demonstrate his thesis that reason is dominant over the emotions by reflecting on the examples of the so-called Maccabean martyrs — Eleazar, the seven brothers, and their mother (see 2 Maccabees 6–7). His discourse may have been associated with the annual commemoration of the Maccabean martyrs ("On this anniversary," 1:10). He praises them as examples of "courage and endurance" and as the cause of the liberation and pacification of the land of Israel in the time of Antiochus IV Epiphanes. He divides his discourse into two major parts: the "main principle" (1:13–3:18), and "their story" (3:19–18:24).

Part One: The Main Principle (1:13–3:18)

A. Some *Definitions* (1:13-30a) provide a foundation for the demonstration that reason is sovereign over the emotions. Reason is "the mind that with sound logic prefers the life of wisdom" (1:15). Wisdom is "the knowledge of divine and human matters and the causes of them" (1:16). Education in the Law (the Torah) is the means by which divine and human matters can be learned (1:17). The last point contains a most important qualification, since for this Hellenistic-Jewish author the Torah provides content and guidance for reason.

Of the four cardinal virtues, rational judgment (what is often called "prudence") is supreme because it is "the guide of the virtues" and is sovereign over the emotions (1:30a). The two principal emotions or passions are pleasure and pain, while anger shares aspects of both. Rather than eradicating the passions, rational judgment serves as the "master cultivator" that "tames the jungle of habits and emotions" (1:29). Having laid out a philosophical framework, the author proceeds to prove his thesis about the sovereignty of devout reason over the emotions by examples from the Torah and Israel's history.

B. *Examples from the Torah* (1:30b–2:23) show how self-control led by rational judgment allows Jews to abstain from food forbidden by the Torah (1:33-35). It enabled Joseph to overcome sexual desire in the case of Potiphar's wife (Genesis 39) and to keep the commandment (Exod. 20:17; Deut. 5:21) against coveting another's wife (2:1-6a). Likewise, reason guided by the Torah enables Jews to forgo exacting interest from other Jews, to cancel debts during sabbatical years, and to leave part of their harvests for the poor (2:6b-9a). Moreover, reason guided by the Law can supersede family obligations and prevail over hostility toward enemies (2:9b-14). Finally (2:15-20), reason can prevail over violent emotions, as the cases of Moses controlling his anger at Dathan and Abiram (see Numbers 16) and of Jacob's censure of Simeon and Levi (see Gen. 49:7) suggest. The author's twofold emphasis on reason and the Torah (2:21-23) is essential for understanding the biblical examples: Reason is sovereign ("as a sacred governor") over the passions, and the Law provides the proper content for living the virtuous life.

C. The *Example of David* (2:24–3:18) illustrates the principle that "reason can provide a way for us not to be enslaved by desire" (3:2). The example is taken from 2 Samuel 23:13-17 and especially its statement that David "desired" water (23:15). The version in 4 Maccabees differs from the biblical episode at several points. In 4 Maccabees David wants water from the enemies' territory rather than from Bethlehem; there are two soldiers rather than three; and the drink is "regarded as equivalent to blood" rather than as "blood." Most important of all, the author takes the episode as an illustration of his thesis that devout reason is sovereign over the emotions. He suggests that David poured out the water on the ground as proof that a temperate mind can overcome the passions — in this instance, thirst. The case of David in turn provides a transition to the cases of the Maccabean martyrs, in which devout reason will overcome the most terrible tortures and even horrible deaths.

Part Two: Their Story (3:19–18:24)

A. The *Background Information* (3:19–4:26) is taken from 2 Maccabees 3–6 (with changes, omissions, and errors) and explains how Eleazar, the seven brothers, and their mother came to face martyrdom before King Antiochus. The reference to "the present occasion" (3:19) suggests that 4 Maccabees was composed for a commemoration of the Maccabean martyrs.

The first part (3:20–4:14) describes how Apollonius (rather than his emissary Heliodorus, according to 2 Maccabees 3) attempted to rob the temple treasury in Jerusalem (which also served as a bank). He was prevented by "angels on horseback" and recovered his health only through the prayers of the high priest Onias. The author attributes the chastisement of Apollonius to "divine justice" (4:13).

The second part (4:15-26) provides the specific background to the persecution of the Jews under Antiochus IV Epiphanes. When Onias's brother Jason purchased the high priesthood for himself, he "changed the nation's way of life" (4:19) by constructing a gymnasium and abolishing the temple service. The "divine justice was angered by these acts" (4:21), and so Antiochus became directly involved in trying to end Jewish observance of the Torah. In the face of the Jews' resistance, Antiochus sought to force all Jews "to eat defiling foods and to renounce Judaism" (4:26).

B. The *Martyrdom of Eleazar* (5:1–7:23) is occasioned by the elderly sage's refusal to eat pork and foods sacrificed to idols — in effect, to perform an act of idolatry (5:1-4). The exhortation to him from Antiochus (5:5-13) focuses on the apparent conflict between the Jewish religion and a universally applicable philosophy. Since "nature" gave us pork as a "most excellent meat," it might appear only rational to eat it and irrational to abstain from it (5:7-8). Moreover, if "some power" watches over Eleazar, he will surely forgive his transgression made under duress (5:13). These two arguments from Antiochus probably echo discussions among Jews

211

and their neighbors in the Diaspora about what were regarded as the peculiar customs of the Jews.

In reply (5:14-38) Eleazar insists that the Jewish religion is governed "by the divine law" (5:16) and teaches the great philosophical virtues of self-control, courage, justice, and piety. He refuses to eat pork because he believes that "the law was established by God" and teaches what is "most suitable for our lives" (5:25-26). He concludes his refusal with a direct address to the "law that trained me" and to "beloved self-control," thus emphasizing the link between the Jewish religion and philosophy. His religious principles are sound philosophy, and he will not allow Antiochus to dominate them.

The torture and death of Eleazar are narrated in 6:1-30 in gruesome physical detail, while also showing his nobility as a true philosopher. Though tortured in body, "he kept his reason upright and unswerving" (6:7) and suffers like a "noble athlete" (6:10). When offered the opportunity only to pretend to eat pork, he refuses on the grounds that such deceit would be "irrational" (6:18). In his last words (6:27-29) he claims to die "for the sake of the law" and gives his death a sacrificial and expiatory interpretation: "Make my blood their purification, and take my life in exchange for theirs."

In the final reflection (6:31–7:23) the author puts Eleazar forward as proof for the thesis that "devout reason is sovereign over the emotions" (6:31). Next in 7:1-5 he compares Eleazar to a skillful pilot sailing into "the haven of immortal victory," to a besieged city, and to a jutting cliff breaking "the maddening waves of the emotions." Then in 7:6-15 he addresses Eleazar in an encomium ("O priest . . . O man in harmony . . . you father . . . O aged man . . ."), and observes that "he became young again in spirit through reason." Finally in 7:16-23 the author returns to his thesis that devout reason is the governor of the emotions. He claims that only sincerely religious persons can control their passions (7:18), and that such persons can endure any suffering for the sake of virtue (7:22). Thus Eleazar emerges as an example of the harmony between the Jewish religion and true philosophy. By following the Torah faithfully, Eleazar allowed devout reason to guide and control his passions.

C. The *Martyrdom of the Seven Brothers* (8:1–14:10) is a greatly expanded version of 2 Maccabees 7. Their sufferings and deaths are presented as further evidence for the sovereignty of devout reason over the emotions. When Antiochus summons the brothers and their mother, he is impressed by their appearance and nobility (8:1-4). In his address to them (8:5-11) he promises great rewards if they agree to eat the food forbidden by the Torah: "Enjoy your youth by adopting the Greek way of life and by changing your manner of living" (8:8). And he also shows them the instruments of torture that await them if they refuse (8:12-14).

Before giving the seven brothers reply, the author presents a set of rationalizations (8:15-26) that could have led them to accept the king's offer: the king's apparent kindness, fear of torture, their youth and their mother's age, the possibility of divine forgiveness, and so on. Rather than even consider these excuses (8:27-29), they reply in 9:1-9 that they will pursue "the prize of virtue" (immortal life with God), while the king "will deservedly undergo from the divine justice eternal torment by fire" (9:8-9).

The martyrdoms of the seven brothers (9:10–12:19) proceed from the eldest to the youngest. The amazing feature is that these young men imitate perfectly the example of their teacher Eleazar (9:5-6) and show themselves as models of devout reason overcoming the emotions. Their physical sufferings are narrated in frightening detail. But what is more important is how by fidelity to the Torah and to reason they are able to withstand the tortures and to die a noble death.

The seven episodes about the brothers (9:10-25; 9:26-31; 10:1-11; 10:12-21; 11:1-12; 11:13-27; 12:1-19) share many features. In almost every case the brother is brought forward and offered forbidden food. On his refusal he undergoes gruesome physical tortures to which he responds with defiant words. He dies a noble death after warning the king that he will suffer eternal punishments. The defiant words involve three major themes: fidelity to the Torah and its food laws, the guidance of devout reason and the quest for virtue, and solidarity with other family members. There is great emphasis on the torments that await the wicked king (see 9:9; 9:32; 10:11; 10:21; 11:3; 12:12-13; 12:18). Though "the prize of virtue" (9:8) is clearly immortality and it is later said that the seven youths were "running the course toward immortality" (14:5), they show even more interest in fighting "the sacred and noble battle for religion" (9:24), suffering because of "godly training and virtue" (10:10), and holding "fast to reason" (11:27).

When the seventh and youngest son in 12:1-19 consults with his mother, the king imagines that he will relent. However, the boy calls the king a "most savage beast" for mistreating other humans and promises him "intense and eternal fire and tortures" (12:12-13). Then he flings himself into the fire, committing a kind of noble suicide when faced with inevitable death due to fidelity to the Torah and reason. The appeal to common humanity and to voluntary death undertaken for the sake of principle serves to enhance the youth's image as a philosopher.

In the concluding reflection (13:1–14:10) the author puts forward the seven brothers as further proof that "devout reason is sovereign over the emotions" (13:1-7). Then in 13:8-18 he gives samples of how they encouraged one another by appealing to biblical precedents (Daniel 3 and Genesis 22), exhorted one another to "put on the full armor of self-control, which is divine reason," and envisioned the prospect of eternal life with Abraham, Isaac, and Jacob. What allowed them to endure and to die nobly were "common nurture and daily companionship . . . general education and our discipline in the law of God" (13:22). So great was the power of the Law and of reason that it enabled them to master even "the emotions of brotherly love" (14:1). The seven brothers are comparable to the seven days of creation and to a chorus surrounding and dissolving "the sevenfold fear of tortures" (14:7-8). The concluding comment "even now we shudder" (14:9) may also indicate that 4 Maccabees was composed for a public commemoration of the Maccabean martyrs.

D. The *Martyrdom of the Mother* (14:11–17:6) emphasizes her sufferings in witnessing the tortures and deaths of her seven sons, as well as the power of her commitment to religion and reason in urging them on (14:11-12). Overcoming the natural maternal instinct for her children's safety that even birds and bees display, she followed the example of Abraham (see Genesis 22) and put her religion first (14:13-20). Given the choice between religion and preserving her seven sons for a time (15:1-32), she "loved religion more, the religion that preserves them for eternal life according to God's promise" (15:3). Moreover, it was devout reason that gave her a "man's courage" and enabled her to witness the tortures inflicted on her sons. Even though their cries moved her (15:21), she remained "more noble than males in steadfastness" and so "withstood the wintry storms that assail religion" (15:32). More remarkable than the old man Eleazar or her seven sons, the mother illustrates the thesis that devout reason — fidelity to reason and to the Torah — is sovereign over the deepest human emotions.

To highlight the mother's nobility (16:1-25), the author reflects on what she might have thought (16:6-10) — about seven births in vain, no prospect of grandchildren, the lonely life of a widow, and no one to bury her. But these were not her thoughts at all. She did not lament because she was "giving rebirth for immortality to the whole number of her sons" (16:13). And so she urged her sons to "fight zealously for our ancestral law" (16:16), and to remember the examples of Abraham and of Daniel and his three companions and show the same faith in God. Her conclusion is that "it is unreasonable for people who have religious knowledge not to withstand pain" (16:23) The author notes in 16:25 that those who die for God live to God as Abraham, Isaac, and Jacob do.

Rather than be taken by the king's soldiers and run the risk of sexual abuse, the mother throws herself into the flames as her youngest son did (17:1). For the courage of her faith, she is praised as "a roof on the pillars of your sons" and as "the moon in heaven" (17:2-6). She and her sons now enjoy the reward of eternal life with God.

E. The *Final Encomium* (17:7–18:24) reflects on the significance of the martyrs' suffering and death. After noting how hard it would be to depict their trial in art, the author proposes an epitaph that commends the martyrs for vindicating their nation (17:9-10). As the "athletes of the divine legislation" (17:11-16), they won the prize of "immortality in endless life."

The benefits of their martyrdoms are manifold (17:17–18:5). They now enjoy eternal happiness with God (17:18). The wicked king Antiochus came to recognize the futility of his efforts "to compel the Israelites to become pagan" (18:5). And the nation of Israel was purified and gained peace, and the observance of the Torah was revived. More than providing a good example, the martyrs exercised a causal effect upon the fortunes of their people. Their death served as "a ransom for the sins of our nation" and as "an atoning sacrifice" (17:21-22; see 6:29). The idea (so important in the New Testament teaching about Christ's death) is that their deaths wiped away Israel's sins and made possible Israel's right relationship with God.

In a final speech (18:6-19) the mother recounts her life as a pure virgin and as a devoted wife and mother, and recalls the biblical passages that her husband taught the seven sons. These passages deal with the major themes in 4 Maccabees: innocent suffering, zeal for the Law, faith in God's power, and hope for eternal life with God.

The book ends in 18:20-23 with a lament over the bitterness of the day on which the martyrs suffered torture and death, as well as a word of consolation expressing the conviction that the "accursed tyrant" will be pursued by divine justice while the martyrs have already "received pure and immortal souls from God."

Significance

The suffering of the Jewish people is the major topic of 4 Maccabees. What is distinctive is the philosophical framework in which the topic is treated. The author evinces no doubt about God's omnipotence and justice, while describing in gruesome detail the sufferings of Eleazar, the seven brothers, and their mother. He is confident that the martyrs will gain the prize of immortality for their fidelity and that the wicked King Antiochus will suffer eternal torments for persecuting the righteous faithful. Belief in rewards and punishments after death is basic to his approach.

One distinctive feature in his approach concerns suffering in the present. With his many descriptions of instruments of torture as well as his psychologically perceptive analysis of how a mother suffers when watching her children suffer, the author forces the reader to confront the reality of physical and emotional suffering. At the same time, he offers a philosophical and theological strategy for dealing with suffering. From philosophy he takes the idea of reason as governing and directing the other virtues and the emotions. From the Jewish theological tradition he takes the concept of the Torah as supplying the divinely revealed content for making a rational decision. The combination of the two traditions in "devout reason" promises to help the martyrs (and anyone else) to deal effectively with the most terrible sufferings.

Another important element in the author's approach is the concept of expiatory or vicarious suffering. As Eleazar dies "for the sake of the law," he prays for the people of Israel that God will "let our punishment suffice for them" and that his life may be taken "in exchange for theirs" (6:27-28). In the final encomium the author interprets the martyrs' sufferings and deaths as "a ransom for the sin of our nation" and as "an atoning sacrifice" (17:21-22). The idea of death "for our sins" can be traced back to the Suffering Servant of Isaiah 53 and of course is a major theme in the New Testament. In the author's perspective, the martyrs were responsible for wiping away Israel's sins, defeating Antiochus, purifying the Temple, and renewing observance of the Torah.

Issues. How much philosophy did the author know? Some scholars regard his knowledge as rudimentary and eclectic, while others view him as fairly well versed in Stoicism. His philosophy was surely not Cynic or Epicurean. The problem comes in determining how "pure" his Stoicism was, and in the extent to which he borrowed terms and ideas

216

from the broad philosophical tradition that began with Plato and Aristotle.

How successful was his effort at integrating philosophy and theology? The author was confident that there is no ultimate contradiction between the two. Since God created nature and reason, there can be no real opposition. For him the faithful Jew is the true philosopher, and the philosopher gets true wisdom from the divinely revealed Torah. The concept of "devout reason" would not have appeared especially strange in the Greco-Roman world. His effort at bringing together philosophy and Scripture has found many imitators in Jewish and Christian history. However, the case on which he spends most of his time and energy — abstaining from pork and meat sacrificed to idols — and his insistence on the rationality of following the Torah indicate that for him the Torah takes precedence over what some might regard as philosophy.

Does the author condone suicide? Both the seventh son and the mother leap into the flames when faced with certain death (12:19; 17:1). The seventh son in effect refuses to participate in idolatry, and the mother protects herself from possible sexual abuse from the soldiers. The Bible's dossier on suicide is surprisingly thin, and here we have cases of inevitable death undertaken for fidelity to the Torah and reason after extreme tortures. For the author, and for his philosophical contemporaries, the deaths of these martyrs would have been interpreted more as instances of "noble death" than as suicide.

Influence. Although 4 Maccabees appears in some Greek biblical manuscripts, it is not regarded as canonical by Jews or Christians. There is a long rabbinic version of the martyrdoms of the seven sons and their mother in *Lamentations Rabbah* 1.50 (on Lam. 1:16; see Hadas, pp. 129-33). The work's emphasis on the martyrs' death as "a ransom for the sin of our nation" and as "an atoning sacrifice" finds important parallels, if not echoes, in Mark 10:45 and Romans 3:21-26 with reference to Jesus' death understood as a sacrifice for sins. The example of the Maccabean martyrs, especially as this is presented in 4 Maccabees, exercised great influence on the development of the Christian concept of martyrdom. And if 4 Maccabees was composed for delivery at a memorial service in honor of the Maccabean martyrs, this work probably contributed to the Christian tradition of venerating the saints as heroes of faith in a regular (perhaps annual) cycle.

For Further Study

DeSilva, David A. *4 Maccabees.* Sheffield: Sheffield Academic Press, 1998.

Gruen, Erich S. *Heritage and Hellenism: The Reinvention of Jewish Tradition.* Berkeley: University of California Press, 1998.

Hadas, Moses. *The Third and Fourth Books of Maccabees.* New York: Harper, 1953.

Henten, Jan W. van. *The Maccabean Martyrs as Saviours of the Jewish People: A Study of 2 and 4 Maccabees.* Leiden: Brill, 1997.

Index

219